Photography Methods for the UFO Hunter
J. Chisholm
Snow Crystal Press
Copyright © Snow Crystal Press
Printed in the United States of America

Library of Congress Cataloguing-in-Publication Data

Chisholm, J.

Photography Methods for the UFO Hunter, J. Chisholm – Volume 1

ISBN-13 978-0-9865629-0-7

Acknowledgement

To Laurie. Thank you for your determination, patience and verve.

Preface

The best questions get asked daily at lunch. Some of the better questions to ask are, what is the best food, what is the best wine, and most importantly, who is going to pay the bill. But, back in 1950, while having his lunch, Enrico Fermi, a famous nuclear physicist and Nobel laureate, had an especially good question when he was asked about life on other planets, in particular, he questioned, "where is everybody?" Fermi's query became known as Fermi's Paradox.

Fermi's Paradox is the viewpoint that if one were to bet on life and its origins, then it is a likely bet that life arose elsewhere in the galaxy, billions of years before humans. And if life arose elsewhere before humans, then from Fermi's perspective, several space-faring civilizations would have had time to colonize part or all of the galaxy. Fermi believed that if these space-faring civilizations were around, they would have introduced themselves to humans. If there were no aliens coming to earth and introducing themselves, then perhaps there were no aliens. Or, so the question and theory went as discussed during mealtime sometime back in 1950. Just a table conversion with no observation, no facts, just a guy sitting at lunch with an opinion and asking a question.

But a good question by Fermi nevertheless. So where is everybody? If one holds the thought that many extraterrestrials are potentially knocking about our universe, then one is also faced with the lack of evidence of aliens, such as repeatable UFO sightings. To date in the public sphere, there have been no repeatable events one can point to and say, aliens are here or not. Either we are wrong about our assumption of life, or our search methods are wrong or flawed. Which brings up the issue of viewpoint with respect to Fermi's Paradox.

The issue here is an assumption in Fermi's Paradox that alien life will somehow communicate with us. Fermi assumed alien life would announce itself upon its arrival on our planet. However, alien life may be following strategies quite foreign to Fermi's human viewpoint.

Even life in the oceans of our planet rests its strategy for survival upon hiding from other life. Imagine if Charles Darwin, who developed evolutionary theory, sat down at that lunch with Fermi. Darwin, who based his theories on years of looking at earth life, would likely have replied to Fermi's lunch time question by saying that a hiding life, is a surviving life, as shown by the creatures in our oceans. For example, octopus survive by changing color and hiding against background coral reefs on the sea floor. In other words, hiding is a good strategy for survival even on our planet. Why should alien life be any different?

This book will explore this hidden world of alien life, by outlining photography and video methods for viewing unidentified flying objects that hide in a stealthy, survival optimized manner in the skies above our planet. This book's aim is to provide the curious reader with a simple and concise set of videographic and photographic methods, using off the shelf computer equipment and software, in order to search for and reveal, hidden UFOs. Videographic UFO hunting is a hobby that can be enjoyed by photography hobby enthusiasts or anyone, using only a few hours of time each day, and can be shared with others on Youtube as video or other popular UFO sites.

Note to the reader: photographic images in this book, due to the book printing process may be different in color than actual photographs captured.

Contents

Chapter 13: Conclusion   130

Chapter 1: Beginnings

Although nature commences with reason and ends in experience it is necessary for us to do the opposite; that is to commence with experience and from this to proceed to investigate the reason.

Leonardo Da Vinci[1]

Writers are supposed to write about what they know. For the author, this was a tricky matter writing on the subject of UFOs, which is a subject completely outside everyone's ordinary experience. To write about strange craft flying our skies is reminiscent of the kind of stories told to reduce fears of noises heard in the dark. Likely that was why storytelling was invented, to tell tales, entertain, and reduce the fear about whatever creature in the dark, was making noise.

This book is not about telling tales. The aim of this book is to show the reader a better way to see into the dark, and to lift a corner of that veil of mystery which surrounds the subject of UFOs. Others can tell tales about the unknown, or adopt a position of disbelief based on opinion.

In particular, this book is about collecting visual facts through photography and video, of the unknown called, unidentified flying objects. This book provides a general set of guidelines that shows the reader how to build the video equipment and use the right software for capturing video of UFOs. Think of this book as a how-to UFO photography and videography book. Additionally, for photographers, the book provides an introduction to an especially challenging area of photography.

I am a great believer in how-to books. The how-to methods outlined in this book are the result of testing video and photographic techniques on actual UFO sightings over several years. The goal of the video and photographic techniques in this book is to provide you, the reader, with a self empowered ability to search for and capture evidence of UFOs on video and cameras. This is a how-to book for people who wish to observe, and sometimes (with a little luck) produce clear photographs and video of Unidentified Flying Objects (UFOs).

The value proposition of this book is to show people how to capture UFOs on video as evidence, and moves away from focusing on looking at old records and eyewitness accounts of UFOs. Capture enough weight of evidence on video of UFOs, and you cannot dismiss the phenomena based on lack of evidence or lack of repeatable evidence.

Eyewitness accounts are too easily dismissed as evidence based on the state of mind of the witness, hoaxes or misperception. For instance, the U.S. Air Force dismissed a particularly large UFO sighting that occurred in Phoenix, Arizona, back in March of 1997, as just being flares. The U.S. Air Force disregarded the UFO sighting despite the UFO being seen by several people and the former Arizona State Governor, Fife Symington III.

As Symington noted, *"As a pilot and a former Air Force Officer, I can definitively say that this craft did not resemble any man-made object I'd ever seen. And it was certainly not high-altitude flares because*

---

1   Leonardo Da Vinci, **Movement and Weight**, from The Notebooks of Leonardo da Vinci, trans. E. MacCurdy, Vol 1., 1938, page 546

flares don't fly in formation.[2]

On the anniversary of a project that for fifty years has searched for alien life and failed, people want answers to the question of whether or not there is extraterrestrial life (ET). This year, 2010, marks the 50th anniversary of the Search for Extra Terrestrial Intelligence (SETI) study (originally called Project Ozma). For 50 years, SETI has failed to receive a radio signal in its search for radio signals that positively indicates alien life in our galaxy.

This book offers an alternative to SETI and can provide some answers to setting up your own search for UFOs and alien life. As an alternative method to SETI, this book suggests guidelines as well as unique ways for people to take a closer look at home, in the search for clues to alien life. In honour of this search, I have named this search for ET: **CLUE**, or **C**lose and **L**ow **U**FO **E**arth study. CLUE's search for alien life is at very short distances, at most a few kilometres, our Mr. Magoo near sighted version of SETI. Far short of the lofty SETI search goal which searches light years away for alien civilizations.

More importantly, CLUE, as a photography method study, unlike the sublime SETI program, is built around you, the home photography hobbyist. As mentioned already, you are in control of your search for sightings of UFOs.

Most of the methods in this how-to book use free, high quality open source software found on the Internet, and a core technology of an ordinary web-cam converted to a near infrared web-cam capture tool for viewing of high speed UFO events. You do not have to spend 438,000 hours (50 years) and millions of dollars searching with a set of radio telescopes for a signal that has not come. This is self-empowered, UFO hunting on a budget.

And as an added bonus, this book contains many never before seen photographs of UFOs and aliens recorded within the North American context from the years 2007 to 2010.

---

2   Symington, Fife, **Special to CNN**, Found at: http://www.cnn.com/2007/TECH/science/11/09/simington.ufocommentary/index.html

Chapter 2: Viewpoint in Seeking Facts

Seeing UFOs for the first time is an amazing sight. The first experience lays to rest doubts about life from other planets and starts the process and opportunity of understanding something truly unknown and unique.

Seeing UFOs with abilities that are technically miles ahead of what we can achieve is also unsettling for people who take a more traditional view on our culture and society. There is no getting around that fact. Philosophically, my take is it is best to maintain cool thinking on the matter of UFO sightings. Calm thought is a good state to have when looking at something that is: (a) not supposed to be there according to the critics; and (b) not of a shape built by man.

No matter the dismissive reports by government agencies, such as Project Blue Book back several decades ago, when you first see a UFO, there is no denying the fact of what you see with your eyes. In fact, when you first see a UFO for yourself, then you are, from that point onward, on the road to gathering information, developing ideas on what you are seeing, and expanding your mind.

Seeing UFOs puts to rest preconceptions on their appearance. UFOs are not the flying saucers of popular culture. UFOs are always blurry, tend to take any shape, and can turn on half a dime. UFOs can shock, and it is not uncommon to see hundreds in a minute flying overhead in video.

Another not uncommon sight: seeing UFOs pull extreme turns greater than 90 degrees within 1/30th of a second between two video frames. These "wow" events happen all the time during video recording sessions. Frequently, UFOs are moving so fast, you only see the object when reviewing motion captured video. As for shapes, UFOs are like looking at modern abstract art doodled with crayons. Seeing those shapes, the thought pops up all the time, "What the heck was that?"

Such thoughts of surprise are often a result of preconditioning by our cultural viewpoint. For example, our minds are preconditioned to recognize dogs, cats and babies, but not UFOs. There is a laundry list we carry in our heads, no matter what country we are from, that defines what we recognize as human beings. However this laundry list of items does not apply with UFOs. When seeing UFOs, you get used to that spine tingle of fear that relates to seeing something totally foreign, and from somewhere beyond our imagination. Common road posts of human thought, such as use of standard ways to build things, does not apply here. UFOs suffer no such standard; UFOs come in any shape.

The truth is, UFOs are beyond our knowledge. We are like a people in a bubble, natives on a small planet with no ties to a larger universe. We have no common birthright with these aliens and their craft. Past records from ancient times of visits to our planet are spotty at best, and records in the past 70 years are too often open to debate, and with too many holes. Clean, fresh photographs and video, collected by people within their own means, is therefore needed. There should be no filter on knowledge. Gaining new photographic and video-based knowledge is so interesting that it can lead to a form of obsession or a cargo culture form of admiration for UFOs. My suggestion is to avoid this type of focus in your photographic study of UFOs.

To obsess about UFOs has even been linked to pop culture. For example, Roy Neary was a fictitious Indiana lineman played by Richard Dreyfuss in "Close Encounters of a Third Kind". In the movie, Neary became obsessed with UFOs after coming across a UFO during a blackout. The foreignness of the experience draws Neary further and further down the rabbit hole, obsessed by the strange shapes, abilities and purpose of UFOs. Near the end of the movie, Neary fulfills his obsession, by boarding a mother ship UFO at the top of Devil's Tower, Wyoming. Obsession with UFOs in real life doesn't work out that way, nor does it provide the grounds for clear advancement in photographic study of any phenomena.

The positive of experiencing otherworldly phenomena is that the experience sets the mind on an expanding journey, a journey that is an enriching affirmation that we are not alone in this universe. Observation driven understanding moves us to a higher plane of thought that is not constricted by opinion alone, but which puts things into perspective determined by experience. As seen from pictures extracted from a few seconds of video clip on January 19th, 2009, at 9:38 a.m., UFOs challenge our minds and our senses with their unknown shapes and purpose (**see two UFOs below**), and second frame from same video (**see next page**) that shows how dramatically UFOs change in shape and color in milliseconds.

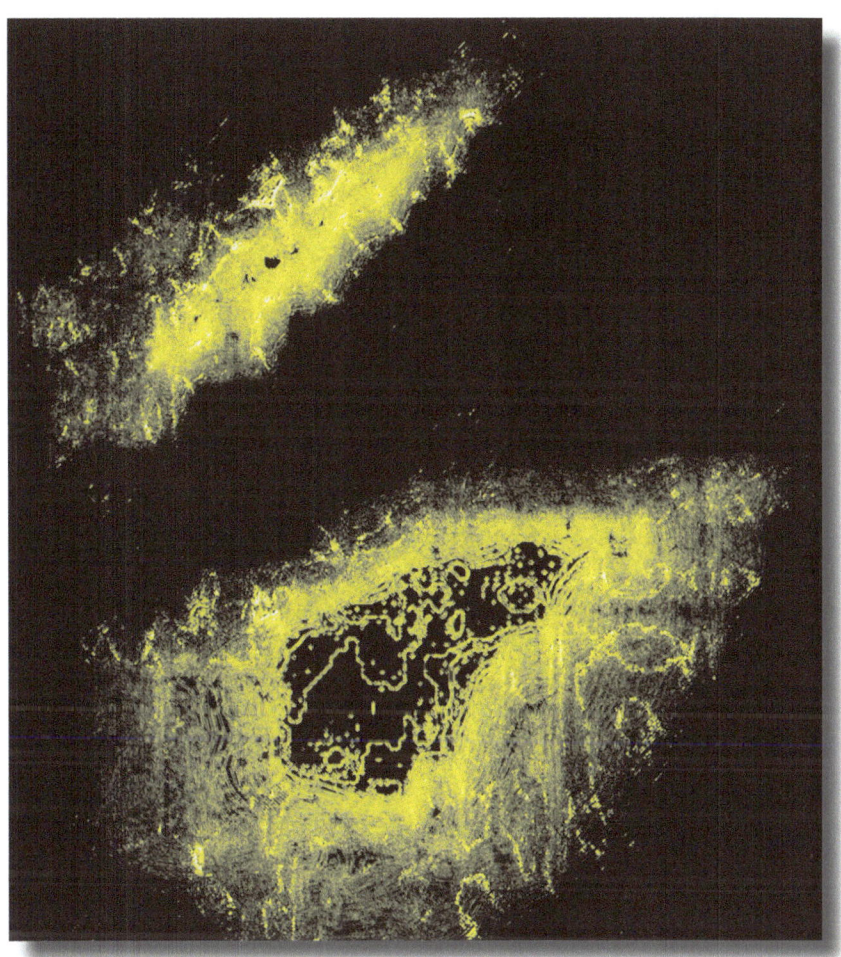

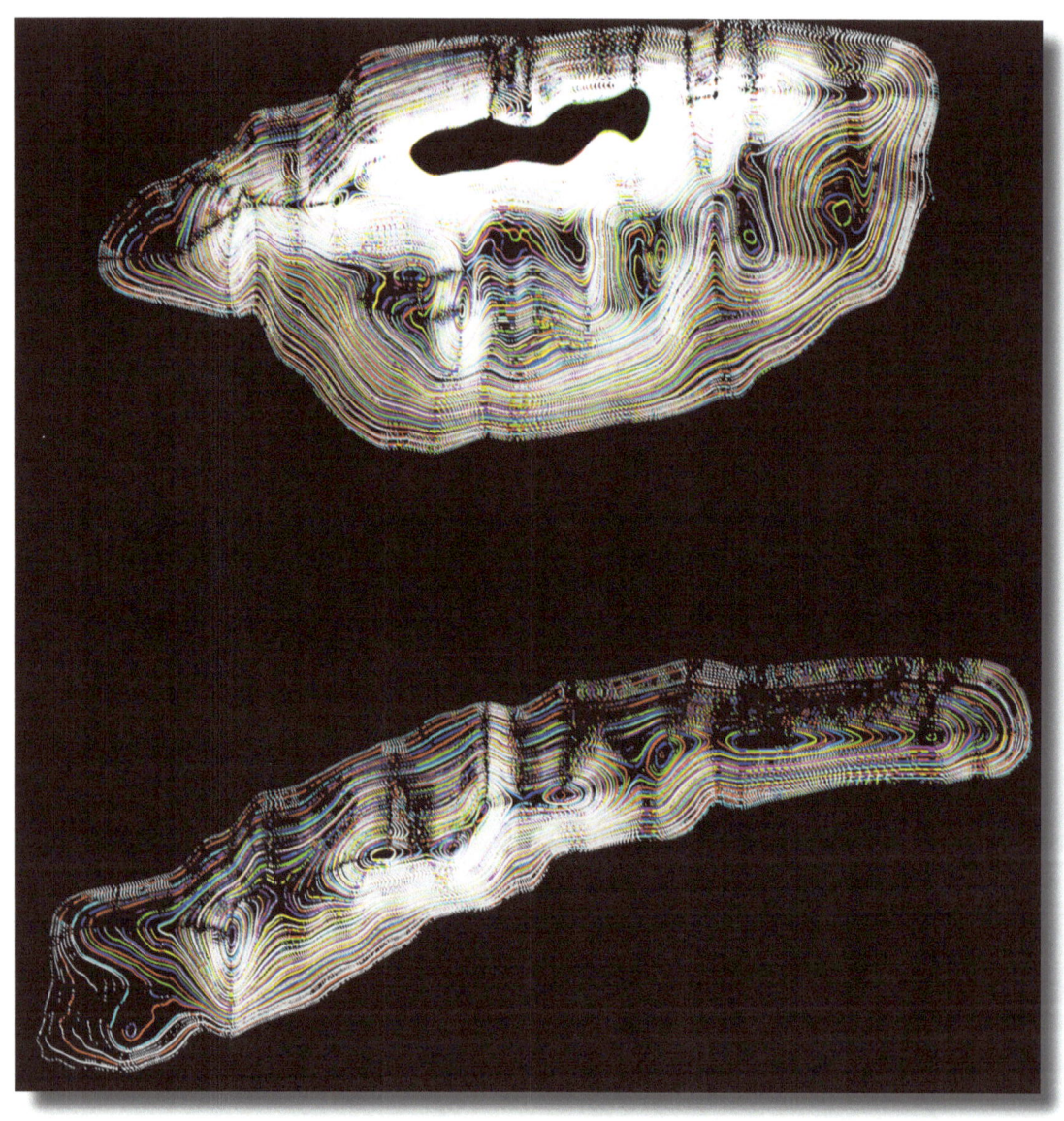

Chapter 3: Where to Capture UFO Images

"Maybe they have looked us over and don't want to come in contact. Or perhaps they have conquered telepathy so they can read our thoughts and feel that is enough. Or maybe we represent nothing more important to them than a termite colony in the jungle."

Professor Hermann Oberth, One of the Fathers of Modern Rocketry discussing UFOs[1]

Where to Start

Where is the best place to set up equipment to see UFOs? Despite Dr. Oberth's opinion, UFOs seem to have man under constant study. Constant study of people by UFOs actually helps quite a bit in figuring out locations where UFOs can be captured on video. It is a logic game in figuring out where UFOs will appear. This logic game is really about spatial logic, i.e. figuring out where UFOs can achieve the best vantage point from the air to see people. It is similar to how pilots back in WW II must have thought when they lined up on ground targets. A UFO, studying people on the ground, must be always jinking and jiving across the sky, trying to find best air flight patterns for seeing people on the ground. Take for instance, tall buildings in the middle of a city. Are UFOs studying tall buildings?

Tall buildings represent a flight obstruction for UFOs. UFOs tend not to hang around the middle of cities unless the UFO is flying above buildings. People walking on the ground below office towers could be a point of interest for UFOs, while office towers stand only as a type of flight blockage for UFO craft.

Other UFO vantage spots for viewing people are at large open public events where crowds gather. UFOs, while looking at us from the air, have the same problem as people who look at aerial photos, which is, finding the best line of sight on objects situated on the ground from the air. I will define "line of sight" as a straight line along which an observer has a clear view when they are sighted at an object on the ground. With too many buildings, and too many trees, UFOs lose line of sight of people on the ground.

Additionally, UFOs would be more likely to appear during sunny, mainly cloudless days. Cloudy and foggy weather reduces UFO viewing opportunities of people on the ground, so there is less motive for UFOs to appear during that type of weather.

Put yourself in a location where there is a lot of people visible from the air, equip yourself with the right tools, and bingo, you may soon see a UFO. Places where large groups of people walk during day light, represent good UFO spotting opportunities. The repeat event of seeing daylight UFOs is greater, for example, near shopping malls, dog parks, and walking paths. Places where there is a lot of "people traffic" are the best areas to set up for the UFO hunt.

So give yourself the chance to see UFOs. Set up a near infrared web-cam combined with the John Bro Wilkie method (both methods described later in this book) in areas where people are visible from the air. The chance of seeing a UFO using the tools and methods described in this book, will go up at events such as football games, large outdoor rallies, or during high ground traffic times when people walk to and from work in major cities. The times around 8:00 a.m. to 9:30 a.m, and 3:30 p.m. to 5:00 p.m.

---

1   Author unknown, **Where Are They Now?,** Newsweek, March 25, 1968 Found at: http://www.mufon.com/znews_oberth. html

are particularly good times to do a UFO hunt.

As an example of a UFO passing over crowds, consider what happened during President Obama's inauguration. In January of 2009, during a CNN broadcast hosted by Wolf Blitzer and Anderson Cooper, a UFO was caught nine seconds into the video, flying at high speed above the inauguration crowd and passing by the Washington Monument.[2] Forty two seconds after the UFO passed over the crowd, Obama's helicopter was seen in the same video flying to the Inauguration which was taking place at the West Front of the United States Capitol building.[3,4]

Nuclear Power and UFO Sightings

UFOs are often observed near and around nuclear facilities. Using 23,000 records from the National UFO Reporting Center (NUFORC), there is a very strong statistical pattern that suggests that UFOs tend to show up near or around areas that have installed nuclear plants fifteen years after the date that the nuclear power plants have started working (**see below**).[5]

Anecdotal stories suggest UFOs also show up near high tension power lines. There has been speculation in the past by others that UFOs use power lines to recharge. I would suggest that what is providing power to these craft does not need a recharge from our power lines. It may be more a matter

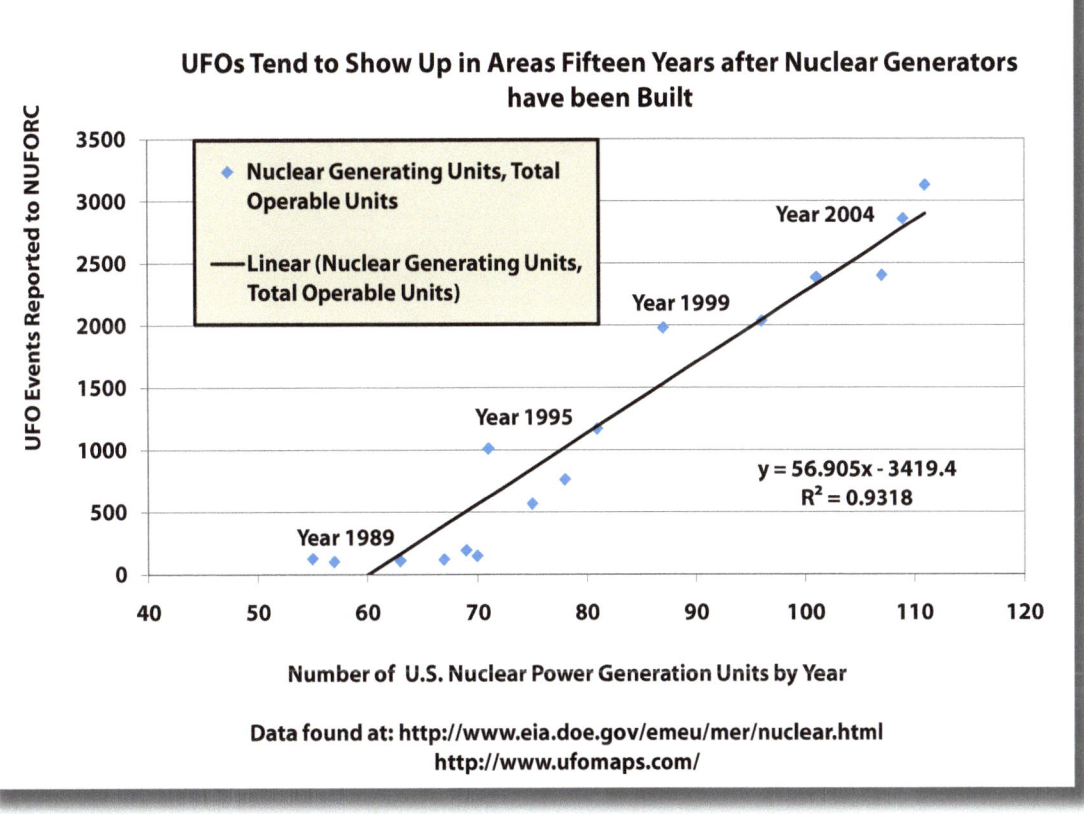

UFOs Tend to Show Up in Areas Fifteen Years after Nuclear Generators have been Built

$y = 56.905x - 3419.4$
$R^2 = 0.9318$

Data found at: http://www.eia.doe.gov/emeu/mer/nuclear.html
http://www.ufomaps.com/

2   Blitzer, Wolf, Cooper, Anderson, Gergen, David, CNN Analysts, **Obama's Inauguration,** January 20, 2009, Found at: Http://edition.cnn.com/video/#/video/politics/2009/01/20/inaug.blitz.gergen.obrien.cnn?iref=videosearch
3   Ibid, CNN Video
4   Various Authors, Found at: http://en.wikipedia.org/wiki/Inauguration_of_Barack_Obama
5   NUFORC Database, Found at: http://www.nuforc.org/

that nuclear power plants are attached to high tension power lines. UFOs may be simply using the fluctuation of power in the power lines to measure whether nuclear power plants, which are attached to the power lines, are in good shape or not in an operational sense.

Whatever the case, there is a clear pattern of UFOs showing up as sightings at certain distances from nuclear power plants. It appears from the scatter plot of data (**see below**) that UFOs seem to be

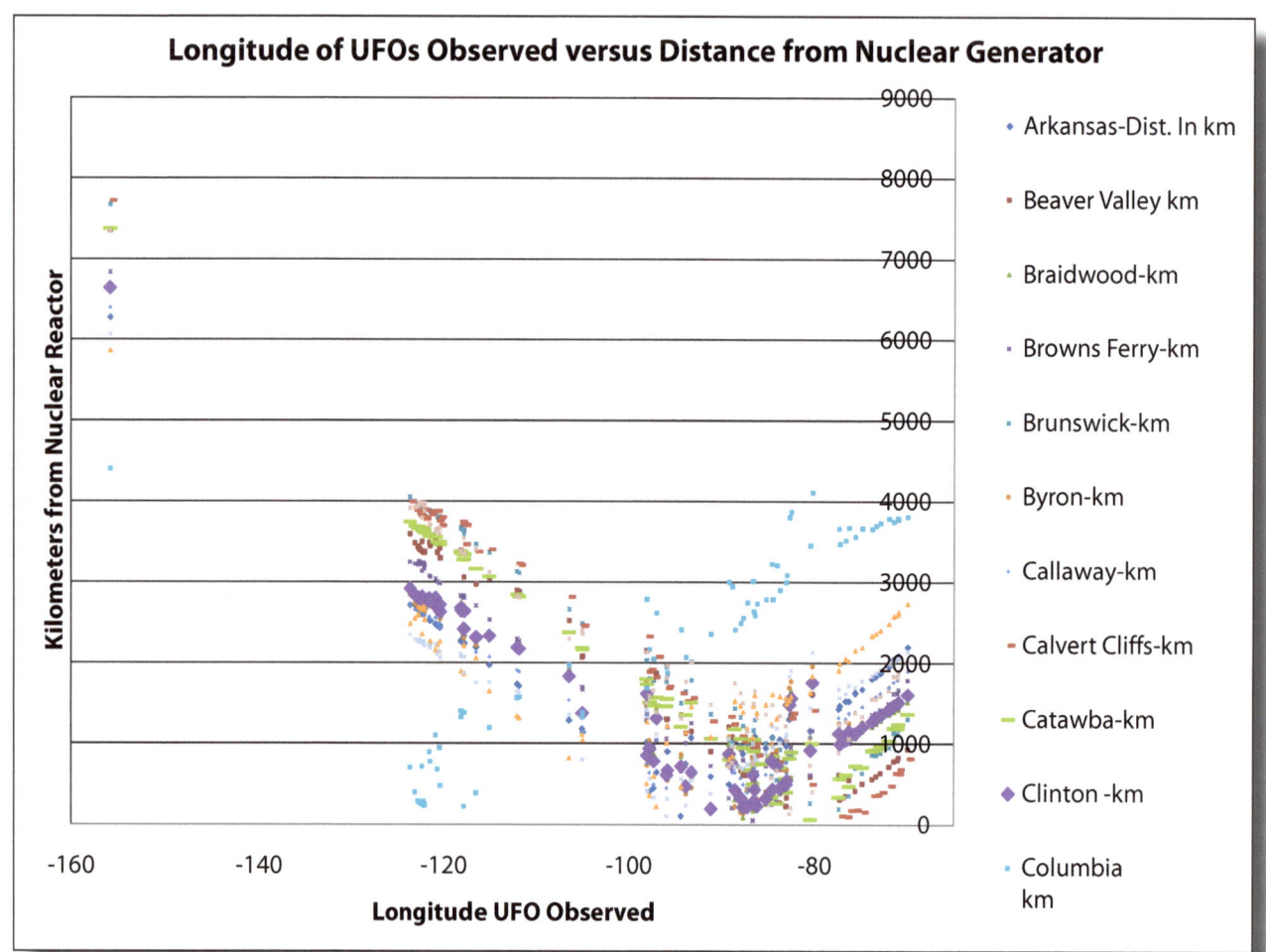

appearing at certain distances from nuclear reactors (perhaps as a survey). Therefore, if one wants to see UFOs, check out areas near nuclear power plants, especially power lines leading from nuclear power plants.

Along the same lines, it should be noted that Area 51 is situated next door to the Nevada Test Site (NTS). Once known as the Nevada Proving Ground, the site, started on January 11, 1951, was used to test nuclear bombs by blowing up about 1,350 sq miles (3,500 km²) of desert and mountain area.[6] The pattern of UFO flights seen near nuclear reactors suggests former nuclear testing sites also draw UFOs. This may account for many UFO sightings near places like Area 51.

And UFOs have had a long history of directly looking over nuclear explosions. Note UFO "anomalies" in one photo taken of the Baker nuclear explosion (**see next page**).[7] The "Baker" explosion, part of

6   Nevada Test Site, found at: http://en.wikipedia.org/wiki/Nevada_Test_Site
7   U.S. Department of Defense, Baker Nuclear Blast, Bikini Atoll, Source: Library of Congress

Operation Crossroads, was the fifth nuclear weapon test by the United States military. The Baker nuclear test was carried out at Bikini Atoll, Micronesia, on July 25th, 1946. An insert false color photo of one UFO is shown (**see right**) in the main photo to the right, as well as some other UFOs, marked with small yellow squares, that are hovering above empty test navel ships parked within the nuclear explosion blast zone.

An alternative explanation to these UFO anomalies are things such as dust motes on the camera lens, flying objects from the explosion, or radiation impinging on the film.

On the other hand, a video of the Baker blast (shown on an upcoming companion movie DVD to this book) shows a UFO flying over the nuclear blast water column, moments after the explosion.

In the next section the subject of near infrared photography will be introduced. Near infrared photography is the method of choice for revealing UFOs in clearer detail.

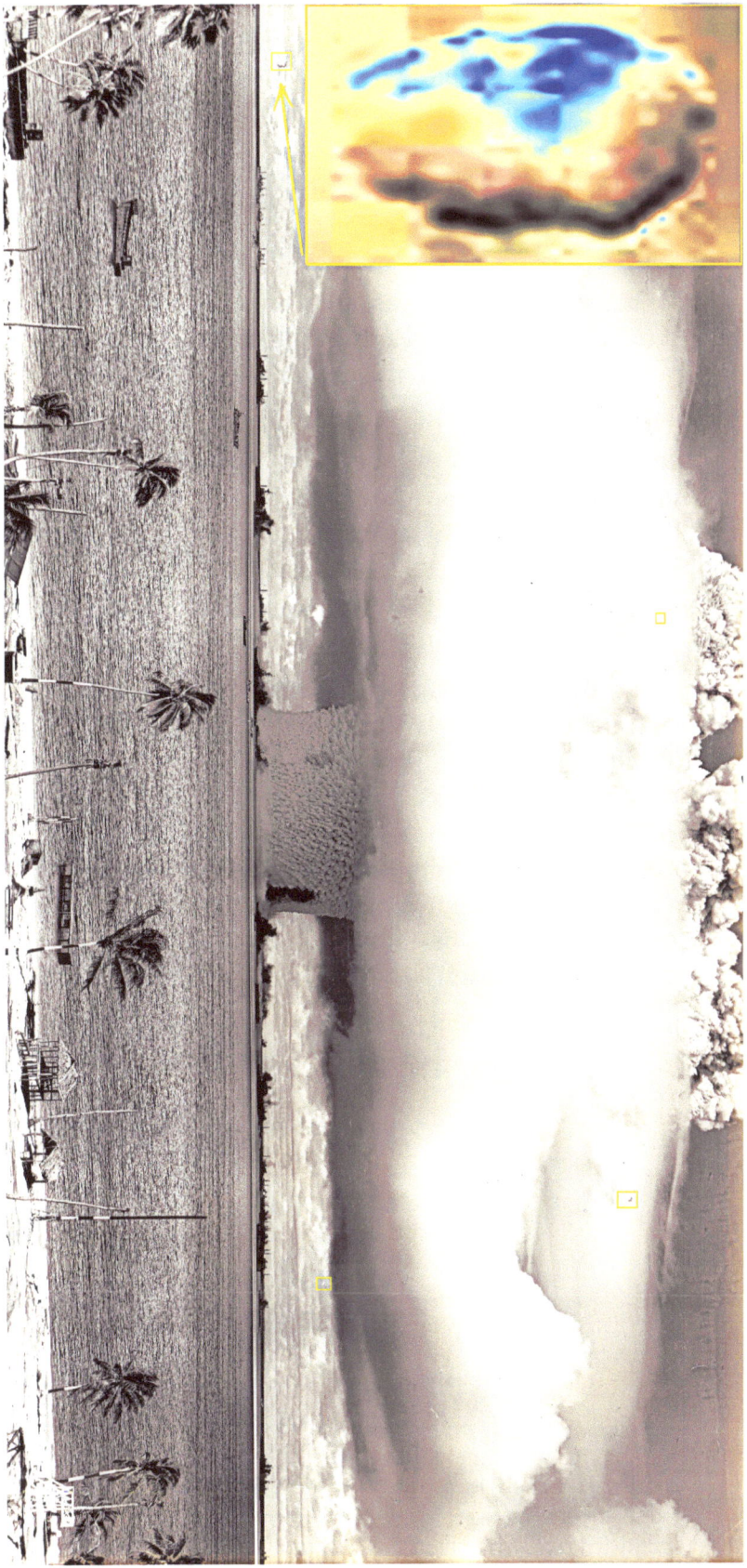

What is Near Infrared?

To understand near infrared light, you first have to understand the meaning of the word spectrum. A spectrum is the distribution of colours produced when white light is dispersed by a prism or diffraction grating. With respect to the spectrum, there is a continuous change in wavelength from red, the longest wavelength, to violet, the shortest wavelength. Seven colours are usually distinguished: violet, indigo, blue, green, yellow, orange, and red. Just beyond the red end of the spectrum, there exists an invisible light, called the near infrared part of the spectrum.

Near infrared spectrum was discovered in science 210 years ago in Britain by an astronomer, William Herschel.[8] In 1800, William Herschel detected the near infrared part of the spectrum (Herschel 19 years before first found Uranus in the night sky using a home made telescope in his backyard).[9]

Recorded notes from the time show that Herschel passed sunlight through a prism to divide white light into the colours of the spectrum. He then used a set of thermometers, where he measured the heat level of each of the spectrum colours (red, orange, green, yellow, blue, indigo, and violet) and found that the amount of heat increased from blue to red. Pushing his test a little further, Herschel placed the thermometer beyond the red light rays where no light was visible. To his surprise, he measured a temperature even higher than that within any of the visible spectrum, and proved for the first time that light unseen to our eyes, infrared, exists beyond the red portion of the light spectrum.[10]

In more modern times, near infrared photos were first done by Robert Wood, an American physicist, who worked for Johns Hopkins University from 1901 until his death in 1955. Wood was the first to publish near infrared photographs, i.e. landscapes, taken in 1910 on near infrared film. In a report to the Royal Photographic Society in 1910, many photographs show Wood's early use of both near infrared and ultraviolet photography. He noted how plants reflected infrared strongly and how blue sky recorded almost as a black. The Royal Photographic Society in a vote of thanks, credited Wood with "opening up two new worlds; the worlds at each end of the spectrum beyond the point of limit of vision". Wood's best near infrared landscapes were shown at the annual exhibition of the Royal Photographic Society in 1911 and were published in the "Illustrated London News" at the time.[11]

The section of the spectrum just outside the visible red part of the spectrum is called near infrared, and it is the part of the spectrum we will focus on to make a set of tools in which to see UFOs.

---

8   Near infrared was discovered on February 11, 1800 by William Herschel, Found at: http://en.wikipedia.org/wiki/William_Herschel#Discovery_of_infrared_radiation

9   Found at: http://en.wikipedia.org/wiki/William_Herschel

10 Found at: http://www.thepathphotography.co.uk/history_of_photography.html

11 Ibid, Williams, Robin and Williams, Gigi, Found at: http://msp.rmit.edu.au/Article_04/03.html

Chapter 4: Tool Setup

Digital Cameras and the CCD Web-cam

Digital cameras and web-cams come with either CCD (charge couple device) or CMOS (Complementary Metal-Oxide Semiconductor) light sensor chips. These light sensing chips are better than the human eye for seeing near infrared light (**see graph below**). Unlike the human eye, CCD sensors are able to see beyond the red end of the light spectrum. To prevent CCD web-cams from seeing this near infrared light, web-cam makers install filters above the CCD sensors to block near infrared light. If a near infrared blocking filter is not installed, people look like boiled lobsters in video. Looking like

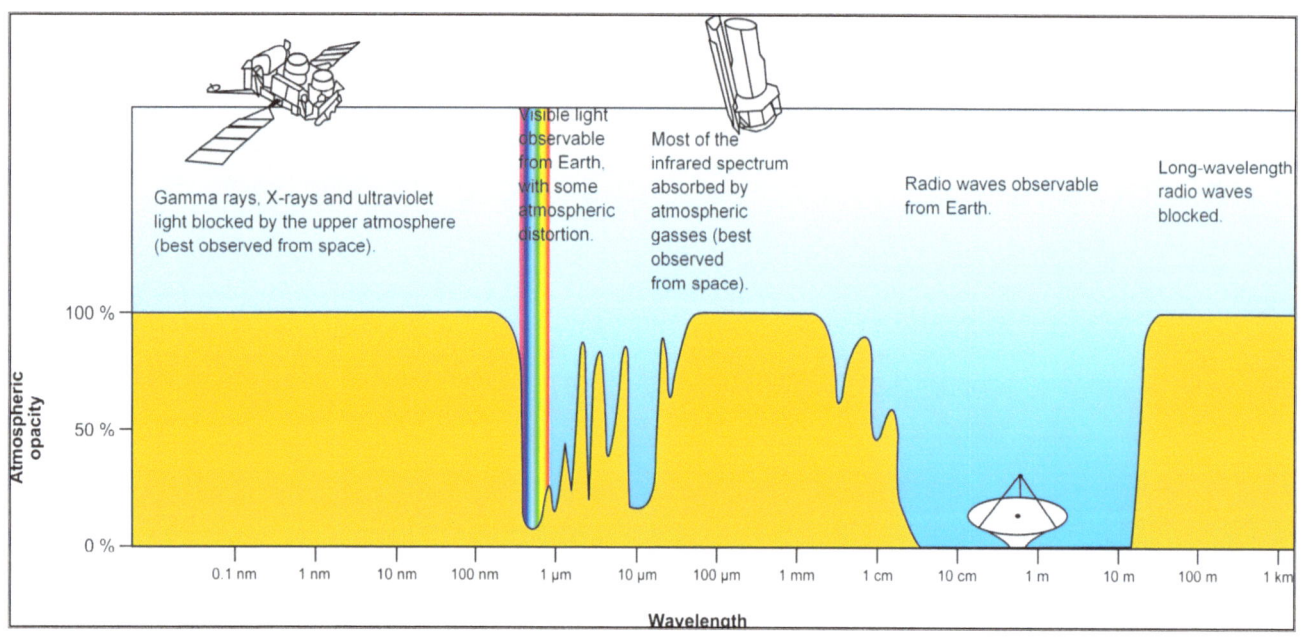

boiled lobster is not a selling feature for a web-cam. So to prevent images from being too red, web-cam builders have worked hard to improve the near infrared blocking filter feature in web-cams. This near infrared blocking filter makes it hard for web-cams to see UFOs. Near infrared web-cams will be discussed later in this chapter, but first let's take a look at near infrared photography with respect to UFO hunting.

Using an Unmodified Camera with a Near Infrared Filter

Using an unmodified camera with an intact near infrared blocking filter, the Canon EOS T1i camera is still able to take near infrared photos. However, the camera is only able to take limited pictures in near infrared. "Limited" here means the DSLR, which is an acronym for "digital single-lens reflex camera", can only take pictures of objects that are still, and is not capable of capturing a moving UFO.

With an intact near infrared blocking filter, a DSLR camera can still see some near infrared light. As a result of there still being a near infrared blocking filter in the camera, longer exposures are needed to take a near infrared picture. A near infrared passing filter (**see below**) combined with the camera's near infrared blocking filter will let through less than 0.1% of the incoming light. A bright scene, requiring 1/500th of a second at F/8 in visible light, will need about 1 second or longer at F/4 on most cameras in near infrared. Unmodified cameras can only work at slow speeds to acquire a picture in near infrared, and a tripod is needed to prevent blur. If the air is not quite still then moving parts of the scenery will be blurry, such as grass or trees.[1] For such a setup, one must wait for a rare event, such as a UFO hanging

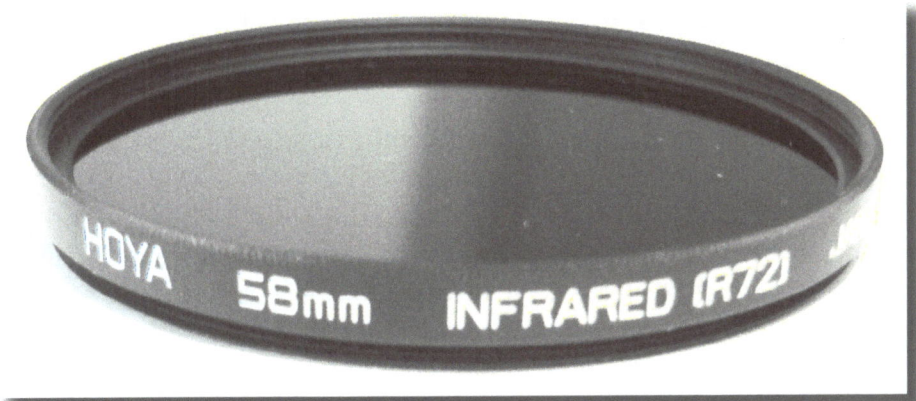

still in the air during daylight. Below on this page, we see just that event.

The following UFO photo was taken using a regular DSLR Canon EOS T1i above a Canadian city. The UFO was captured as a photograph using a regular DSLR Canon EOS T1i on Sept. 23rd, 2009 at 11:45 a.m. (**see photo below**) using a Hoya R72 Filter (**see above**). A Hoya R72 near infrared filter was screwed onto the 55-88mm kit lens that came with the regular Canon EOS T1i camera.

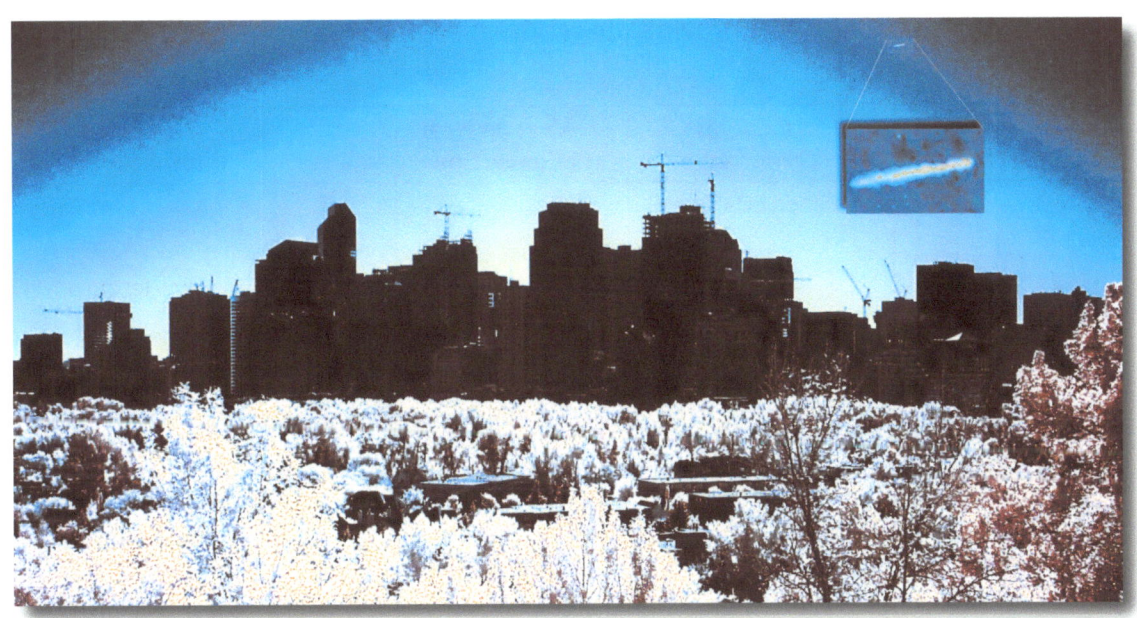

---

1   Wrotniak, Andrzej J., **Photo Tidbits, Infrared Photography with a Digital Camera**, Found at: http://www.wrotniak. net/photo/infrared/

If this UFO had moved during the photo capture, the UFO would have vanished with the slow shutter speed of the camera. As noted on the previous page, it takes a while for a DSLR camera to gather enough light with an intact near infrared blocking filter combined with a near infrared passing Hoya R72 filter. Specific details of the picture: a Canon EOS T1i (aka EOS 500D) was used, 32 mm focal length, center weighted average bias for metering mode, with a F-stop set at 4.5, an exposure time of 0.6 seconds, ISO was set at 1600 with an exposure bias of +0.7 step on the camera. A Hoya near infrared R72 filter 58 mm wide filter was screwed onto the Canon camera lense to take the picture. Free software, IRIS, was used to blow up the UFO image by 60 times. The insert inblown-up image of the UFO was then inserted into the first image using GIMP software. Using a quick colour change in GIMP (a free photo tool which is an open source clone of Photoshop), red colors in the picture were exchanged for blue colors to increase contrast in the picture. The UFO is sitting still in the air and can be seen in the upper right of the picture, in the boxed area. Note that sky in daylight, in near infrared, is usually grey to black, but depending on your camera's software, sky color may be interpreted by the camera's software as red, purple or blue-grey. Canons tend to color the sky red in near infrared but in fact the sky would be black.

Near infrared black skies have been used in the past in film-making to shoot in daylight but make the scenes appear as if they are done at night. Back in 1941, Hollywood shot the film "The Bride Came C.O.D." in near infrared. This film starred James Cagney and Bette Davis, and the film was shot using near infrared movie film to make day time shots of scenes appear like they were taken at night. This was done in order to work around the limits of filming at night.[2]

Using a Camera Fully Converted to Near Infrared Viewing

To fully convert DSLR gear for UFO work is costly (**see the table below**). Using companies to change a DSLR camera to a near infrared modified camera costs close to one third to one half the cost of a DSLR camera. Some companies that provide the service of changing DSLR to near infrared cameras are listed below on the table:

Company Name	Cameras Converted	Cost for Near IR Conversion	Internet Location
LeZot	Canon EOS Digital Rebel (EOS 300D), EOS Digital Rebel XT (EOS 350D), or EOS Digital Rebel XTi(EOS 400D)	$325	www.lezot.com
Digital Silver Imaging	All Brands	$149 for "point and shoots", DSLR type cameras $299, Full Frame DSLR cameras converted for $349	www.digitalsilverimaging.com
Lifepixel	All Brands	$300 and higher	www.lifepixel.com

The services will remove the near infrared blocking filter glass and replace the glass with a type of

---

2 Warner Brothers Pictures, **The Bride Came C.O.D.** , Found at : http://www.imdb.com/title/tt0033432/

glass that allows only near infrared light to pass through to the CCD or CMOS sensor. These services install either a threaded near infrared filter or place a near IR passing filter inside the camera that will block all visible light but allow near infrared light to pass to the sensor. Various filters block more or less deeply into near infrared light. Various threaded near infrared filters that can be installed on cameras are: the Hoya R72 near infrared filter, Wratten #89B, Wratten #88A, Wratten #87, Wratten #87C filters and the 88A filter from Harrison and Harrison.

To convert a DSLR to near infrared yourself is tricky. A camera warranty is voided when the camera is opened by the owner. A twelve hundred dollar DSLR can become junk if you attempt to convert the camera yourself. It is best to have a DSLR changed to near IR by using someone who knows the proper way to convert this equipment. LifePixel offers services to convert a camera to a near IR camera but also shows people on their website how to convert a camera into near infrared. You can see how to change a Canon camera to a near IR camera at the Lifepixel website, at: **http://www.lifepixel.com/IR.htm**

Lifepixel offers great advice for changing a DSLR to a near IR camera. And unlike other services, Lifepixel shows the home hobbyist, in step by step fashion on their website, how to convert their own DSLR cameras to near IR for the Fuji Finepix, Nikon and Canon cameras.

However, it is better value to convert either a web-cam or a camcorder to near infrared (near IR). Recording UFO sightings is a volume game meant to capture a quick event. To capture quick events, some form of video, recording in a constant manner, is the best method to record UFOs. To make this hobby convenient, all you want to do is capture the UFO on video, without having to look at a lot of empty video. UFO video tied to motion capture software gives you the event of a UFO without looking at a lot of boring video with nothing happening.

Reducing the volume of recorded video is one issue, but the other issue is dealing with spotty lighting conditions. Good video is hard to come by when lighting conditions make it difficult to obtain the best video. Difficult lighting conditions break down into the following areas:

- Low contrast subjects hidden against blue sky, as well as flat surfaced objects in the air.

- Subjects in low light.

- Stripes and other patterns where contrast is only in the level plane.

- Under a light source whose brightness, color, or pattern keeps changing.

- Night scenes or points of light.

- Under street lighting or where the light flickers.

- Extremely small subjects which are poor reflectors.

- Subjects that reflect light in a strong manner.

- Subjects which move within the AF (automatic focusing) point, and AF confused by camera shake or subject blur under low light.

- Auto-focusing while the subject is way out of focus.[3]

In later chapters, I will break down in step-by-step manner, ways to deal with the above lighting issues. The major thing to take away from this is that UFO hunting is a volume game. Recording video provides the volume, and is carried out by constantly taking video of only a certain area of the sky. Tie that volume of video recording to motion capture software and the motion capture software saves immense amounts of your time by dumping video when nothing is happening. Constant video capture with motion sensing software is the most effective way for you to capture UFOs when they pass by the camera. This volume of video and motion capture method works even if UFOs are passing by in thin little slices of time, from 1/30th to 1/3rd of a second. The volume game works for daytime UFO hunting, but hunting for UFOs at night is a game which requires different tactics. At night, UFOs can and do slow down, and have been known to hover. Techniques to capture UFOs at night on video and as pictures will be discussed in the chapter on nighttime UFO hunting techniques.

Now, time for a little digression on what is the meaning of near infrared and deep infrared. People tend to get these two areas of the infrared spectrum mixed up. Deep infrared equipment can record heat, and will show objects at night, lit up with their own heat. Deep infrared gear is very expensive, and cost wise is not within the reach of the average hobbyist in the search for UFOs.

Near infrared equipment discussed in this book does not see heat. The near infrared passing filters are black in color, and do not pass a lot of light. Near infrared equipment is only really useful for daytime hunting of UFOs, unless you want to lug around a near infrared spotlight. Pointing a near infrared spotlight at a UFO in the sky might not be wise. I tend to lean towards the camp that captures UFOs on film and video without shining a bright spotlight on the alien craft. But be my guest if you want to do some near infrared UFO spotting at night with a 1,000,000 candles of near infrared illumination. However, you have to keep in mind, when you go from quietly recording UFOs with no lighting system at night to a lighting system pointed at a UFO in the air you may find yourself going from recording an event to becoming an event, such as an adductee / contactee. Which brings us to an aside on Sony recording gear, which is very good equipment for near infrared UFO spotting.

Back in 1998, Sony pulled "Nightshot" video camcorders off the market because these camcorders could often see through clothing in daytime conditions when set on Nightshot mode. Nightshot mode works by moving the near IR blocking filter from the path of light going to the CCD sensor in the camcorder, allowing full near IR light to hit the CCD sensor. As it stands, many Sony video cameras are better at seeing near infrared light due to the SuperHad CCD technology which is put into Sony camcorders.

However, times have changed since that era. Sony camcorders today are not supposed to be able to do that Nightshot mode in daylight trick now. After 1998, Sony disabled video features allowing full near infrared video recording during daytime (a sensor in the lense area disables Nightshot during daytime). But when some of these camcorders before the 1998 era are used during daylight with Nightshot mode on, often people have noted UFOs travelling across the sky in near infrared recordings. One company has gone into the business of converting modern Sony camcorders into day time "night shot mode" enabling camcorders. This company can be found at: **http://www.maxmax.com/**

---

3   Various authors, **<u>Canon EOS T1i Manual</u>**, Page 115

Using a video camcorder is good choice. But, cheaper methods, which cost around one hundred dollars, will deliver you a near infrared field tool for viewing UFOs that allows motion sensing of UFOs when recording. The cheaper choice, one that delivers concise video of UFOs flying by, is to convert a web-cam to a near IR web-cam. And this conversion of a web-cam to a near IR web-cam is within the skills of a person like you!

Tool List to Convert a Web-cam to a Near Infrared Web-cam

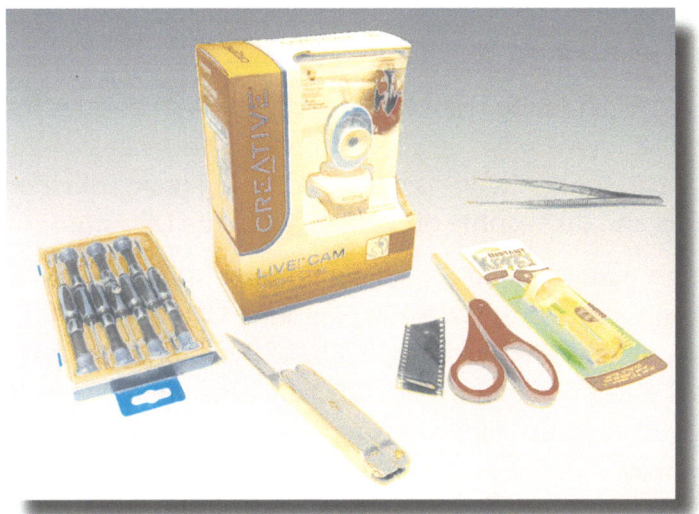

It is easy to equip yourself for the near infrared web-cam UFO hunt. The best tool to start with is your eyes. With respect to equipment (**see equipment list photo to left**), the list is short and does not take long to collect. Equipment needs are broken down into the following list (note the author has no relationship with the software makers listed below):

• A CCD web-cam (do not use a CMOS based web-cam).

• A laptop that runs on Windows XP, Windows Vista, or Windows 7 is a primary piece of equipment.

• The author used a CCD based Creative Live! CAM Video IM (VF0350) web-cam for this book. The web-cam was obtained at Walmart for less than forty dollars U.S. This web-cam was then converted to a near infrared web-cam (**instructions to convert the web-cam to near IR shown later in this chapter**).

• Free QE Super-resolution software or other astronomy image stacking software, such as Registack. Stacking and super-resolution are explained later in this book. For ease of use, QE Super-resolution is the recommended software to use. This program will improve images taken on a CCD web-cam immensely, and is found at: **http:// download.cnet.com/QE-SuperResolution/3000-2169_4-10392416.html**

• IRIS – Free astronomy software to enhance pictures, downloaded from: **http://www.astrosurf.com/buil/us/iris/iris.htm**

• GIMP, a free photo program which works like Photoshop, and is more ideal for enhancing stealthed UFOs. Download GIMP at: **http://www.gimp.org/windows/**

• HandyAvi – commercial meteor motion detection software capable of recording lightning bolts, meteors, and UFOs. This software can be found at: **http://www.azcendant.com/**

• Old film negatives (used to make near-IR web-cam filters, explained later in the chapter). 35 mm film exposed, then processed, can also be used.

- Crazy Glue

- Tweezers

- Sharp Scissors

- screwdrivers (**see set of screwdrivers, previous page and close up of Phillips screwdriver below**).

In the next section, we will break down the steps in making a near infrared web-cam.

Out of the list above, HandyAvi is a great tool for UFO hunting. HandyAvi is the only item besides the web-cam that will cost you more than thirty dollars. HandyAvi will save you uncounted hours of looking through video for fast UFO fly by events. You want to use HandyAvi, as looking through reams of video can be tedious and takes some of the fun out of the UFO hunt.

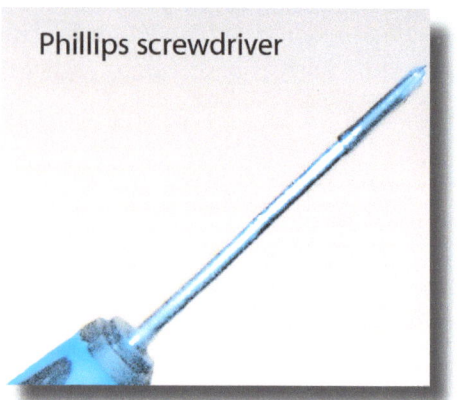

Phillips screwdriver

After testing many motion detection software suites, HandyAvi came out on top as the clear winner in capturing UFO events. Note that HandyAvi is not perfect with respect to UFO capture. HandyAvi captures birds and bugs along with UFOs. These items have to be removed from video clips captured by the motion sensing software. However, in the end, finding UFOs flying by is far easier using HandyAvi, especially during sunny, cloudless days.

The other item on the list that will cost you money is the web-cam. The web-cam used for this book was a Creative Labs Inc. Web-cam "IM", Model VFO540. This web-cam was bought for thirty dollars U.S. at a local Walmart. The Creative Labs Web-cam IM takes about two hours to convert to a near-IR web-cam if you follow the steps outlined in this book. Software which comes with the Creative Web-cam IM is also a good choice for UFO spotting purposes.

An older model, Creative Labs Inc. web-cam "Chat" (Model VFO330) can also be used, but the casing of this older web-cam requires the use of a knife to split open the web-cam case. The newer Creative Labs IM, features a web-cam casing that has screws in the casing, which makes the process easier to change the web-cam to near infrared. This book will describe the method to convert the newer Creative Labs Inc. Web-cam "IM" (Model VFO540) to near infrared use (**see next section**).

With respect to UFO hunting, note that web-cams should have a true CCD based VGA (**video graphics array**) sensor inside. CCD VGA sensors are much more reactive to near-infrared light than CMOS chip based web-cams. The box that the web-cam comes in should state that it is a true VGA sensor. CCD sensors are one of the keys to UFO hunting. In fact, 80 percent of the light spectrum, both visible and non visible to the human eye, is seen using a CCD based web-cam or camera. CCD chips are more tuned to near infrared light than CMOS based sensors.

How to Convert a Web-cam to a Near-Infrared Web-cam

True VGA web-cams, such as the Creative Web-cam model, are almost ideal for UFO spotting. Web-cams use a barrel lens which is easy to remove and can be adjusted for focus on distant objects. It is an easy matter to remove the near IR blocking filters on these barrel lenses to replace the near infrared blocking filter with a near IR passing filter. Near IR filters allow infrared light to pass through them, and near infrared light is the spectral light needed for UFO hunting. These near IR filters can often be very costly. To buy a near infrared glass filter can cost as much as three hundred dollars. What is a surprise is that a very economical, yet excellent form of near infrared passing filter exists that can be used instead of costly glass near infrared filters. The black ends of film negatives, make first-class near infrared passing filters, seeing a deeper near infrared, around 830 nanometres and above into the near infrared spectrum. Earlier, we described the near infrared spectrum, however below is a more detailed explanation.

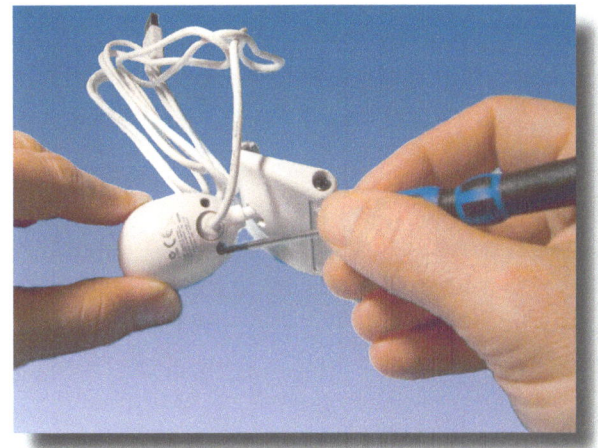

A typical human eye will respond to wavelengths from about 380 to 750 nanometers.[4] A nanometer is one billionth of a meter (a meter is just over a yard in the English system). Near infrared, which is "next door" to the visible light spectrum and beyond the red end of the visible light spectrum, ranges from 750 to 1200 nanometres, a range of light invisible to the human eye. Near infrared wavelengths are an ideal area of the spectrum where UFOs can be seen, especially around 830 nanometers and above. To achieve a distinct visual viewpoint in near-infrared, a web-cam needs to be first converted to near infrared viewing.

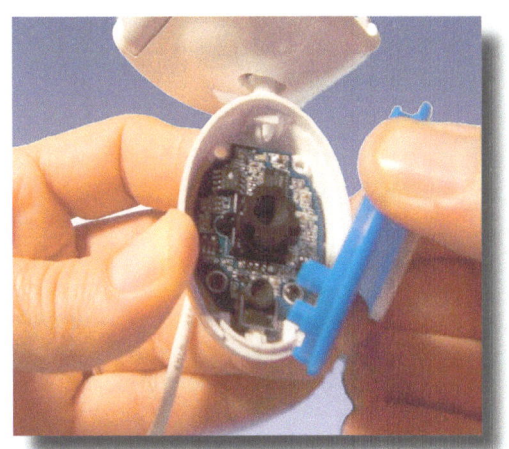

The following is a series of steps needed to convert a CCD Creative Web cam IM into a near-infrared UFO spotting tool. Remove the Creative Web-cam IM from the product package, look at the back of the Creative Web-cam IM, and you will note two fine small screws at the back of the web-cam. These screws require a fine Phillips head screwdriver to remove them (**see top figure left**). Fine screwdriver sets can be found at your local hardware store.

After removing the Phillips fine head screws, pry open the casing of the web-cam (**see left**). We can see the blue casing being pried off in the figure to the left. Open the case by prying with your fingers, to expose the black barrel lens which is screwed on above the CCD chip element.

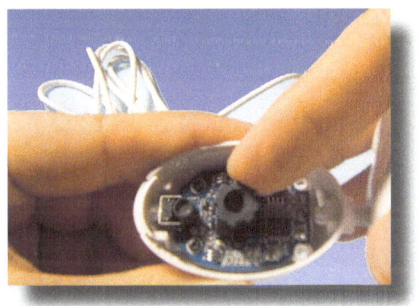

Note the barrel lens (**see left**). The finger is on the barrel objective lens in the picture. Unscrew the barrel lens counter clockwise and flip the bottom of the barrel lens upwards when the barrel lens is removed (the side facing the circuit board of the web-cam is the bottom of the barrel lens). You should now be able to now see a square, reddish purple plate of thin glass on the back of the barrel

---

4   Various authors, **Whole Spectrum**, Found at: http://en.wikipedia.org/wiki/File:Atmospheric_electromagnetic_opacity.svg

object lens you have just removed. This thin plate of glass blocks out near infrared light (this is the near infrared blocking filter) from reaching the CCD sensor chip.

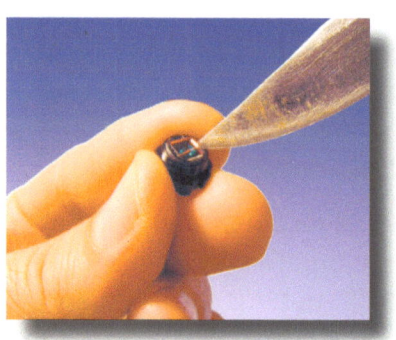

We want to see near-infrared light with the web-cam. So remove this thin square plate of glass (**see left**). Pry off the thin piece of glass with a sharpie or use a sharp knife. Set the near-infrared blocking filter aside in case you decide to convert the web-cam back to regular use later. Store the blocking near infrared filter in a plastic bag to keep off dust, or discard it.

With the barrel lens and glass near-infrared blocking filter off, we need to obtain a near infrared passing filter. In case you do not have the black ends of old developed photo negatives to use for near IR passing filters, then do the following.

Expose a photo negative canister to direct sunlight. Take the undeveloped 35 mm film and pull the undeveloped film out of the plastic canister. Use your fingers. Grab the edges of the unexposed negative with your fingers to pry it out of the canister so finger oils do not smear on the unexposed film negative surface. Place the film in a dust free area where it is exposed to the sun for twenty minutes to expose the 35 mm film fully. Again, be careful to keep dust, grit or naturals oils from your fingers off the film by holding the film on the edges of the film, not on the flat surface part of the exposed roll of film.

Roll up the now exposed photo film. You may wish to use the container the film came in to store the exposed film when you transport it to be processed. Now take the exposed film to your local Walmart or film processing center, and ask the technicians to process the film. The film technician may give you a few strange looks, but you may wish to tell them you are into near infrared photography, and that this is a cheap way to get a near infrared filter for near infrared photography purposes. Typically, a near infrared filter of this grade can cost up to three hundred dollars, so yes, a near infrared filter made out of two dollars U.S. worth of 35 mm film, is an economical alternative.

Now you have the processed exposed negatives which make excellent near infrared passing filters which you can size for the back of the barrel lens of the web-cam (**see right figure**).

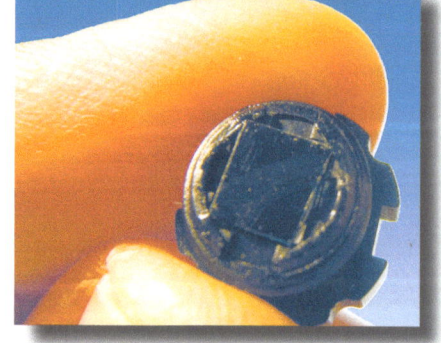

Cut two squares from the black exposed film negative that are approximately the same size and shape as the glass near-infrared blocking filter you have just removed from the web-cam. Use tweezers to lift up the squares and handle them so that you avoid marring the filters with finger oils. You can also handle the exposed photograph negatives with dustless neoprene gloves while handling the film to prevent marring of the filters. Neoprene gloves can be found in the paint section of a hardware store and are non-allergenic.

Again, one method to size the near-infrared passing filters correctly for the back of the barrel lens is to take the IR glass blocking filter that was originally in the web-cam, and use this glass filter as a template guide to cut two squares of exposed photo negatives that are the right size and shape. You could use a sharpie knife or sharp scissors to cut the film negative squares. As a practice run before gluing, carefully place each of the two filters in the place where the infrared blocking filter

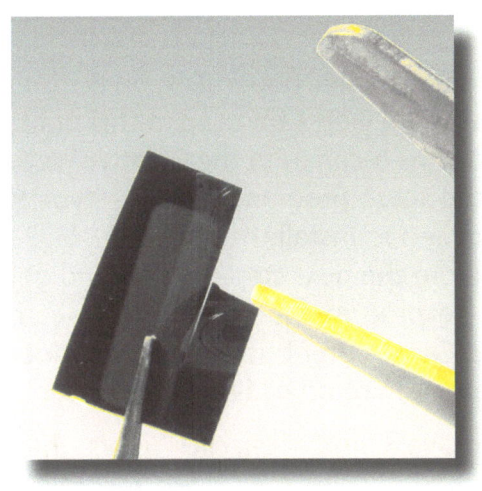

used to be, trimming the filters as necessary to make an exact fit (**see trimming process left**).

Now carefully use tweezers (the filters are delicate) to hold the edge tips of these near IR passing filters, again in order not to smear or mark the filters with either finger oils or imprints from pressure from the tweezers. Imprints will show up in web-cam pictures, so gently handle the film negatives with tweezers.

For each black photo negative near-infrared passing filter, pour a very tiny pool of Crazy Glue on the cap of the container for storing the Crazy Glue. The pool should be no wider than the letter "t". Carefully dip two opposing edge tips of each filter square quickly into the Crazy Glue and place the filter in the spot that was formerly occupied by the glass plate infrared blocking filter. You only need a minute amount of glue on each filter to make this work. Less is more in this case.

Wait one hour before placing the second exposed black film negative filter into the barrel lens on top of the first negative in order to avoid glue smearing and the possibility of glue vapor re-depositing on the web-cam lens. Repeat the gluing procedure above. Wait two hours after the second near-infrared passing filter is installed to make sure the glue is dry. Reinstall the barrel lens back onto the web-cam. Failure to wait sufficient time before reinstallation of the barrel lens can result in a glue vapor problem outlined below (this happened to the author).

If you do not wait for the glue to dry, what potentially happens is glue vapor from the glue can form a blurry film on the glass lens that is under the glued-in black negatives now installed on the barrel lens. To avoid this problem, it is best to wait a few hours before reinstalling the barrel lens back onto the web-cam to make sure that the glue is hard and dry.

If you do not wait, you will get a blurry image on the video even after tuning the barrel lens for focus, whereby glue vapour forms a blurry film on the inner barrel lens. To fix this problem: remove the barrel lens, and then remove the recently installed near infrared passing filters. Then you need to remove the blurry filmy coating on the glass lens of the barrel lens using acetone cleaner. Note that acetone is found at hardware stores in the paint section. You can then clean the lens by using very tiny amounts of acetone on a lens cloth to remove the glue deposit off the lens. Use a gentle circular motion to clean the barrel lens. This process may have to be repeated a few times to rid the lens of glue. Finally, look at the lens side on, under a strong light to see if any glue or dirt is present after cleaning. If there is still a milky film on the lense, more cleaning will be needed.

You can then cut new exposed and processed film negative filters, repeat the gluing of filters to the barrel lens, and reinstall the barrel lens, with the filters added only after waiting a suitable time for the glue to dry. You are now ready to set up the software.

Software Setup for Web-cams

Software setup for your web-cam, will not be the same for each web-cam, depending on the one you end up using as a near infrared web-cam. For the Creative IM web-cam used in this book, the following short steps cover the set up of software for this brand of web-cam. Put the Creative Web-cam IM installation CD into your laptop CD/DVD player and run the setup program. Choose "typical installation" within the Creative Web-cam setup wizard. Then proceed to install the software. Make sure that the Creative Web-cam IM is plugged into a USB port before the next step. You should get a warning screen from the Creative Web-cam IM setup asking to plug in the Creative Web-cam IM. After software setup, you should be able to click on the Live! Cam Center button located under Windows XP/Vista in the following spot: "**Start; all Programs; Creative; Creative Live! Cam Center**"

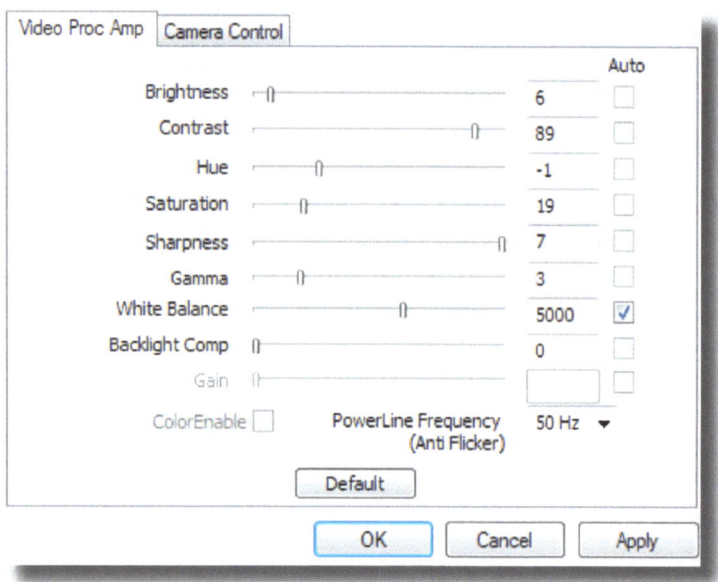

In the Live! Cam Center, click "Tools", then settings and choose the "video recording" tab at the top. Click on the option for file format and make sure it is on "wmv format" or "AVI format". Under the box "WMV Options", choose to save at a higher file size. Click "OK" to get out of that screen. Click on the main tab "Video Recording" to see if your web-cam starts up. Then, select "My Settings" on the Live Central button console and make the following changes to the web-cam manual settings to set the near infrared web-cam for ideal near IR daylight viewing of UFOs (**see left**). Setting the web-cam in this manner allows for a sharp picture, with high contrast. Set the auto balance for outside or outdoors (**see bottom figure, next page**).

An Automatic Way to Capture UFOs on Video

By using the right motion detection software, the web-cam will only record when motion is detected. Using motion detection means you do not have to sit through days worth of video just to capture a fast event of a UFO passing by the web-cam. The other upside is you do not fill up your laptop with endless reams of video shots. Paying for motion detection software that is capable of catching a UFO passing by the web-cam is a worthwhile investment.

The majority of the motion detection software on the market is far too slow to capture UFOs. As mentioned, the best piece of software for the task is a software called HandyAvi. HandyAvi is designed for high speed motion capture for meteors and works equally well for motion capturing UFOs in video. For UFO video capture, HandyAvi is the clear winner. This software, when installed and working with your web-cam, can capture an in flight UFO, lightning bolt or a meteor passing through the air.

You can download this software from: **http://www.azcendant.com/**

When you purchase this software for $35.95 (U.S.), you get a very capable piece of software that is ideal for UFO hunting in clear, cloudless skies. You can install the software from the internet site provided above. After downloading and installing the software, click on the option for "Capture", then click on "Meteor Trail Images", followed by clicking on the "Video Format", which is seen on the upper left hand side of the "Meteor Trail Capture and Detect" screen. Click on this button.

A screen will open called "Properties". On this screen, you set the frame rate box to 30 frames a second, and the resolution of the picture to "640 by 480" pixels (**see right**). You can also set the Creative web-cam to record at a frame rate of 15 frames a second (a rate Windows Vista will allow) with the Creative web-cam recording at a size of 800 by 600 pixels. The recording rate against picture size is a toss up between better pictures at the front end for less recorded UFOs passing by per unit of time, versus higher volume of footage recorded when UFOs fly by the web-cam recording at 30 frames a second (at lower picture quality).

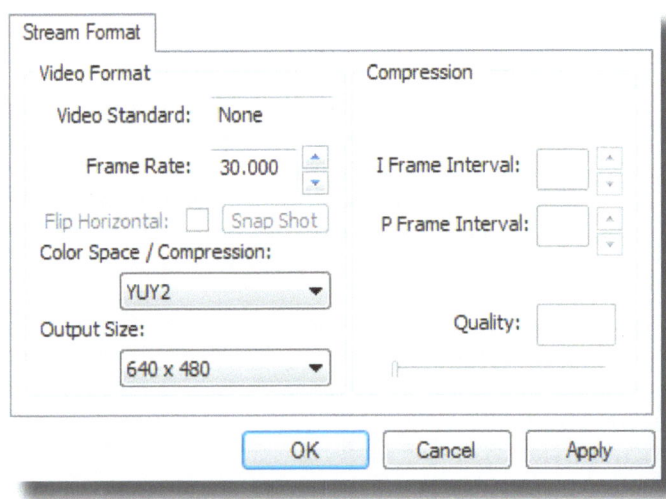

Set the web-cam for outdoors (**see right**) mode in HandyAvi (if this has not been set already as discussed previously inside the web-cam software). Setting the web-cam to outside mode prevents light values going up and down in the video recording. If the webcam is **not** set for outside, the picture light levels will tend to go up and down in strong sunlight. The recorded picture will tend to flare white periodically. This will make it hard to observe UFOs. So it is important to set your video web-cam mode on outdoor light levels, and this problem will not occur.

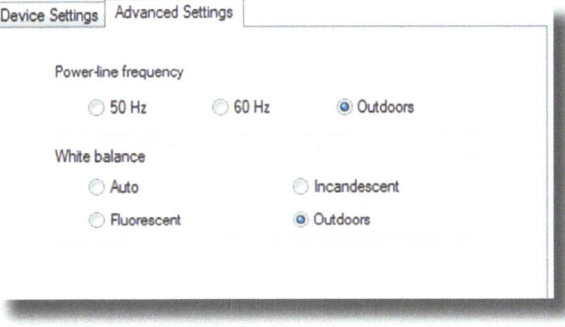

Set the pre-frame and post-frame rates on the meteor capture screen according to the settings shown in the figure (**see next page**). These settings will capture a UFO in video during sunny days. Set the sensitivity to 77 or greater during cloudless days. On cloudy days, the setting should be in a range of 30 to 55 to prevent motion capture of clouds rather than UFOs with HandyAvi. On days with clouds, keep adjusting the sensitivity setting downward until the motion sensing software is not set off by cloud movement. UFO capture will tend not to occur very often during cloudy days in any case.

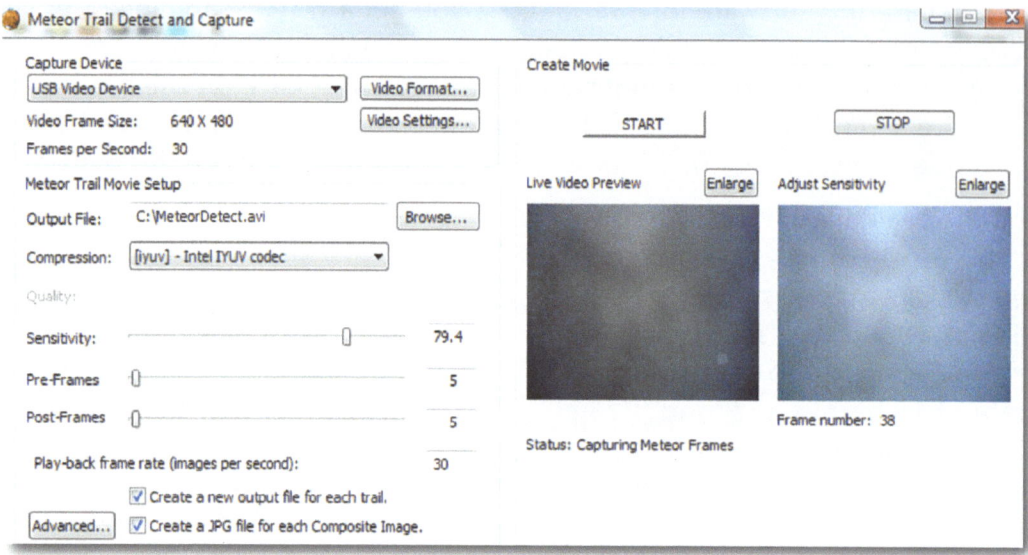

Scanning for UFO Motion in Previously Existing Video

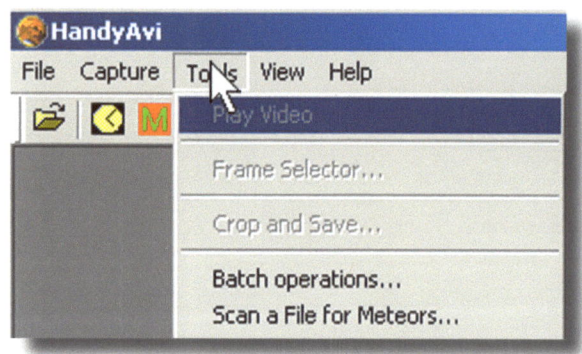

A great feature of HandyAvi motion detection software is it can be run on pre-existing video to find UFOs. Go back to the main screen and click "Tools" on the upper palette menu. Under "Tools", you will find "Scan a File for Meteors" (**see left**).

Click on that menu item and a screen will open up that is like the "Meteor Trail Detect and Capture" screen seen before in the previous section. The change in this screen is that there now is an option to input an AVI movie file, under "Scan AVI for Meteors".

Note that the movie file must be an AVI format that is converted from "Windows Movie Maker". Windows Movie Maker is found under "Program Accessories" in Windows XP, and Movie Maker is found under "Programs" in Windows Vista. In the section on processing, we will explain how to convert movies into proper DV-AVI (NTSC) format, a format which allows you to both input movies into HandyAvi to check UFOs, and also to input movies for improved detail using "QE Super-resolution".

Click "Open" the AVI Movie. Click on a check box at the bottom of the screen "Create a New Output File for Each Trail" and "Create a Jpeg for Each Composite Image". "Trail" normally refers to "meteor trails", but in this context it works equally well to map out trails of UFOs crossing the sky. The composite picture (**see right**) shows how many UFOs and their flight tracks were found in one 10 minute video file. Wow! In the next section, a manual tuning method to focus the web-cam will be discussed.

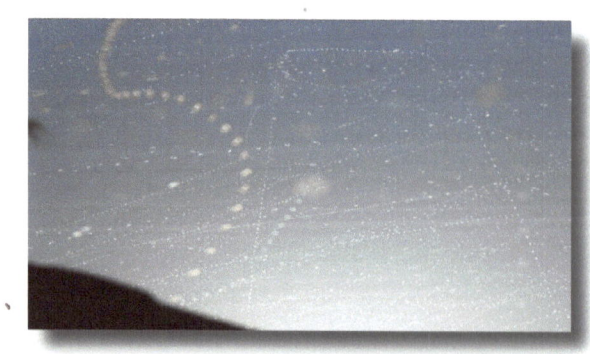

Tuning Your Web-cam Optics for Ultimate Clarity

You have set up your web-cam for near-infrared and are waiting like a kid to start viewing UFOs. However, the image is quite blurry and unfocused. This is because you have not yet spent the time to achieve careful focus of the web-cam eye for distance. How do you get the best focus for distance out of a web-cam? After all, what is wanted is a very clear and detailed picture of UFOs. The answer to this question is found in a web-cam focusing trick: tune the web-cam at night to the most distant streetlight that is seen with the web-cam (**see left image, initially unfocused web-cam image on street lights**). After the sun sets and the street lights turn on, focus the web-cam on a distant streetlight until the light coming from the streetlight looks square (**see focused web-cam lower left**). Yes, square. Web-cam CCD light sensing chips are square in shape. A distant point source of light, such as a streetlight, should appear square if the web-cam is tuned to an exact focus. The person tuning the web-cam image against a distant streetlight will get a square light coming from the streetlight with just about no "blur" coming off the square edges of the web-cam image. The figure on the next page shows how a tuned web-cam on a streetlight looks one third of a mile down the road.

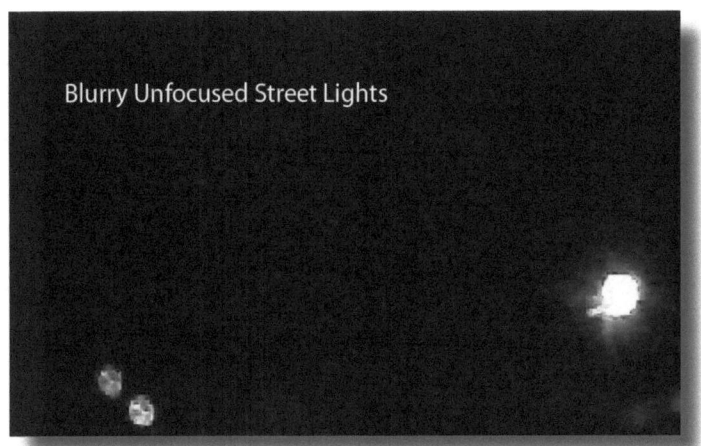

Blurry Unfocused Street Lights

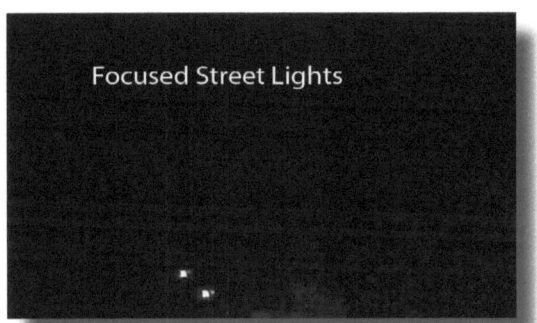

Focused Street Lights

Compare the badly tuned image of the streetlight from the previous page, against the tuned image in the focused street light figure. The tuned web-cam has streetlights that appear square. If you do this trick, you will have a perfectly focused web-cam for distance.

UFO Camouflage

You will get used to the fact that a UFO will appear blurry when captured on video despite very careful focusing of the web-cam. The problem with focus is not the web-cam focus if you follow the procedures in the previous section. A UFO will be seen as blurry in the air by design. This is something you have to get used to as a UFO videographer. This section and the next section will explain why UFOs are blurry, and why they will always appear unfocused when first captured in video or as photographs.

UFO craft have the capability of emitting light in sequences of red, blue and green. The UFO rotates between red, blue and green light rapidly in a sequence, which forms a white colored light. It is this white light that mixes into the background blue sky, which makes the craft disappear when seen from a distance.

This is not a new idea (even if used by UFOs). In the 1850s, James Maxwell proved white colour is a mixture of colours by showing how light from blue, green and red filtered lanterns converge

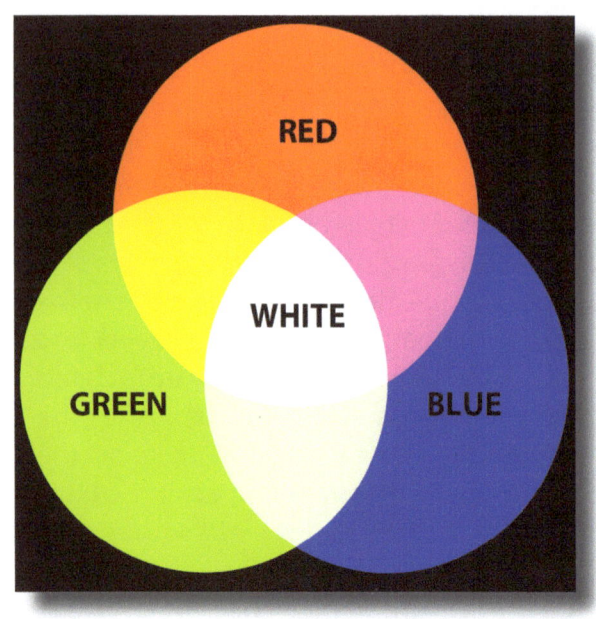

on a screen to form white. Dimming or brightening individual lanterns re-created all the colours of the spectrum, while an equal mixture of the three primary colors formed a patch of white (**see left**).[5] The next section explains this concept in detail with regard to UFOs.

A Christmas Tree

The purpose of emitting light as red, green and blue (across the surface of the UFO) is to make it hard to spot a UFO against clear sky. I will explain this concept by way of an analogy. What if a Christmas tree were erected, and back dropped by the skyline. This Christmas tree is lit up by several red, green and blue bulbs. The bulbs on this Christmas tree are very bright bulbs, and emit a strong light which is about the same intensity of color in each respective primary color.

If an observer were to look at the Christmas tree standing at the skyline against a blue sky backdrop and if the observer were far enough away from the Christmas tree, then in daylight the individual green, blue and red light bulbs would tend to mix together and form a blurry white color at a distance. The Christmas tree bulbs would form a white color from a mixture of colors, much like the color wheel in the figure (**see above, red, green, blue circle diagram**). It is the white light against a blue sky background that makes the Christmas tree disappear against the sky.

UFOs use a lighting system that acts as a form of 3-D television screen to achieve the same effect of emitting green, blue and red light. When UFOs want to vanish, the UFO will emit red, green and blue lights that mix together to form white light. With a blue sky background, the UFO will disappear from our sight.

Another form of stealth UFOs deploy, is a kind of contour like series of etched surfaces on these craft. These etched surfaces tend to make light reflect away from the craft in a dispersive pattern rather than reflect back to the eyes of the person seeing the UFO. That sounds complicated. But the effect it achieves is not difficult to visualize. Think of how a bathroom window looks after a shower, with a foggy film of water droplets on the window. That is a dispersive light coating on the window, i.e. the water droplets disperse light randomly. The etchings on the UFO surface, otherwise known as optical gratings, achieves the same effect as a foggy window. So people looking at UFOs always see them as blurry.

The optical grating surfaces reflect light away from the UFO in almost random directions which tends to make the UFO blurry in the air even when the active lighting system is turned off. The optical gratings have lights, or light elements called pixels, of green, blue and red which are intermixed with these etched surfaces or which show as colored lights emitted from these surfaces. It is these red, green and blue lights that mix to form white light at a distance. When these lights are turned on, they

---

5   Langford, Michael, and Bilissi, Efthimia, **Langford's Advanced Photography**, Pages 69 and 70

emit or flicker at a certain rate between red, green and blue light. The other aspect of the lights is they can act like television pixels on the surface of the craft. These red, green and blue lights will emit colors in red, green and blue that form 3-D pictures. This forms a further layer of stealth for the craft, but is also used to communicate with other UFOs using alien symbols mixed with flight path data (**this flight data is seen later in the book**).

For example, the picture (**see top of next page**) is of a UFO, captured on February 12, 2010, at 4:49 p.m. Here the UFO shows etched contour-like surfaces with light elements (pixels) buried into the surfaces of the etchings. Light elements, or pixels, are part of each surface, and emit colors in red, green and blue.

> **Definition: A pixel (from the word pix, for picture, and element) is the smallest element on a video display screen. A screen contains thousands of pixels, each of which can be made up of one or more dots or a cluster of dots. On color screens, three dot colors are included in each pixel-red, green, and blue.**

However, the UFO in this case is only emitting solid red (for the outer UFO surface) and blue (in the window part of the UFO). The background wall inside the window is also an etched surface. This window background etched surface also reflects incoming sunlight in random directions.

UFOs can project red, green and blue symbols on the window portion of the UFO, i.e. the window pane operates as a HUD on the craft, completing the almost perfect optical stealth of the craft when the craft is viewed at a distance. Variations on this theme also see UFOs actively projecting holograms

> **Definition: A head-up display (HUD) is any transparent display that presents data without requiring the user to look away from his or her usual viewpoint. These systems are used on modern jet fighters, such as an F-18, and also apparently UFOs, to project flight data in front of the pilots eyes.**

which project primary colors (red, green and blue) as an analglyph hologram (discussed and shown later in this book) and as holograms that project flight path data around the entire UFO craft. There are several variations on a theme here with respect to stealth technology, but the central scientific idea is the same: UFOs, no matter the technique of camouflage used, deploy red, green and blue light in a mixture forming white light to optically hide the craft against a blue sky.

I used GIMP software to cut the green color from the picture for clarity. By removing the green color from the picture it prevents the red, blue and green colors in the picture from mixing to form white light. A pilot, if present in the window portion (it is hard to tell in this particular picture), will wear a suit which has shaped dispersive elements In the suit that matches, somewhat, the etchings of the background wall inside the window. The suit the pilot wears will also emit green, red and blue lights, allowing the pilot to blend into the overall UFO craft camouflage.

In the next section, you will begin using software to help you increase the clarity of UFO images extracted from video.

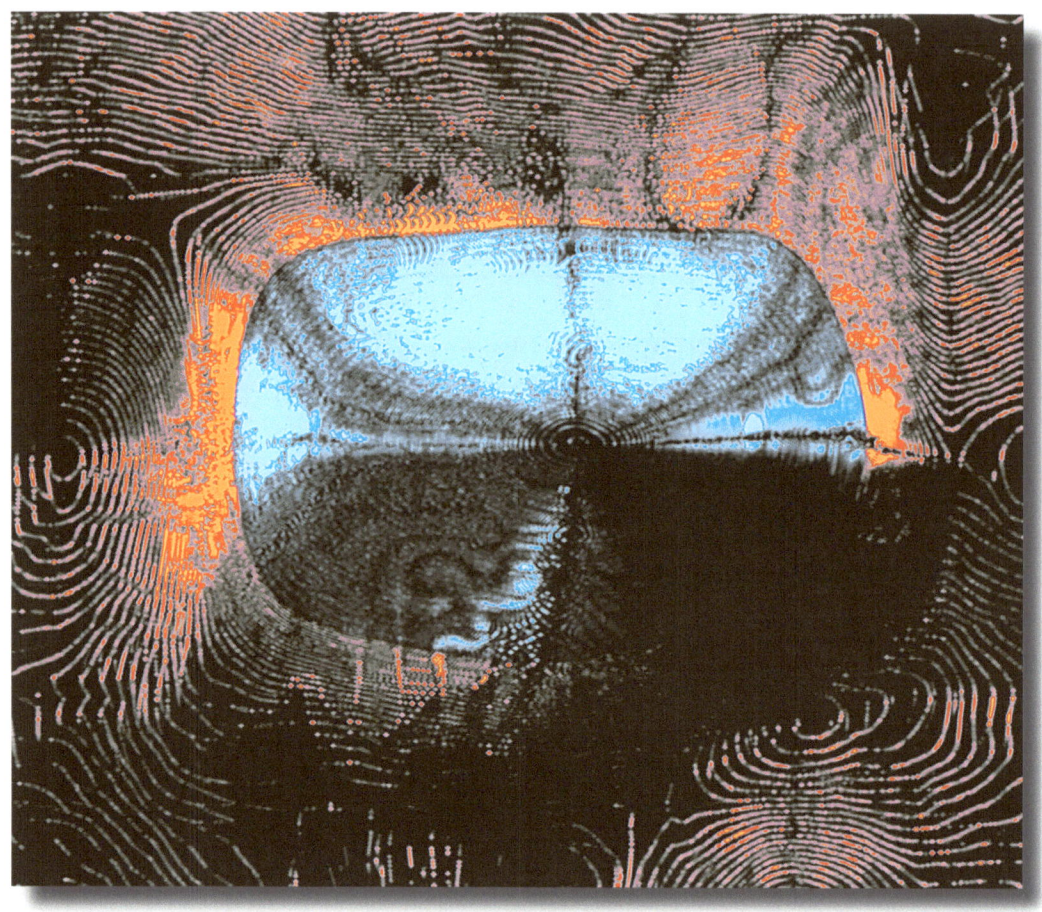

Beginning Steps to UFO Image Processing

UFO processing starts with the "Windows Movie Maker Program" which takes the raw footage recorded in Windows Movie Maker format (WMV) filmed by your near-infrared Creative Web-cam. Next, open up Windows Movie Maker, which is found under Windows XP desktop under "Start; All Programs; Accessories". In Windows Vista, Windows Movie Maker is found under "Start; All Programs". Click on the Windows Movie Maker icon and open up the program (**see right**).

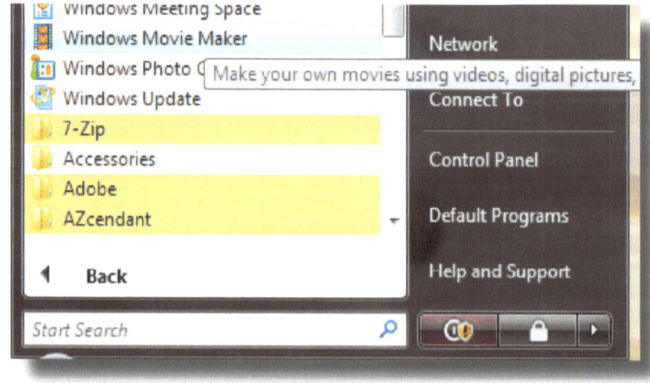

The motion capture software, HandyAvi, was used in conjunction with the web-cam to capture UFOs on video. Because HandyAvi is very efficient at the task of capturing UFOs on video, the video clip WMV file has been reduced down to the exact length of the UFO flying by the web-cam. The WMV file now has to be changed to an AVI file as preparation for later input into another program, QE

Superresolution. Windows Movie Maker, which comes with Windows Vista and Windows XP base operating systems, is ideal to change a WMV file to an AVI file. The AVI format produced by HandyAvi is not suitable for QE Superresolution, so this extra step is needed.

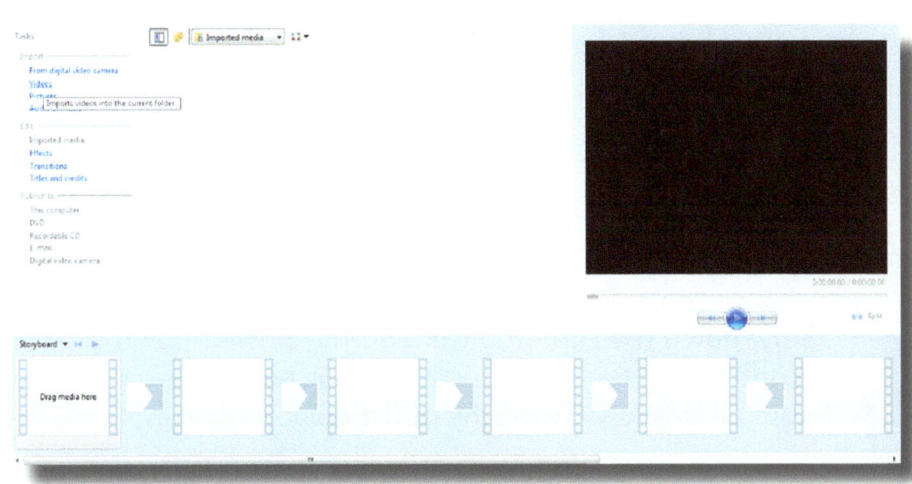

The version of Windows Movie Maker we use is the one installed by default in Windows Vista. First, you have to locate the video clip that has been recorded by your web-cam (**see left**). In the case of using a Creative IM web-cam, the Creative web-cam will default to record videos by date, for example, hover your mouse pointer over the lower left Windows symbol on the bar at the bottom of the Windows desktop. This symbol is the "Start" button. Click on the right mouse button with the cursor over the start button, and choose "Explore" from the menu that pops up, then browse to, and look for, the date you recorded the video in the directory. HandyAvi defaults to store the video files in the base "C:" drive. You can change this default to another video storage location. The next step is to import the video into Windows Movie Maker by clicking the "Video" function located in the left pane window in Windows Movie Maker, and then navigating to your video, open the video file (**see right**) in Windows Movie Maker.

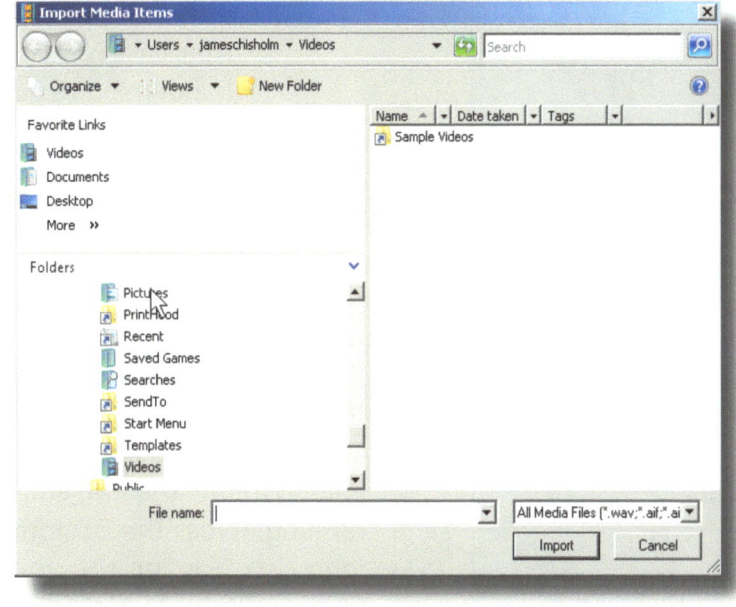

Next click on the video that is imported into Windows Movie Maker. Drag the Windows Movie Maker "Monitor" vertical drag bar (this bar divides the left and right halves of the video screen window and the window where input video files are stored as a window in Windows Movie Maker) to the left to expand the screen, i.e. expand the image to 800 by 600 pixel size.

Now drag your imported video clip down to the lower left hand film strip labeled "Drag media here". You can now edit your video (**see top figure next page**). If you have not used HandyAvi, you will likely have recorded a lot of empty video along with UFO events. To isolate the UFO events, play your movie in the Monitor screen by using the "play button" controls found below the movie monitor screen of Windows Movie Maker (**see left figure, play button surrounded by grey box**). Go to the first point

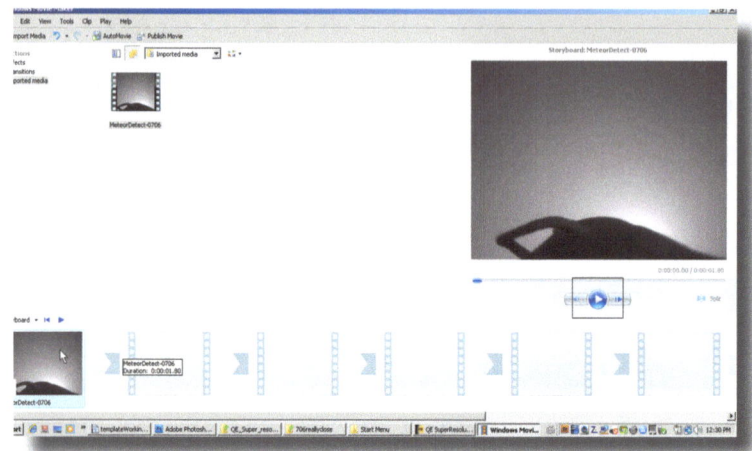

where you started to record the UFO, and use the "split" button to cut and edit the film to just before the UFO enters the frame.

If the UFO is too fast to be seen clearly (this is likely), then slow down the clip by adding a slow down effect. To add a slow down effect, right click on the movie clip within the film strip, pick "effects" from the pop up menu (**see lower left**), and within effects, scroll down to the selection called "Slow Down, Half", and click the "Add" button 3 to 5 times to slow down the clip. You can edit the slowed down clip for length using the "split" function, as you now have a clip where you can clearly see what the UFO is doing in slow motion.

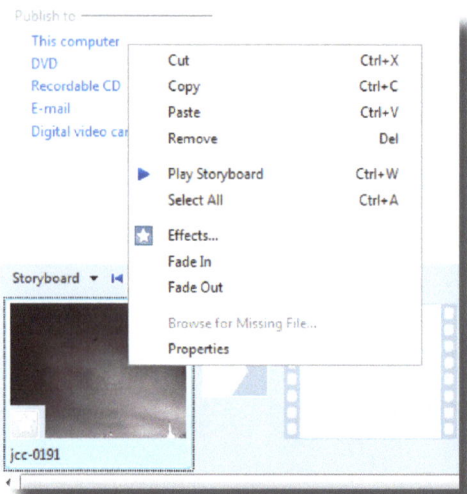

You should now have a chunk of film starting with your UFO entering the frame. Play the clip until the UFO leaves the frame. Use the "split" function again to isolate the UFO part of your movie from the rest of the non-UFO containing video.

If you are using HandyAvi motion capture software, the usual case is that you will have only the UFO fly over itself. You do not need to go through the process outlined in cutting and editing the video for length. Which is neat, and saves time!

As mentioned previously, another option with Windows Movie Maker is to take a clip of the film, and convert that clip of film into something which can be used by a software program that can further increase the quality of an extracted picture. A program that offers the option of increasing picture detail using the extracted UFO film clip is called QE Superresolution. Before you can use QE Superresolution, you must convert the movie into an AVI picture format that is suitable for input into QE Superresolution. Using Windows Movie Maker, we can go back to the UFO picture clip, make sure the clip is in the editing frame (the film editing frame looks like a group of film negatives running across the bottom of the Windows Movie Maker frame). You then click "File" on the upper left hand side of Windows Movie Maker.

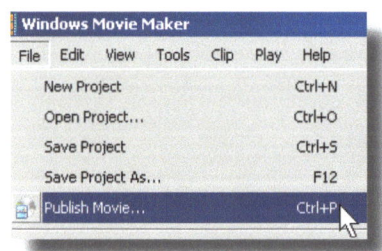

Choose "Publish Movie" (**see upper left figure**). Under "Publish Movie" choose the option titled "This Computer: Publish for Playback on this Computer" and click on the "Next" button. Now choose the destination directory you will save the movie to and click on the "Next" button again. Choose the radio button option "More Settings" and then choose the setting titled "DV-AVI (NTSC)" and yet again click on "Next" (**see previous

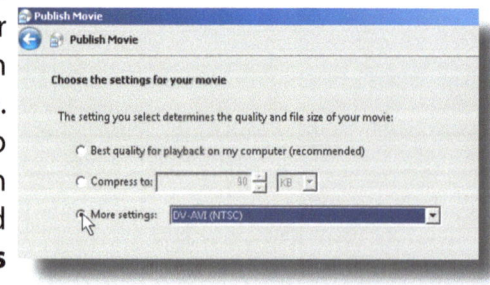

page bottom right figure). Then click "Publish". This will publish the video clip into a format which is suited for input into QE Super-resolution software. In QE Super-resolution, we can increase detail and clarity of pictures despite the blur that surrounds UFOs. But first, super-resolution itself should be discussed.

Super-resolution

Super-resolution is a technique to increase clearness and detail of an image using mathematical image averaging and composite techniques to process many images of a scene, into one main picture, for example, many video frames merged together to produce one picture of superior detail and clarity. The term "Super-resolution" first came into use around the 1990s in the astronomy field. Since then, this method has become one of the tricks used by amateur and career astronomers to increase detail and clearness of pictures taken of the sky.

The mathematical techniques in super-resolution actually originated from a historical technique, stacking, which was used by astronomers back in the days when actual photographs through telescopes were taken of the sky. Stacking is a method to increase detail on an image. The first image stacks were just that — photo negatives or slides stacked on top of each other. When these stacks were viewed on a light table, or printed, the result was a photo with much higher contrast and detail. Details that were not visible in any single original photo negative became easier to see when several negatives were stacked on top of each other. Super-resolution is basically the same thing as stacking, only super-resolution uses mathematical formulas to carry out a form of stacking inside computer software.

When the famous "Hubble Deep Field" photo was taken it captured more than 1,500 distant galaxies in a tiny patch of sky, $\frac{1}{30}^{th}$ the diameter of the full moon. The Deep Field project shot 342 images over 10 days and stacked 276 pictures to create one very detailed image. Of course, the Hubble team used computer graphic techniques to achieve stacking. But the basic idea is the same. Take many pictures and combine them to produce one picture for more detail and contrast. Overall, super-resolution is just a fancy buzz word for "stacking", when images are stacked using computer graphics math-based methods rather than photo plate negatives.

The idea here is that on the rare occasion when a UFO pauses for a microsecond during daytime, or when a UFO hovers at night, this allows a few frames of video to be stacked (super-resolution) to achieve a composite photograph with better detail and contrast. In the next section, I will explain how QE Super-resolution can be used to apply super-resolution to UFO video.

QE Super-resolution: Software for Super-resolution

QE Super-resolution is free software used to achieve super-resolution of a picture from a video clip. The software is easy to use and designed for the average photographer.

Along with QE Super-resolution software, there is other software that can do stacking, such as Registax. However, my experience has been that QE Superresolution, when applied to video and web-cam recordings, produces better super-resolution of resulting photographs than Registax. QE Superresolution can be downloaded in beta form from the Internet.

Try searching for QE Super-resolution in Google or at CNET, found at: **http://download.cnet.com/**

At the CNET site, under the search engine at the top of the screen, type in "QE Super-resolution 0.1.0.550". Choose this program at CNET online, and download QE Super-resolution.

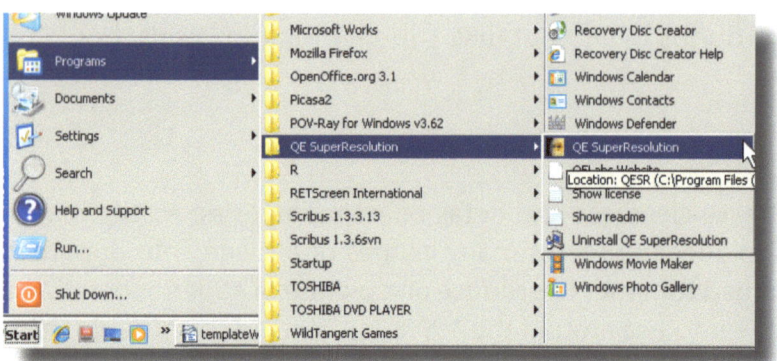

In Windows Vista or XP, click on the "Start" button on the lower left hand side of the Window screen, then click on "All Programs", then click on "QE Super-resolution". Open QE Superresolution here after installation in Windows Vista and Windows XP (**see left**).

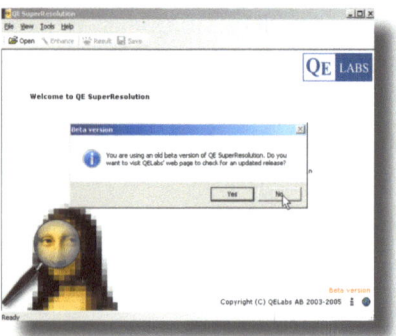

The program, every time you open it, will ask you if you wish to go to the home page for the QE Super-resolution developers (**see left**). Answer "No" and proceed onward. Click on "Open" which is located underneath "File" on the upper right hand side of the welcome screen. Now locate your movie that has been converted to AVI using Windows Movie Maker. Note that if the movie has not been made into AVI format using Windows Movie Maker, then QE Super-resolution may or may not be able to load the video. If you follow the steps of converting the movie into AVI format from whatever native format the movie was recorded in by using Windows Movie Maker (**using the method to convert files to AVI format that is outlined a few pages back**), you will then have an AVI video that is suitable for input into QE Super-resolution. Using QE Super-resolution, now select your movie that has been converted to proper AVI format. In QE Super-resolution, find the open file function under "Open" located underneath "File" in the function bar at the top of the QE Super-resolution window, and click on "Open" (**see lower right**). Find the movie you have just converted into AVI format and import the movie into QE Super-resolution. Open the video into QE Superresolution and now click on "Enhance" and choose the option for "Create Image for Printing, i.e. high resolution. Wait a minute or two for the software to work, and when the picture has been enhanced from the video, choose "File" on the upper toolbar and then choose "Save Enhanced Image" as a bitmap file. You now have a bitmapped image that has increased detail suitable for further image processing with GIMP, Paint Shop Pro and other image processing software such as IRIS.

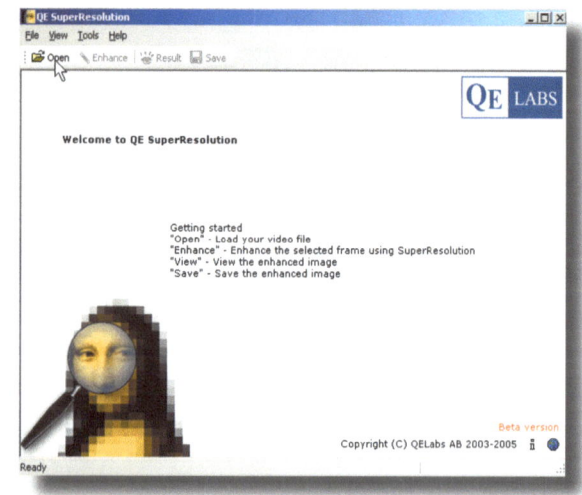

There is one program claimed to carry out and produce super-resolution on video streams rather than video super-resolved to photographs, but the program has not been tested by the author. This program, called "Deemon SuperResolution", is a super-resolution plugin for Adobe After Effects and Premier Pro, and the plugin is made by Dee Mon Software. This super-resolution plugin can be found at: **http://www.thedeemon.com/**.

Chapter 5: Timing and Equipment Position

As mentioned previously, UFO video hunting is best carried out during daylight hours when the skies are clear and there are no clouds. Depending on UFO activity, your results will vary so think of the following discussion on times, as general guidelines for UFO activity. During the evening, between the periods of 6:00 p.m. and 7:30 p.m., UFOs appear less frequently. However, UFOs become more active after this time of night. In the evening, UFOs move slowly in the air showing red, green and blue lights as rotating colors. On occasion, alien occupied UFOs will sometimes have a yellowish light mixed in with these other colors, while some UFOs themselves will hang still in the air, appearing as lights in the sky which emit green, blue and red lights. Some UFOs will move slowly across the sky, at roughly the speed that appears to emulate planes in appearance, but will often sport a blue light that is not seen on planes. Standard aviation lights are red and green, while plane landing lights appear as a glaring white light. Planes create a challenge in working out whether or not you are viewing a UFO or plane.[1]

During nighttime viewing, to figure out if you are seeing a UFO, is a process of removing the usual suspects from the list. The list normally consists of stars, airplane lights, planets, comets, meteors, etc. Only when these known suspects are removed, is there a case for a UFO being present. Nighttime UFO hunting will be discussed further in the chapter on night time UFO sightings.

Note that the author prefers the daytime hunt for UFOs over nighttime sightings. Daytime UFO hunting can reveal UFOs flying by at great speeds and these objects often can be clearly seen in video. At night, near infrared gear does not work well, providing only dim images of UFOs. Using near infrared gear with near infrared lights at night is not a suggested approach for UFO viewing as mentioned previously. Viewing a UFO with active near infrared lighting, i.e. a near infrared spotlight, may cause a UFO craft to change how these craft moves, or how it deploys stealth. The UFO may tend to avoid your area if you are seen using active near infrared light systems or as a potential scenario may abduct you.

How to Place and Point Near IR Web-cams out a Window

When UFO hunting during daylight, and before placing and pointing web-cam gear from a house window, thought should be given to using regular glass windows that are not a "low E" variety of window. Modern homes in northern climates use low E windows to retain heat in homes. Low E windows tend to block and reflect near infrared light and can create the condition of blocking the part of the near infrared spectrum where UFOs can be seen by a near infrared web-cam. Therefore, regular window glass, which does not block near infrared light from reaching the near infrared web-cam, should be used if at all possible, for UFO hunting out of a house window.

A near infrared web-cam should be pointing out a window that is shaded from the direct glare of the sun. In fact, the sun should be blocked from the web-cam in a manner as described later on in this chapter as per the Solar Obliteration method. By blocking the near infrared web-cam according to the Solar Obliteration method, this will improve the quality of UFO video captured in near infrared.

For recording purposes, the near infrared web-cam should be pointed out a window that is clean.

---

1   Various authors, **Aviation Light Signals**, Wikipedia, Found at: http://wn.wikipedia.org/wiki/Aviation_light_signals

Clean windows lower the chance of minute particles obscuring UFOs passing by in the sky and aid in the rapid identification of bugs as false positives. During early morning and late evening, bits of dirt on windows can obscure viewing small objects in the sky, especially when the window is in direct sunshine. Clean windows give you a much clearer view on UFOs.

Birds, Bugs, and UFOs

Objects that fly can set off the HandyAvi motion detection software, therefore these flying objects must be noted for what they are and removed from captured video as false positives.

Bugs will show up most often as black objects in near infrared and will not resemble a UFO glowing white in near infrared. However, in cloudy weather, UFOs can sometimes appear as black, blurry objects when seen against clouds. Birds flying across a web-cam field of view will show as quickly moving objects which flap. Seagull wingtips will appear to have glowing white tips in near infrared and can be confused with a UFO in a near IR web-cam. If you live near where many birds nest, HandyAvi motion sensing software for UFO events, will not be an ideal way to see daytime UFOs. The author will often run a second regular web-cam to ensure that seagulls are not confused with near infrared glowing UFOs when reviewing footage. Good due diligence is to run a dual near IR and regular light web-cam setup, i.e., have

> **Definition: A scan line is one line, or row, in a raster scanning pattern, such as a video line on a cathode ray tube (CRT) display of a television or computer.**

one laptop recording in near IR and another laptop recording with a regular web-cam.

Another aspect of UFOs seen in video that can be mistaken for bird wings is a energy field that sweeps as a dark line around the UFO, making the UFO flicker. The function of this field is unknown, but it does have a known effect on video recording equipment.

This oblong field could be mistaken for bird wings at a distance, but it is an entirely different phenomena. This field flickers around the UFO at a rate of speed and can be seen in near infrared video. If a web-cam or video camera is recording at or near the rate of how fast the UFO field flickers, one tends to see a scan line in video recordings. This scan line appears to be part of the stealth of the UFO, but, also may be part of a field which provides flight to the UFO.

Scan lines are produced if one points a camcorder or web-cam camera at a TV screen and records the image of the television screen. When you play back the recorded image of the television screen on a web-cam recording, a black bar will run up and down the picture due to the lack of synchronization between the television scanning lines and the rate that the web-cam records.

If a web-cam records at 15 frames a second, but a TV records pictures at a rate of 30 frames a second, straight scan lines will appear and travel across the screen of the TV set being recorded by the web-cam or video equipment. If the rates are very different between the TV screen and the video recorder, scan lines will move quickly across the recorded image of the TV set. If the screen refresh rate is nearly the same between the TV screen being recorded, and the video recorder, scan lines will move slowly. If both the TV and the video recorder are in sync, the scan line will hold still in one spot on the recording or not appear at all. UFO scan lines appear to work in a similar fashion.

Scan lines can appear around UFOs in a manner similar to a TV set being recorded in video, except that the scan line around a UFO appears to be in 3-D. When you expand the video picture of the UFO, you find this scan line forms a 3-D motion around the UFO. Imagine this 3-D scan line appears like a stitch line on a football as the football spins through the air. This scan line reflects the fact that there is a 3-D field of unknown function around the craft and this field has a rate of generation which interacts visually with the web-cam recording rate. This interaction causes the scan lines that appear in recorded video.

A UFO scan line field pattern will rotate around the UFO craft. This 3-D field cycles around the craft at a certain cycle rate, and may provide a UFO with a way to fly above the earth. There is no information on what the function of this field is which is being generated at a rate around the UFO, only that this field can be seen around the craft in near infrared during the daylight when UFOs pass by a near infrared web-cam. Finally, this field obscures a UFO if the web-cam video rate is not close to the rate at which the field cycles.

John Bro Wilkie's Solar Obliteration Technique

On June 28, 1995, John Bro Wilkie read an article titled "Sky Dancer" by Bill Hamilton. Hamilton's article discussed a UFO witness who described how the UFO tended to move into the glare of the sun to hide itself from view.[2]

> **Definition: Photosphere, the visible bright surface of the sun.**

Along with this article, Wilkie had also noted the July 11, 1991, Mexico City sightings, where Mexico City experienced a wave of UFO sightings. According to hundreds of eyewitnesses, a bright object hovered over Mexico City for almost thirty minutes through the interval of a solar eclipse where the moon was blocking out the sun's photosphere. This UFO event was videotaped by seventeen people in different parts of the city.

From this article and the Mexico City sightings, John Bro Wilkie deduced a new method to observe UFOs. Much like how WW II pilots flew out and towards the sun's direction to hide from view, UFOs more or less do the same thing according to John Bro Wilkie. By blocking out the sun disk, or photosphere, using an interposing object such as a house eve, or some other object, Wilkie determined one can see UFOs hiding themselves in the sun's glare (**see figure next page of eclipse, and UFOs seen in penumbra**). By using Wilkie's method, you can block out the direct sunlight from the sun's photosphere and video record UFOs hiding in the glare of the sun during a clear, cloudless day or near cloudless day. UFO hunting using this technique, is best carried out using a house eve or other shaded area to block out the sun. This method works best during high noon.

In the Words of John Bro Wilkie

> *Back in June of 1995, while pondering the Mexico City sightings, then reading a published article entitled 'Sky Dancer' by Bill Hamilton - I stumbled upon the 'Solar Obliteration' method for videotaping what can only be described as UFOs. They are unidentified, moving around up in the atmosphere and are apparently objects. In its truest sense, this is the correct definition.*

---

2   Wilkie, John Bro, **The Solar Obliteration Technique**, Found at: http://www.michigansotherside.com/Articles/UF0_ Solar_ Oblit2.htm

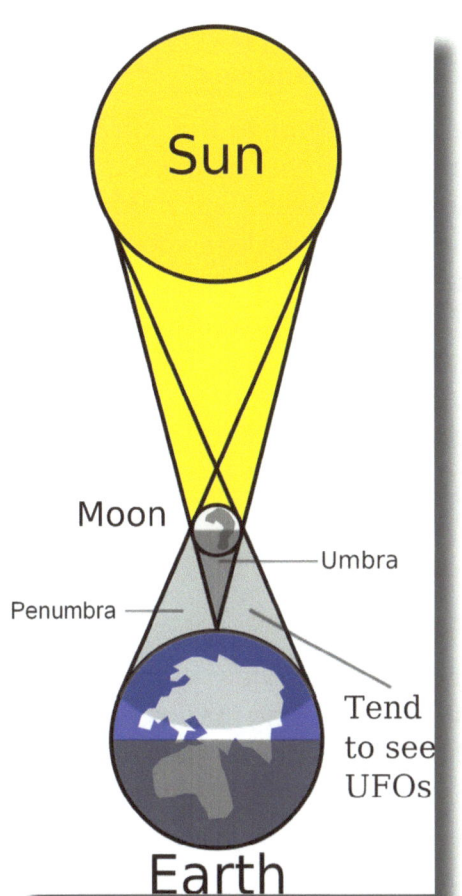

Sun

Moon

— Umbra

Penumbra —

Tend to see UFOs

Earth

Within a few days, I had drawn up the original diagram of what I simply called 'The Technique' (for videotaping unusual aerial anomalies).

'The John Bro Technique' as it has also become recognized, was only meant as a 'beginner's trick' for those that were new to the field/hobby of Ufology. I truly believe that many objects in the sky are not seen because of the 'daylight stealth' techniques they employ, intentionally or naturally. The removal of the direct light in one's line of sight greatly reduces glare.

I found that if I could look up right next to the sun without the blaring brightness coming into my eyes or camera lens, some things that I would otherwise not have seen became apparent. It is akin to the difference that is made when donning a pair of Polaroid sunglasses on a sunny day. What a thrill and life-changing experience it can potentially be, to actually witness an unexplainable phenomenon for one's self.

John Bro Wilkie[3]

The solar obliteration method is meant to recreate or emulate a solar eclipse. Rather than have the moon block the sun's photosphere, objects such as house eves or what have you are used to block the sun disk while leaving the glare around the sun visible to be seen. It is in this area of glare where UFOs tend to hide (**see eclipse figure above**).

Before setting up a tripod and pointing your video equipment in the direction of the blocked sun's photosphere, tune the web-cam or video gear optics on a distant object on the ground, for example a distant street lamp post. Focus the web-cam on the object. If you have automatic focusing on the video gear, turn off this automatic focus and manually focus for infinity. Now direct the web-cam towards the direction of the sun where the sun is blocked by a house eve or a building crest (**see right**).

You should never look at the sun through a view finder or with your eyes. Looking at the sun through

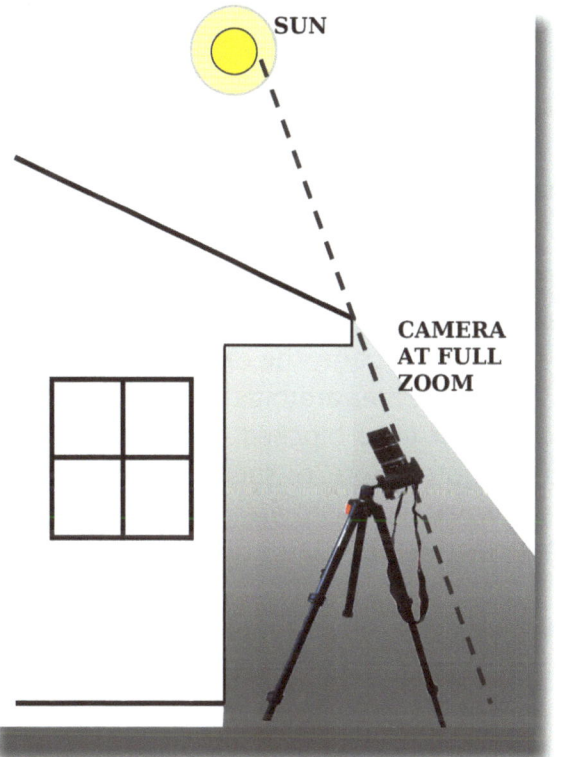

SUN

CAMERA AT FULL ZOOM

---

3   Ibid, Found at: http://www.michigansotherside.com/Articles/UF0_Solar_Oblit.htm

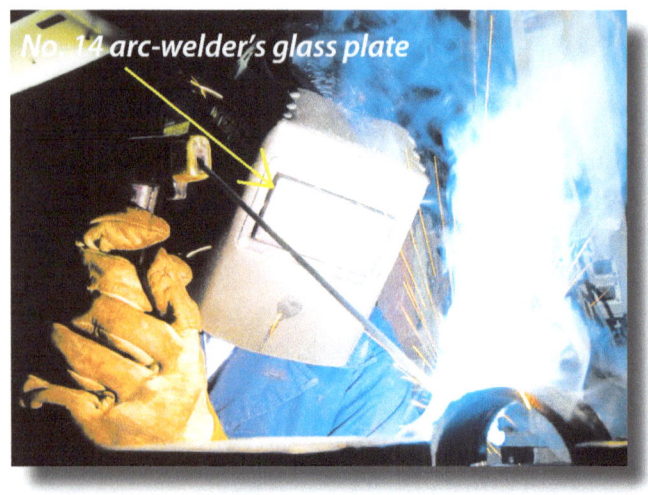
No. 14 arc-welder's glass plate

the telephoto of a DSLR using a view finder can result in eye damage and blindness.

If you feel the need to look at the sun to help direct the equipment for the solar obliteration method (**see figure left showing arc welder glass plate in welder's mask**), then pick up a cheap No. 14 arc-welder's glass plate. This plate is what is normally inserted in front of a welder's mask to protect the welder from arc-weld brightness. This safe solar filter material is found at some welding-supply stores (**check the yellow pages for a local dealer**) in convenient four inch wide pieces that allow viewing the sun with both eyes in a safe manner.[4]

You can also buy some safe Baader AstroSolar Safety Film to view the sun. This film is found at:

http://www.baader-planetarium.com/sofifolie/sofi_start_e.htm

Another safe way to adjust gear is to use "Live View". Canon cameras have a "Live View" mode, which is a small screen on the back of a Canon EOS camera that displays live video feed. Using the live video feed displayed on the Live View screen, position the camera to emulate the photograph shown (**see below**). You see the bright area around the sun's photosphere using the LCD screen on the back of the camera.

However, do not expose the web-cam or camera to direct sunlight, as you can burn out the CCD or CMOS sensor in the camera. Your camera should be shadowed from the sun's photosphere, which imitates how the sun is blocked during a solar eclipse.

As you can see from the photograph (**Solar Obliteration method photograph see right**) and the 2-D side schematic on the previous page, the camera is pointed at the glare area around the sun while the camera itself is blocked from seeing the sun photosphere, or sun disk. Note that a normal video camera can see UFOs in this manner, but later photo processing

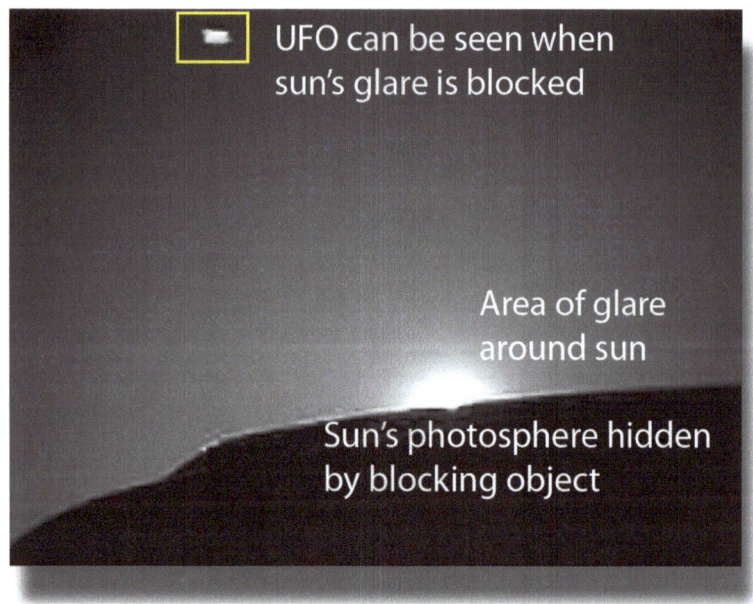
UFO can be seen when sun's glare is blocked

Area of glare around sun

Sun's photosphere hidden by blocking object

in GIMP will never be as good as using a near infrared web-cam or near infrared video recorder. Near infrared recordings capture clear details ordinary video cameras cannot pick up with respect to UFOs.

Other steps you can take using this method involve going outside your home with a laptop and

---

4   Medkeff, Jeff, **Safe Solar Observing**, Sky and Telescope, found at: http://www.skyandtelescope.com/observing/objects sun/3309106.html

attached near infrared web-cam. You can then arrange equipment under a house eve (power pole, tall building or wall, etc.) that cuts off direct view of the sun. Point the web-cam in a manner where the web-cam "eye" is just in the shadow. The full sun should be hitting the top of the web-cam casing but the lens part of the web-eye should be in shadow. Use the laptop screen, which is being fed live web-cam video to help point and adjust the web-cam to only the area of glare around the sun. If you are doing the previous steps right, you should get a picture similar to the bottom photo on the previous page. This is more or less the "solar obliteration method/technique" which was created by John Bro Wilkie.

Once the web-cam is pointed in a correct manner, turn on the HandyAvi motion sensing software and wait to see if a UFO passes by the web-cam and is captured on video. HandyAvi will capture anything passing by the web-eye. Adjust the web-cam's aim on a 20 to 30 minute schedule to maintain the near infrared web-cam position pointing into the glare around the sun.

Using the near infrared web-cam allows you to better break UFO stealth when used with John Bro Wilkie's method. The near IR web-cam is able to view UFOs in any area of the sky. However, your best opportunity to spot UFOs are those UFOs which tend to hide in the sun's glare. Therefore, you increase your chance of seeing a UFO by pointing a near IR web-cam in the sun's direction.

What is Seen Using the Solar Obliteration Technique

Using the solar obliteration technique, one sees a few things. On the one hand, you may be seeing in video sequences, dust, bugs, grit and flying pollen. On the other hand, you may capture images of aerial objects that are UFOs. Note again that this method can be used with regular video gear. But, with normal video gear, it is much harder to process images for clearness and detail. Near infrared web-cams often captures details of UFOs that a regular video cannot capture. Near infrared web-cams are able to break through part of the UFO stealth by using near infrared wavelength light as a recording medium.

With respect to how far away these objects are from the recording gear, we can judge distance roughly by using some simple relative measures. For example, if one waits for a few clouds to come into web-cam view, I have noted many UFOs appear to be moving around, through and above the clouds, with some objects appearing below the cloud base and closer to the web-cam. Checking cloud base height with your local Internet weather program will often give you the cloud base height particulars, allowing you a relative measure of how high UFOs are flying.

It should be noted dust, pollen and bugs would not be viewed in video traveling above the clouds when the web-cam is focused for distant objects. Using this method, UFOs can be seen to travel in formation, which is not possible for dust, leaves and pollen in the air. Often fleets of UFOs can be seen in video, diving into and out of the sun's glare, moving as a group in formation, or in a display of chaotic flight, filled with acrobatics that our planes cannot imitate. John Bro Wilkie's method is a new take on the old saying that, seeing is believing.

Lastly, and again to emphasize this point, John Bro Wilkie's method can be applied with any camera or video machine (the author took movies of UFOs using a HD recording CANON EOS T1i coupled with a zoom lens, in my case a Canon EF-S 55-200 mm kit lens for the Canon T1i). A better choice is to use a near infrared web-cam, where images can be put through a process later that exposes clear details.

Sun Dogs and John Bro Wilkie's Solar Obliteration Technique

"Dazzle mine eyes, or do I see three suns?" [5]

William Shakespeare, Henry VI, Part 3[6]

Sun Dogs are an optical illusion that form around the sun. Sun dogs are called Parhelia or "Mock Suns" and are most easily seen when the sun is low. If you have not seen a sun dog before, then there is a chance that sun dogs can be mistaken for UFOs that are hiding close to the sun.

One thing to note when observing UFOs using the John Bro Wilkie method, is that UFOs fly at an angular distance that can be much closer to the sun than is possible for sun dogs. You can tell a UFO from a sun dog by the fact that sun dogs show up 22° degrees (22° is about the same as an outstretched hand at arm's length from sun to sun dog) to the left and right of the sun and at the same height as the sun. Sun dogs are formed by plate and hexagonal shaped ice crystals in high and cold cirrus clouds or during very cold weather by ice crystals called diamond dust, which tend to drift in the air at low altitudes.

In the instance when the sun is higher, sun dogs appear further away, i.e. "the sun dog" is red coloured towards the sun and can grade into green and blue colors further out from the sun. Sun dogs can be very bright while at other times, they are mere colored smudges in the sky. They are visible all over the world and at any time of year, regardless of how hot or cold it is at ground level. In Europe and North America, you can see a sun dog about twice a week.[7]

In short, Sun Dogs are unlike UFOs which hide in the sun's glare (**see picture of sun dog, next page**). It is easy to point out a sun dog in comparison to a UFO: Sun Dogs are non moving, do not perform aerial stunts beyond our science, and do not reveal alien shapes and beings when you process the pictures.

---

5   Shakespeare, William, Character Edward, **Henry VI**, Part 3, written in about 1590
6   Various Authors, **Sun Dog**, Found at http://upload.wikimedia.org/wikipedia/commons/8/88/Fargo_Sundogs_2_18_09.jpg
7   Found at: http://www.atoptics.co.uk/halo/parhelia.htm

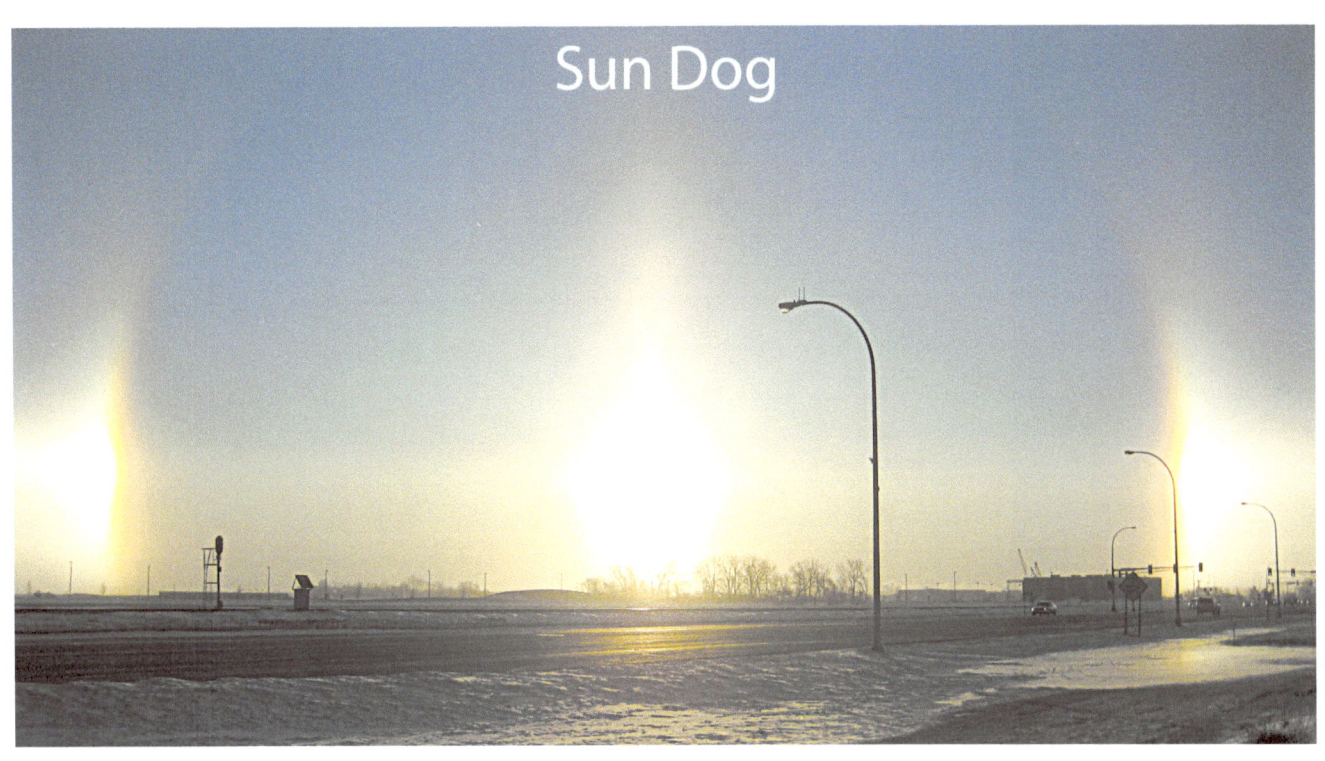

Sun Dog

Chapter 6: Dealing with Confusing Images

The creative act lasts but a brief moment, a lightning instant of give-and-take, just long enough for you to level the camera and to trap the fleeting prey in your little box.

Henri Cartier-Bresson[1]

Many times when you are seeing something alien, it is just plain confusing. Confusion can happen even when the images are visually clear. These confusing aspects to alien images are discussed below.

For instance, sometimes you have a situation where you are left wondering if you are seeing a projection of an alien on the UFO, or if it is an actual alien.

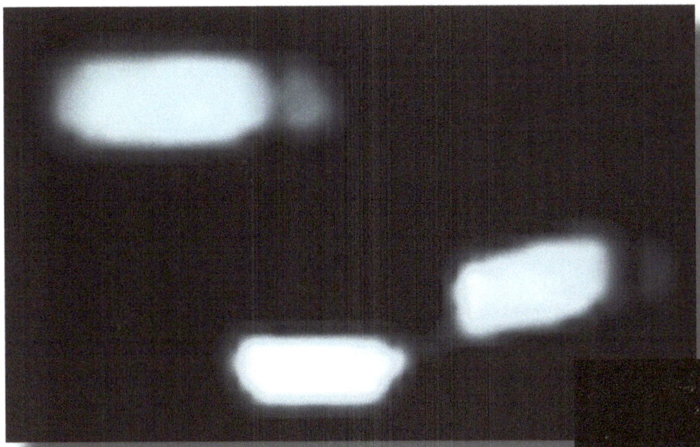

In the photograph, I have taken the initially blurry near infrared image of three UFOs (**see left**), and processed the images for clarity (**see below right**). The images come from a near infrared photo that was extracted from a near-IR web-cam video showing a busy street intersection in a Canadian city. The image was cleared up in GIMP software, using a series

of processing steps.

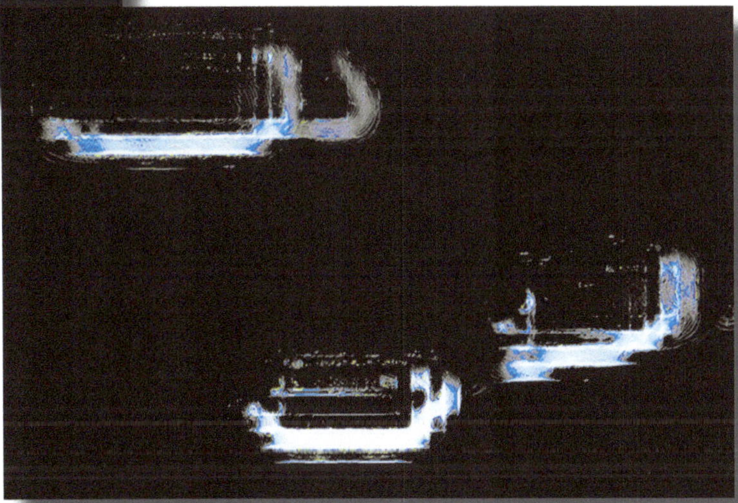

In the processed image, there is an alien figure riding a UFO which appears to be an open boat-like craft, that in video, is moving in and out of the cloud base in a formation with two other UFOs. This formation of UFOs is moving faster than a jet aircraft.

I have surrounded the alien figure with a yellow box (**see next page top figure**). The figure in the yellow box has been further blown up, showing more clearly an alien which appears to be wearing some sort of nosepiece (**see bottom figure next page**).

On one hand, this figure may be some form of 3-D image imposed upon a part of a larger UFO structure.

---

1   Cartier-Bresson, Henri, **Quotes**, Found at: http://www.brainyquote.com/quotes/quotes/h/henricarti107208.html

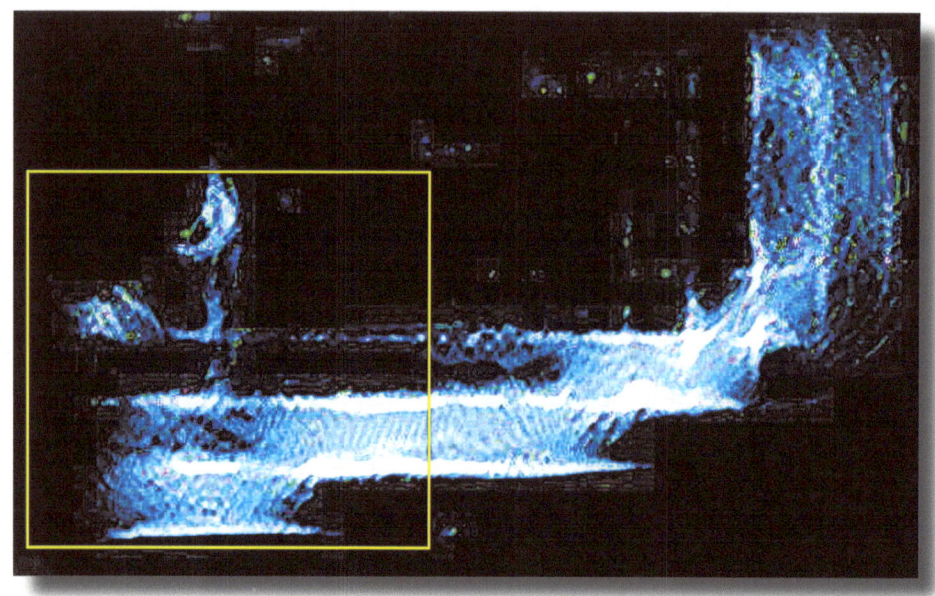

Or, on the other hand, this is an actual alien, driving a craft that appears to be open and travelling at a speed faster than a jet.

How is this possible? Well, I can only speculate that what appears to be an open boat-like craft, might be a window on a much larger craft, and the alien is inside the window. Or, perhaps the alien is being protected by some form of force field (a force field is a science fiction concept with no present basis of reality in our science and technology). And finally, the alien might be an image or projection on the craft, like a calling card sign that the UFO belongs to a certain species.

It is hard to tell from our vantage point, how an alien can be riding an open craft at a fatalistic speed, without having some form of serious protection. For example, the formation of the UFOs is moving at a speed where wind would tear apart any biological life form. So my point here is that even when images are clear, it is hard to figure out what is going on in the photos.

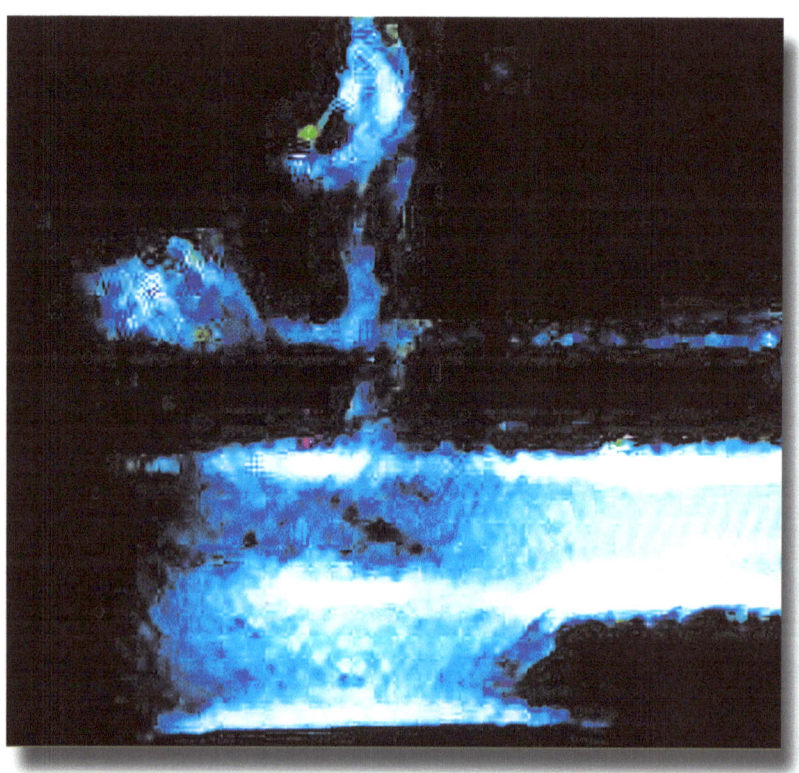

Do Aliens Wear Optical Stealth Suits?

Below are three photographs extracted from a near infrared video taken on December 6th,

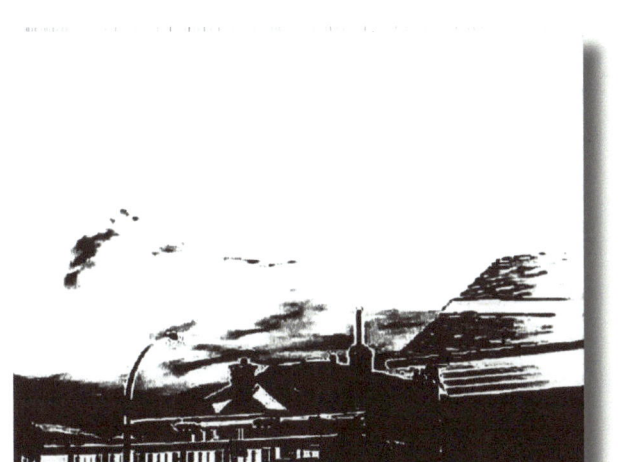

2008 at 1:42:00 p.m. The near infrared photograph (**see left**) presumably shows an alien floating above a busy intersection.

The photograph has been inverted in GIMP to bring out details.

IRIS was then used to zoom the picture 40 times, while GIMP was used to extract details from the picture to produce the detailed photos below. This photograph was extracted from a five minute video, and shows a floating alien, attached to a line like object, moving from west to east across an intersection (**see lower left**). The insert photograph (**to the lower right**) shows the presumed alien's head inside a camouflage suit.

The suit appears to work using the same general principles of camouflage as outlined in Chapter 4.

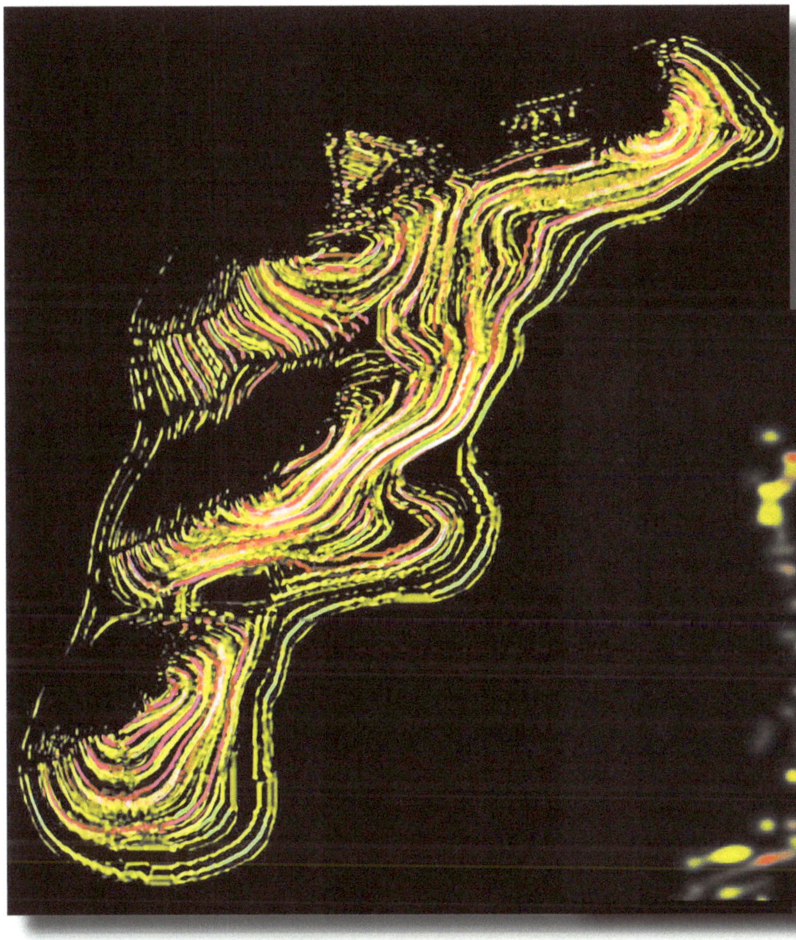

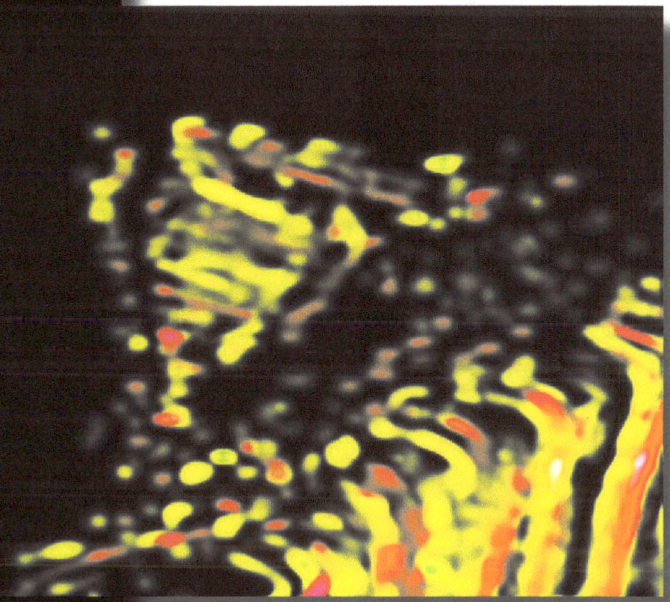

The Three Eyed, Bug Eyed Alien

There are more confusing images. Take for instance the photograph of two side by side craft (**see below left**) which was taken by a near infrared web-cam. These are two open boat type UFOs which appeared in the skies above a major Canadian city around October of 2008. There are two alien figures, who are labeled in the photo to the left. The UFOs paused for half a second in flight, allowing clear stacking of about five frames of video. These UFOs then sped up to a relative velocity which appeared above jet aircraft speeds.

Note the lines that appear in the

picture that relate either to the stealth aspect of the UFOs, or it is a field of force that is providing lift and motive power for these craft. There appears to be some sort of field coming from the bottom of the craft which is seen in near infrared light. The alien figures in these two side by side craft may be projections, except a close up of the figure furthest from the web-cam, argues against this notion. This alien figure (**close up of Alien B, see right**) appears to be working on a device beside its craft, by hanging two ultra long arms over the side of the craft. The alien appears to be wearing goggles for three eyes and is working on some device with fingers that are not shaped like human digits. There is quite a bit of raster to the picture as the craft is several hundred meters away from the web-cam eye, and high in the air. Zooming the picture by ten times, using IRIS software, reveals the figure with three eyes with much better detail. And if you look hard enough at the zoom picture, you can see that the left hand of the figure has an opposable thumb.

UFO Pictures and Strange UFO Sensors

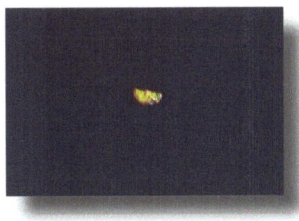

UFOs have been seen to deploy sensors outside UFO craft windows. These sensors, which project out of UFO windows, can add significant confusion to UFO pictures. Take for instance this image (**see left**). The photo was taken on January 27th, 2010 using a Canon EOS T1i at an F-stop of 5.6, ISO-1600, a plus exposure bias of 0.3 step, at a focal length of 232 mm, with the Canon set on center weighted average metering mode.

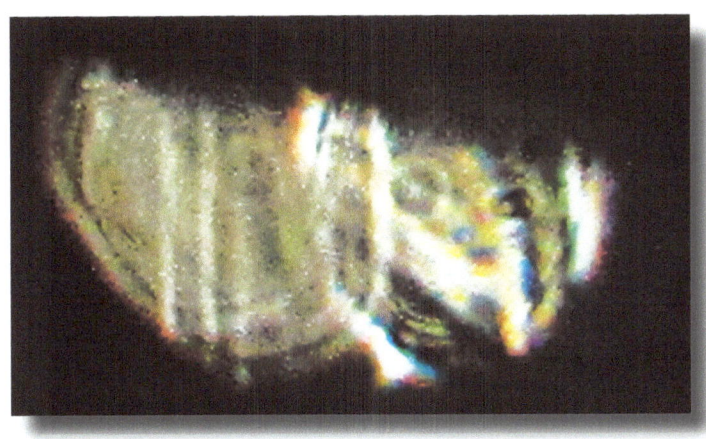

The picture was expanded 20 times (**see left**) and revealed what looked like an alien looking out of a portal on the craft.

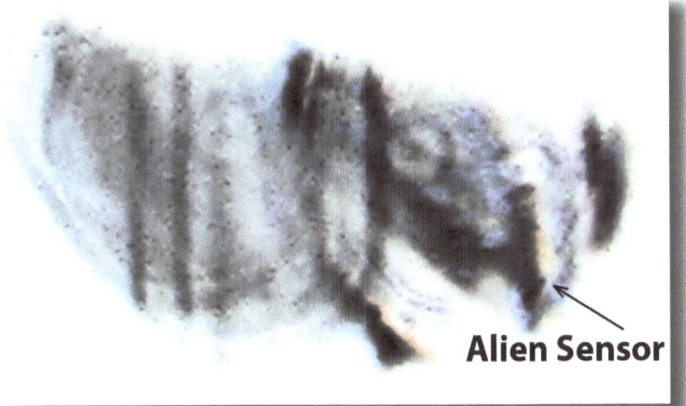

Alien Sensor

However, when the image was inverted in GIMP, further detail comes out of the picture which shows some sort of sensor pointed out the open port on the UFO craft. Sometimes using inverted picture images shows more detail which clears up confusion in alien photos (**see left**). On these occasions the UFO photographer should try inversion of UFO images using the image inversion function in GIMP software, to clear up confusion with respect to what is going on in the photograph.

Chapter 7: UFO Display Systems

Daylight Command and Control UFOs

One of the most confusing aspects of UFO witness accounts relates to descriptions of UFO craft changing shape. UFOs changing shape have been a common theme in the field of Ufology ever since witnesses first began to describe alien craft. Which begs the question, how exactly do UFOs change shape? The answer to this question really boils down to understanding that the 3-D display around the UFO is changing shape, and not the UFO craft itself.

The 3-D display around a UFO is constantly changing shape with the terrain over which the craft flies. Whether the UFO is flying over a city or countryside, this 3-D display is being used for several functions. The first function of the display is for giving the UFO pilot or other robotic craft visual information showing ideal pathways through the air to avoid collision with other UFOs and airplanes. Images processed from UFO sightings, show these 3-D displays, where you can see the symbology of the 3-D displays showing miniature images of other UFOs, contour like flight paths, and sometimes, even miniature images of aliens. So the internal function of the 3-D display as a navigational tool for the pilot or robotic flight system, is apparent because of the symbols displayed.

Another function of the 3-D display is to emit this navigation information as red, green and blue colors. The red, green and blue colored navigational display items serve the dual function of both navigation and acting as camouflage for the UFO during daylight hours. These colors, as explained previously, blur together to form white at a distance, and this coloration makes it difficult to see the UFO pilot and the UFO craft during daylight. At night, the navigational display surrounds the craft and from a distance, the blue, green and red colored navigational display blurs together to form white. This white mixture of primary colors allows the UFO to assume a starlike appearance at a distance during night hours.

The third function of the 3-D navigation display is to show information to other UFOs as to the changing shape of recorded information on the ground movement of people. Ground movement of people is constantly changing through a daily and nightly cycle. For example, this observation based deduction is supported later in this chapter in an image of a 3-D picture map projected from a UFO showing a high concentration of people walking in a city park and another series of images which shows a park is under study.

Usually, one UFO appears to fly lower than other UFOs, is brighter, and displays the most navigational data in comparison to other UFOs. It is this lower and brighter UFO that I call a "command and control UFO". These command and control UFOs appear to direct other UFOs in flight paths that avoid air collisions. Command and control UFOs appear to fulfill an analogous function to how air traffic controllers direct airplanes over airport airspace.

The following picture is what I consider to be a command and control UFO (**see top photograph, next page**). It is a very bright UFO that is constantly changing shape and appears to be closest to the ground when compared to other UFO craft. This photo was extracted from a video taken with a Canon EOS T1i camera which was set on high definition video mode. An EF-S 55-250 zoom lens zoomed to 250 mm was used. The DSLR was mounted on a Manfrotto tripod. All the other functions on the DSLR were set on automatic.

The picture of the command and control UFO was blown up 80 times and shows the 3-D flight data around the craft as a blurry area (**see below**).

Again, a command and control UFO works in analogous fashion to a control tower at an airport, controlling local flight paths of other UFOs. But in this case, the command and control UFO is sending other UFOs to areas where people can be seen walking on the ground.

To say which UFOs are command and control craft in photos is straightforward when groups of UFOs are seen. As noted, these UFOs are the ones closest to the ground during sightings and tend to fly in a direction counter to other less bright and higher up UFOs. However, the best way to tell these are command and control UFOs is to process the UFO picture for detail. In GIMP software, when you click on "Colors" on the top menu, then "levels", and "automatic levels", and then apply a few strong sharps found under "Filters>enhance>sharpen", and lower light levels with the curves function (use an inverted curve) found under "Colors>Curves", 3-D symbols will start to appear in the picture. Using the

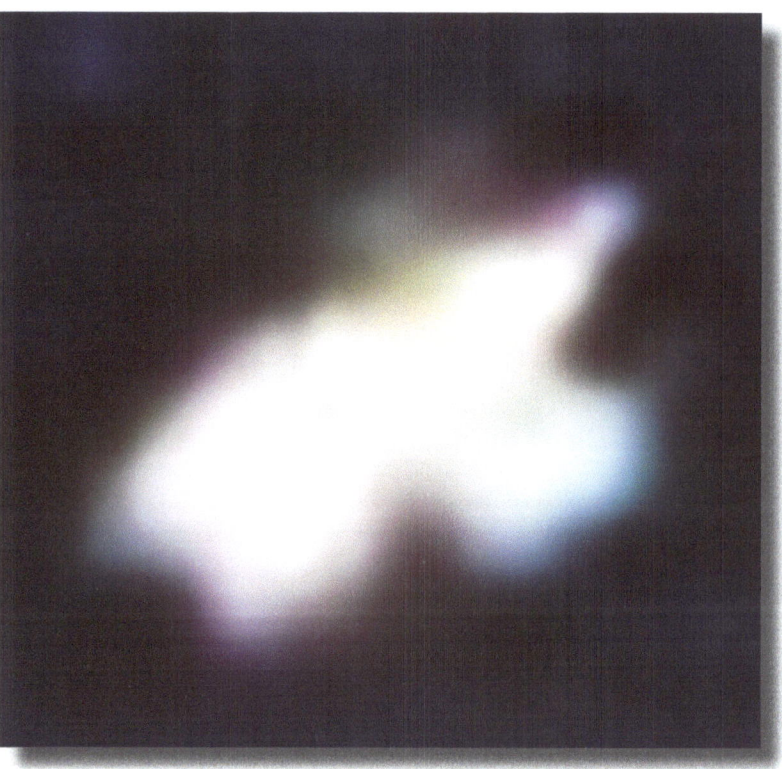

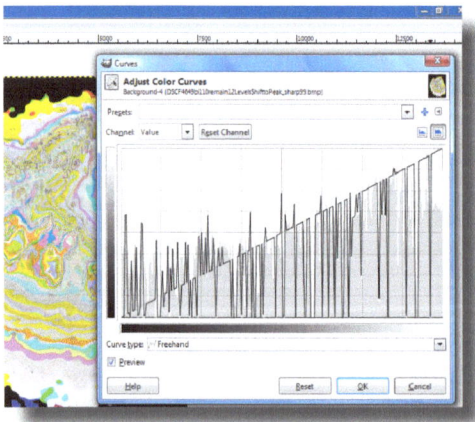

Curves function in GIMP, a histogram of the light from the UFO will show a series of spikes in the light at certain frequencies (**see left, freehand curves adjustment in GIMP**). When you match the light spikes by adjusting peaks in the curves function under GIMP (**in the manner shown left**), you can extract the 3-D imagery around the UFO that is displaying navigational data. When you look, distinct peaks of light in the image are seen. These distinct peaks of light shown on the histogram (**see left**) display geometric messages coded to

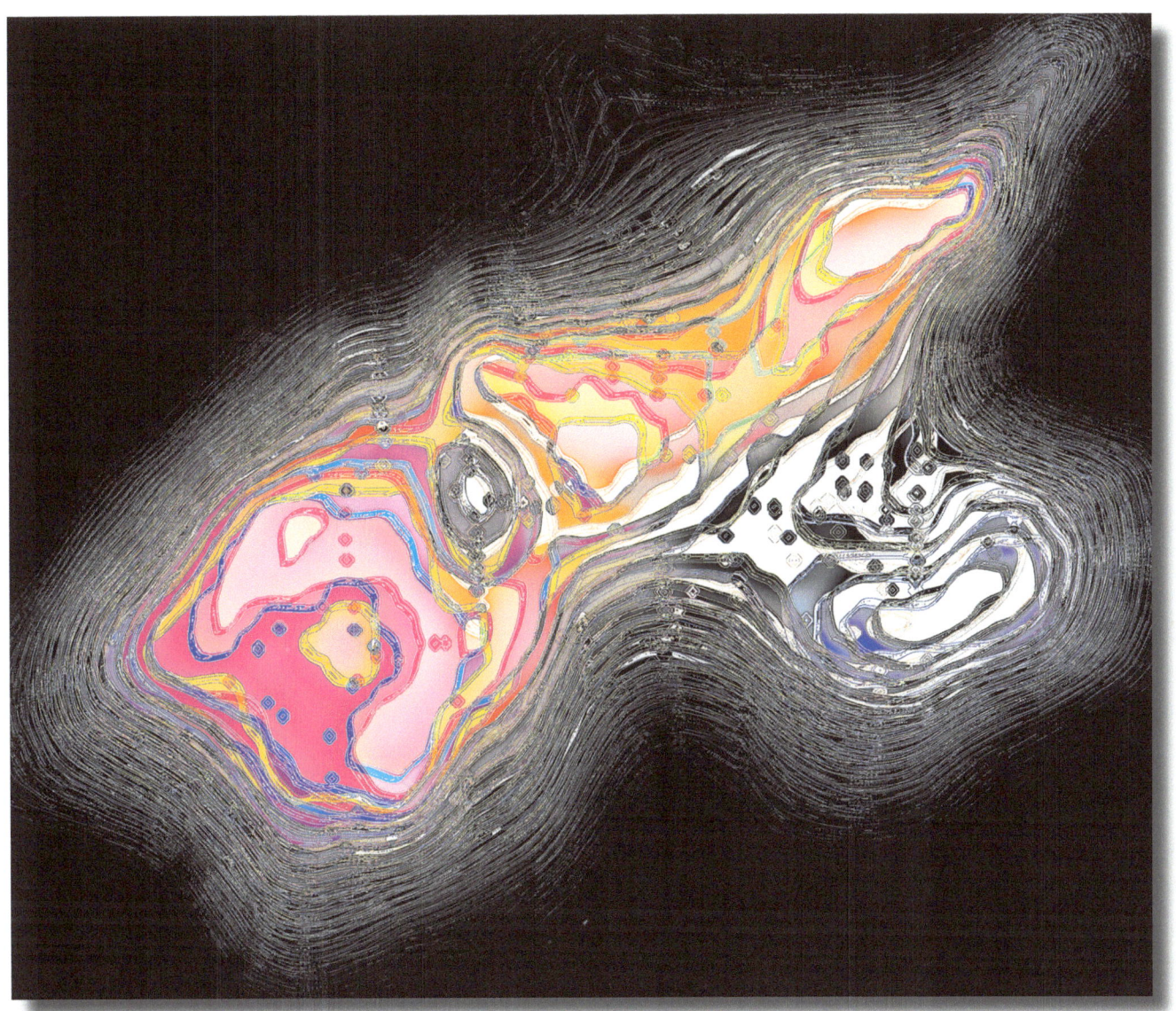

tight light wavelengths. Again, the idea behind these symbols seems to be that the symbols relate to air movement of other UFOs and to the study of human population density changes on the ground. You can take the ground related 3-D map being projected by the command and control UFO, and reapply this 3-D projection to things on the ground such as landmarks, i.e. paths people frequent and elevations of the ground. An example of this type of image from a command and control UFO being re-projected onto the ground will be discussed and shown later.

The middle figure from the previous page was processed further to show the alien symbols projected around the UFO (**see above**). The picture above was blown up ten more times to reveal alien symbols with unique geometric shapes (**see photo next page**). Changing the "hue" setting within GIMP software will reveal in the photo 3-D symbols buried in layers of different hues. For example, you can see symbols coded into separate layers of the 3-D image projected around the UFO craft, with each layer coded to a specific wavelength of light and color. By tuning the picture with GIMP towards certain wavelengths, you can extract to an extent, layers of symbols from the 3-D image.

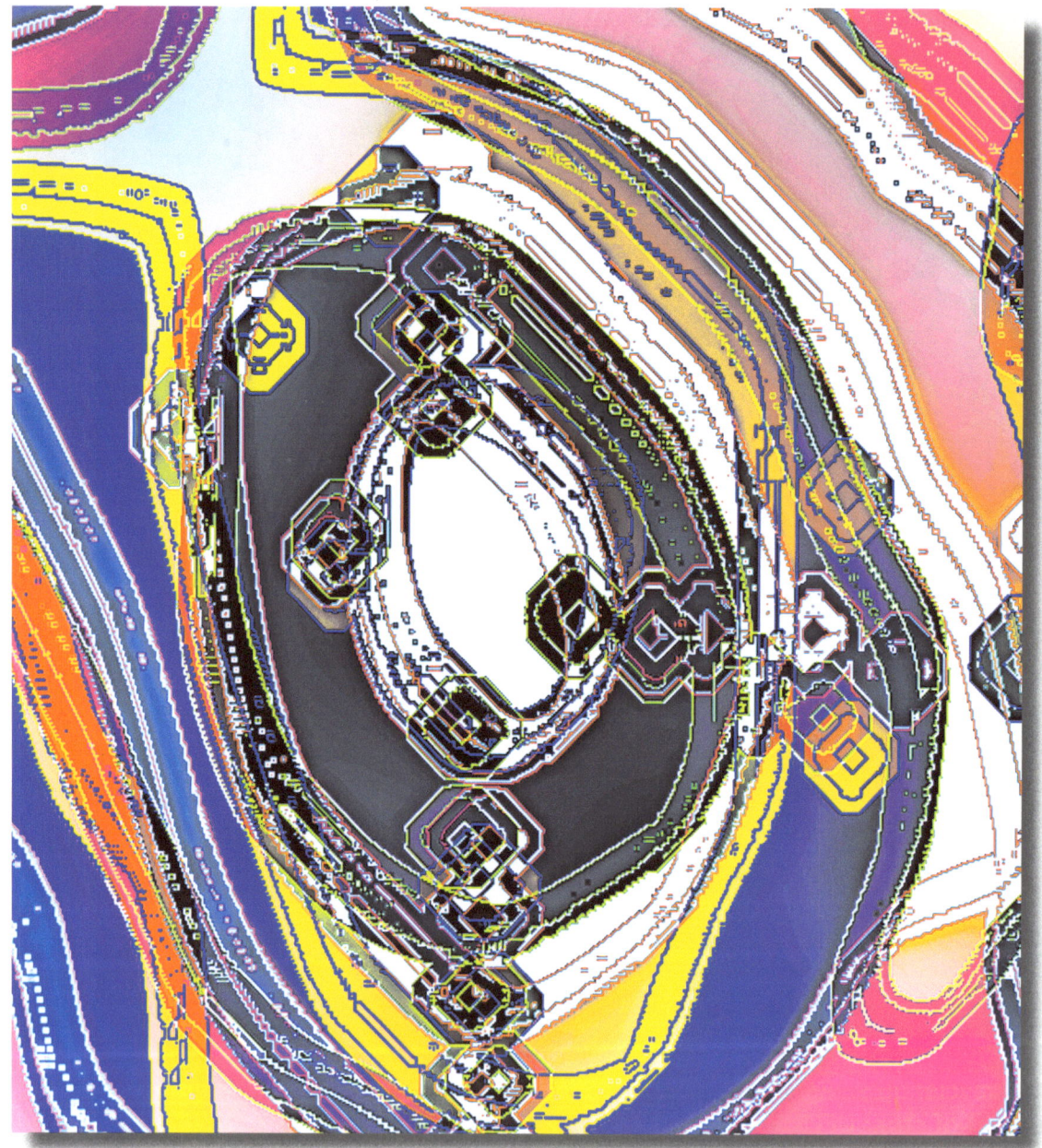

UFO Projection Systems Remapped to Earth Contours

As noted, sometimes command and control UFOs will display a projection that relates to landmarks and movement of people on the ground. As a photographer, you can extract these symbols and contours as seen on the UFO 3-D displays, and remap these landmarks onto local ground topography as shown in Google Earth. This exercise will give you an idea of what is of actual interest to the UFO displaying the data.

Re-projecting or remapping these 3-D symbols being projected from command and control UFOs, is the best puzzle in town, with the challenge of matching alien contours and symbols to ground features

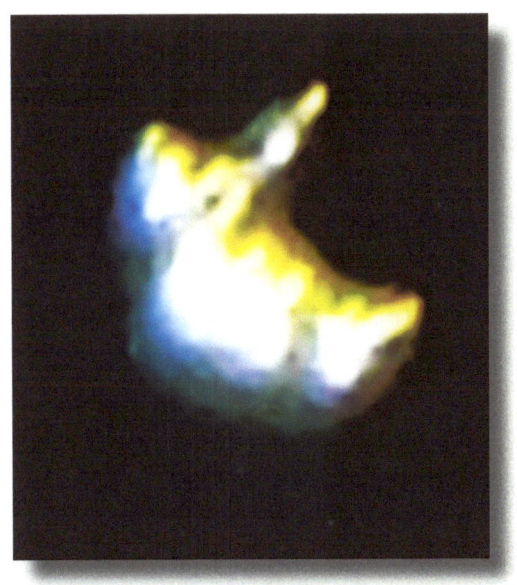

displayed on Google Earth. Google Earth can be found at: **http://earth.google.com/**

By using Google Earth's photo function, you can overlay UFO contour map symbols you have processed out of a UFO photo and apply the contours and symbols over frequented landmarks such as pathways, rivers and hills. Places such as pathways, rivers, small hills, etc., which will allow you to orient the UFO map symbols to what exactly the UFO is looking at on the ground. Play this map puzzle game right, and you find that contours from the command and control UFO match where people go on the ground (**see previous page UFO projection showing symbols on ground**).

As an example of this kind of contour map, here is an unprocessed photo (**see left**) by the author of one such command and control UFO taken using a Fujifilm Finepix E510 point and shoot at 6:57 p.m. on January 8th, 2009 and blown up 110 times.

The Fujifilm point and shoot cameras are known to be some of the finest night cameras. The Fuji takes great night photos, and seems to be an ideal UFO hunting tool for night photography. After processing the picture using GIMP, using functions discussed previously, the image resolves into a 3-D contour map projected around the UFO (**see below**).

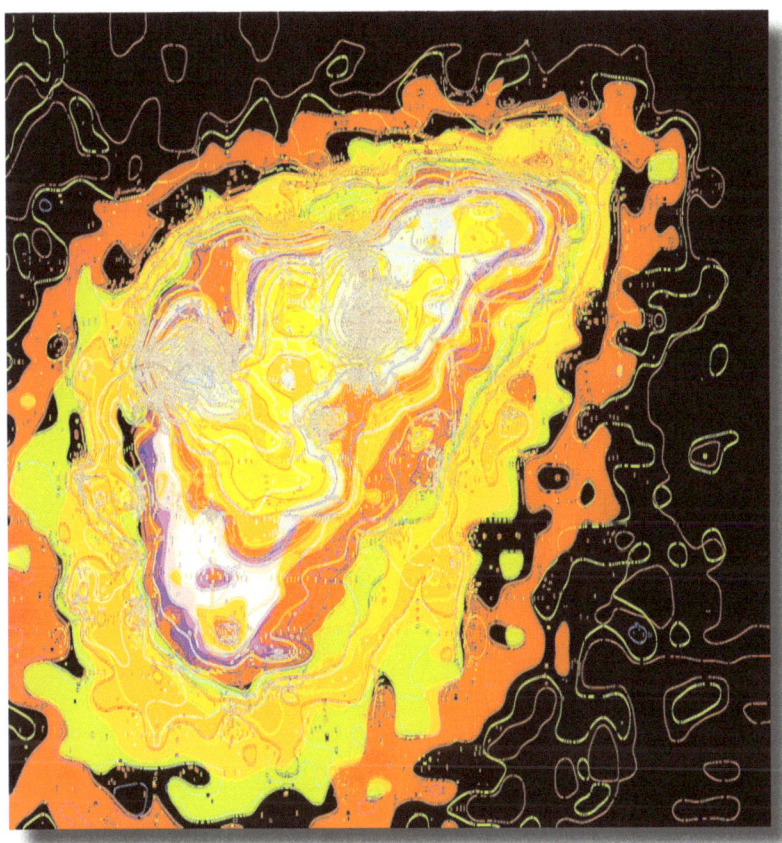

Note: as this UFO photo was captured right above a walking park, I downloaded a digital 3-D contour map of elevations of the park, and reprojected the 3-D map from the UFO onto the 3-D contour map.

In this particular case, I used a free program called 3DEM to reproject the UFO image (**see next page**) onto the city park elevations, rather than using Google Earth software. With 3DEM, the program can project digital elevation map sheets (DEMS) underneath the photo images. This great piece of software can be downloaded for free from the Internet: **http://freegeographytools. com/2009/3dem-website-is-gone- but-3dem-still-available-here**

Also note, 3DEM accepts digital elevation maps, or DEMs, from free Canadian and U.S. government sources. DEMS can be downloaded for particular areas in Canada from this site: **www.geobase.ca.** In the U.S., you can obtain free DEMs at: **http://seamless. usgs.gov/.** By loading the 3-D UFO image and the DEM into 3DEM, I was able to obtain what looks like a color coded map from the UFO of people walking along paths in the park (**see below image from UFO reprojected onto park gully contour map**). Later in this book, I will show another UFO map being projected onto a satellite photo of the same park. In the image produced, line patterns around the park gully suggest flight paths for UFOs moving over the park while studying people walking inside the park gully. The below UFO map image is overlaid onto a Canadian digital elevation map sheet.

People who wish to download digital elevation map sheets from other parts of the world (**Europe, Asia**) should consider using the NASA Aster DEM data found at: **https://wist.echo.nasa.gov/wist-bin/ api/ims.cgi?mode=MAINSRCH&JS=1**

Finally, although the author has not used this Aster DEM site, the website listed above does cover most of the world in fine detail with digitial elevation maps. A much more in depth set of steps on how to load DEMs and apply an image to a DEM is a complex subject. This subject will be explained in my next book which will examine or discuss more intermediate UFO photo methods and processing techniques.

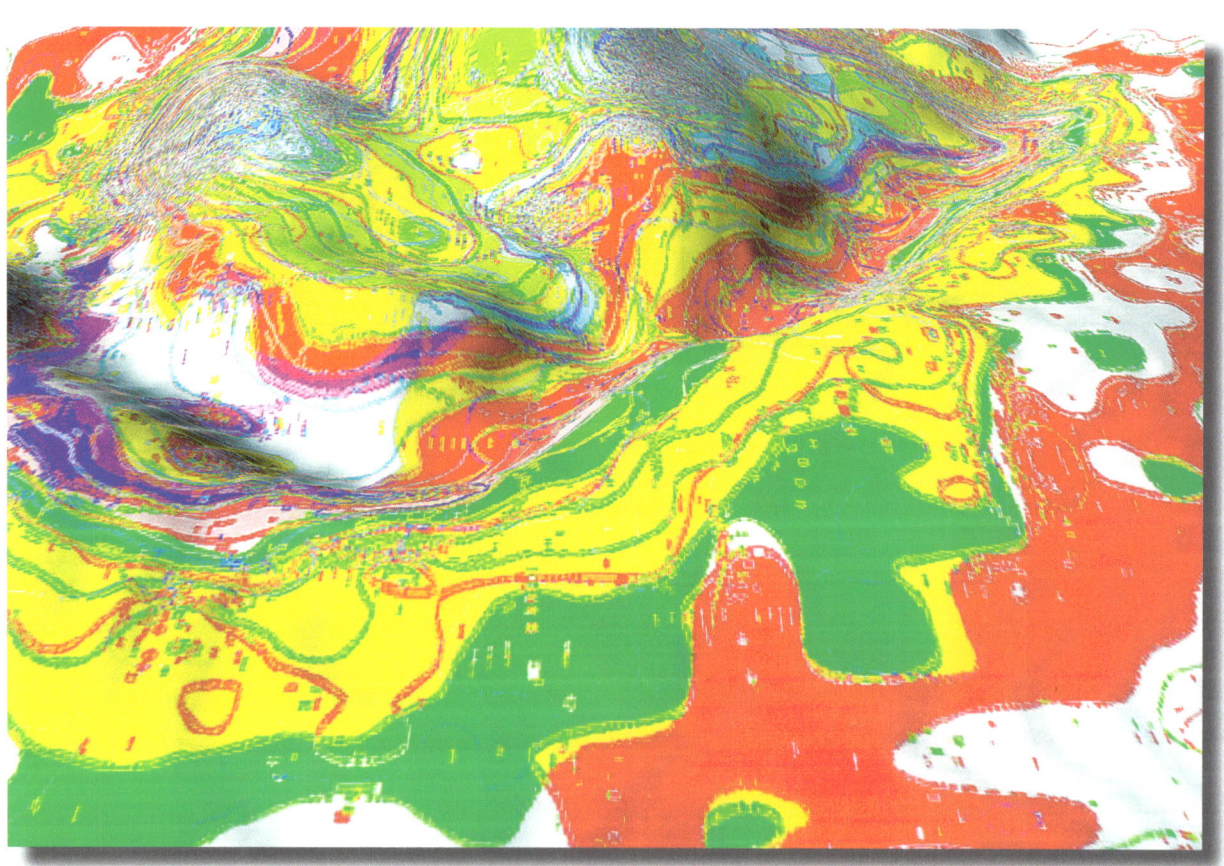

Chapter 8: Connecting Web-cams to Telescopes

The Next Generation Space Telescope, which will be located much further away from the Earth than the Hubble Space Telescope presently is, will also explore the infrared part of the spectrum.

Claude Nicollier, first astronaut from Switzerland and has flown on several Space Shuttle missions[1,2]

Web-cam methods described in this book have borrowed in a direct way from the field of web-cam astronomy, where for the past decade, amateur astronomers have used CCD web-cams for taking pictures of planets and stars. Using CCD web-cams hooked into telescopes, astronomers have used CCDs to achieve clear images of the night sky. What is surprising is that with all the clear images that were taken, why are UFOs not being seen by people who on a regular basis observe the sky?

So why is it that astronomers do not see more UFOs? Is peer pressure from other astronomers the reason that UFOs are not being detected? Is there perhaps a technical reason why UFOs are not being detected?

My theory is that astronomers do not see UFOs because astronomers almost always use near infrared blocking filters on web-cams and cameras designed for astronomy use as a way to improve picture quality. By blocking out the near infrared part of the spectrum, astronomers block longer wavelengths of light, and it is this practice which reduces halo effects in photographs, thereby improving photo quality. However, this practice of installing filters to block near infrared means astronomers are "blind" to seeing UFOs in the world of astronomy. For example, you can even see this push to use near infrared blocking filters in ads targeted at purchasing web-cam filters for astronomy use (**see advertisement below**).

Ad for Typical Astronomy Filter

1.25" IR and UV blocking filter

Our high-quality "hot mirror" infrared and ultraviolet blocking filter is designed for use with modern web-cam and CCD imaging cameras. If you use a web-cam with almost any telescope except a well-corrected Newtonian, you are to encounter halos around stars and a problem often referred to as "fuzzy focus". This happens because any telescope that employs any form of lens in the light path is unable to bring the whole light spectrum to a single well-defined focus. The UV and IR parts of the spectrum will be brought to different focus points to the rest of the spectrum, hence the loss of resolution and halo effects.[3]

Despite the use of near infrared blocking filters which makes this field of science blind to seeing stealthed UFOs, web-cam astronomy offers a means of attaching near infrared web-cams to telescopes to capture distant UFOs with more detail. Web-cam parts can allow you to connect web-cams via

---

1   Found at: http://en.wikipedia.org/wiki/Claude_Nicollier
2   Found at: http://www.brainyquote.com/quotes/quotes/c/claudenico265392.html
3   Found at: http://www.astro-engineering.com/CCD%20%26%20WEBCAM/ccdandwebcamacce.html#cover

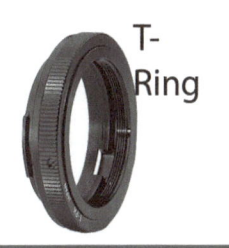

Web-cam 1.25 inch Telescope Adapter

adapters to telescopes. Telescopes combined with web-cams are useful for viewing UFOs close up. For instance, you can find a webcam adapter for a 1.25 inch eyepiece, the most common telescope eyepiece diameter for a telescope at: **http://www.agenaastro.com/**

However, to use a webcam with a telescope adapter (**see left**), you should remove the barrel lens as per the steps discussed in Chapter 4. To do this, you need to cut to shape and add two near infrared passing filters (black film negatives) and place these near infrared filters inside the large end of the telescope adapter tube (rather than putting a near infrared filter into the barrel lens which has now been removed). You then screw the male end of the adapter into the web-cam in the spot formerly occupied by the barrel lens.

T-Ring

You now have a near infrared webcam/ telescope mix suitable for long range UFO sightings. Just slip the adapter tube into the telescope and you have a webcam/ telescope that can record UFO video at long distances.

You can also connect a camera body to a telescope where the telescope effectively replaces the camera zoom lens. This is the preferred method for coupling a SLR (**Single Lens Reflex**) or Digital SLR (**DLSR**) camera to telescope. Normally this requires both a camera adapter and a T-Ring. The camera telescope adapter (**see right**) connects the telescope focuser to brand specific camera, i.e. Canon, Nikon, etc. It is the T-Ring (**see T-Ring left**), which in turn connects to the camera body as if it were a lens to the telescope adapter. The "T" in the word T-Ring refers to a standard thread. Camera adapters feature a male T thread and T-Rings feature a female thread.

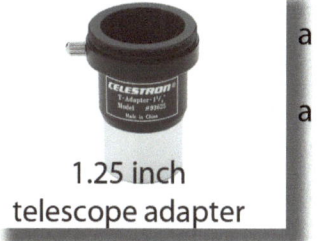

a

a

1.25 inch telescope adapter

As discussed previously, to mount a near infrared camera, you first would have to have a regular camera converted to a near-infrared camera by using a vendor such as Lifepixel, and then add a T-Ring adapter for the brand of camera used (Canon, Nikon, etc.). If you do the previous steps, then you can join the near infrared camera to a telescope using a T-Ring and 1.25 inch telescope adapter.

If you wanted to telescope mount a near infrared video camcorder such as a Sony Nightshot, the most common telescope adapter mount is a C-mount (**see right**) 1.25 inch telescope adapter. You have to check your camcorder for the specific thread type and size.

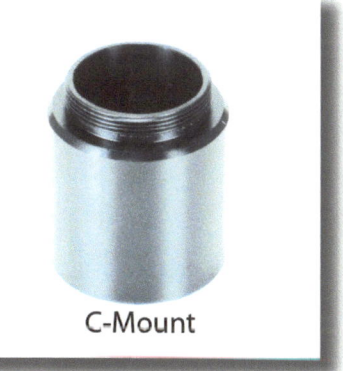

C-Mount

The writer used a near infrared web-cam and 60 X spotter telescope to take this image extracted from a video of a mothership seen at high altitude (**see next page**) on November 3rd, 2008. Any photography novice, photography expert, hobbyist or person with an astronomy background could do the same by utilizing near infrared web-cam equipment and a telescope 1.25 inch adapter described in this chapter to view long range UFOs in near infrared.

Chapter 9: Near Infrared UFO Images

Actually, I'm not all that interested in the subject of photography. Once the picture is in the box, I'm not all that interested in what happens next. Hunters, after all, aren't cooks.

Henri Cartier-Bresson[1]

What is a UFO photography method book for the UFO hunter without a lot of photos of near infrared daylight UFOs! The following pages illustrate what can be achieved using equipment and techniques outlined in the book. Note, these UFO images have been video captured in near infrared and the printed quality of these photos does not match the actual photos when seen on a computer screen. Printed photos have a much more limited color space that does not capture color detail like computer screens and video. For a better understanding of this concept, in the near future I will be producing a companion DVD which shows UFOs in a better color space, the color space of computer screens.

By using only a web-cam and HandyAvi software to capture video, images from video were then extracted, and processed further using IRIS astronomy software and GIMP (a free Photoshop clone).

All the pictures in this chapter were taken during daylight hours in near infrared using the John Bro Wilkie solar obliteration technique (a black coloured barbeque top was used to block the sun) with a near infrared webcam pointed at areas of interest in the sky (**see left photo of a UFO**).

The web-cam used in the photograph has an additional feature: a 5X Fujifilm lens was adapted to replace the barrel lens. This Fujifilm lens was taken from a broken Fuji E510 camera. The lens was used to effectively capture UFO images higher up in the air, while maintaining a wide field of view. To reduce glare while using the solar obliteration method, a LEE Filters number 208 Full C.T. Orange +0.6 neutral density gel filter was used to reduce light down two F-stops.

If you want to obtain the free LEE Filters sample set, you can get the free filter designer set from any high quality camera store or write LEE Filters directly and ask for a free LEE Filters Designer Edition sample of gel filters. Or, buy this neutral density filter sheet.

I used the solar obliteration method in combination with a near infrared web-cam to obtain the image above. In the image, we see a UFO plunging by the sun on October 25th, 2009, at 12:00 pm. This webcam with the Fujifilm lens was set up below a black barbecue top, and the webcam was in shadow from the barbecue top. The black heat paint from the barbecue top lowers reflected glare in the photo.

1   *Cartier-Bresson, Henri quote, found at:* http://www.brainyquote.com/quotes/authors/h/henri_cartierbresson.html

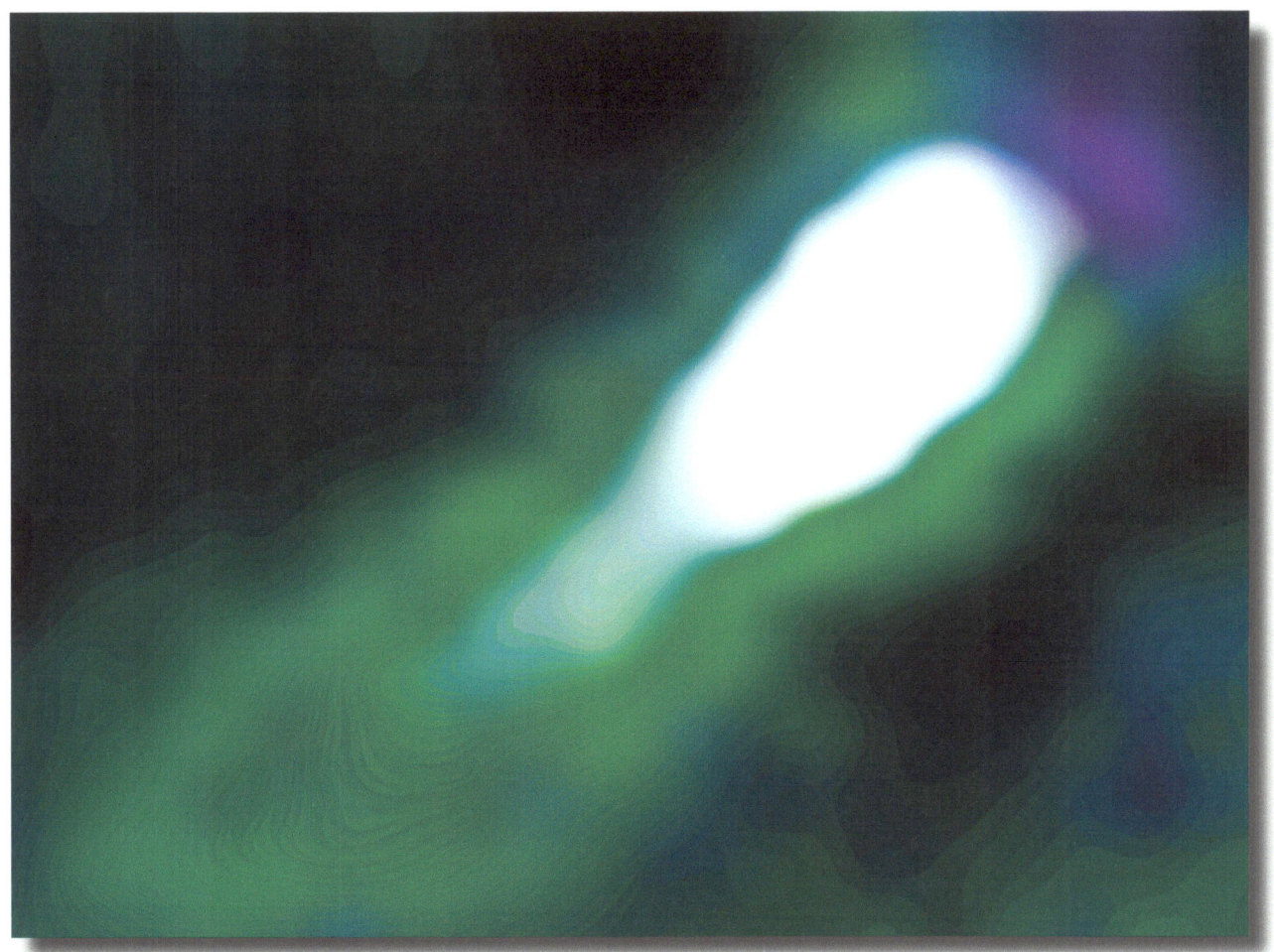

The UFO image was then expanded 130 times using bi-cubic resampling in IRIS to produce a blurred image of a UFO. The blurry image did not have enough contrast (sky is black in near infrared), so the sky was eventually contrast adjusted in GIMP to black. The work done on this stealthed UFO image took the approach to first sharpen the image in GIMP, and then apply an edge extraction algorithm, i.e. NEON (found in GIMP). After NEON was applied, a series of directional blurs were applied in GIMP in order to "disable" the stealth blur around the UFO. This is always a tricky and complex procedure to process a photo this way and an entire book would be needed to describe this method in detail. However, using the above method on pictures, you can obtain on occasion, the actual UFO craft underneath the stealth (**see above unprocessed photograph, processed photograph top of next page**). Overall, the UFO bears no resemblance to any earthly craft when you look at the processed photo on the next page. You can note that there are parts of the craft that are absolutely black, which indicates that some parts of the craft are showing up in near infrared, whereas other parts of the UFO are not showing at all in this part of the spectrum. Note the UFO was travelling by the webcam at a rate where only one frame of the UFO was caught by the webcam eye for later processing.

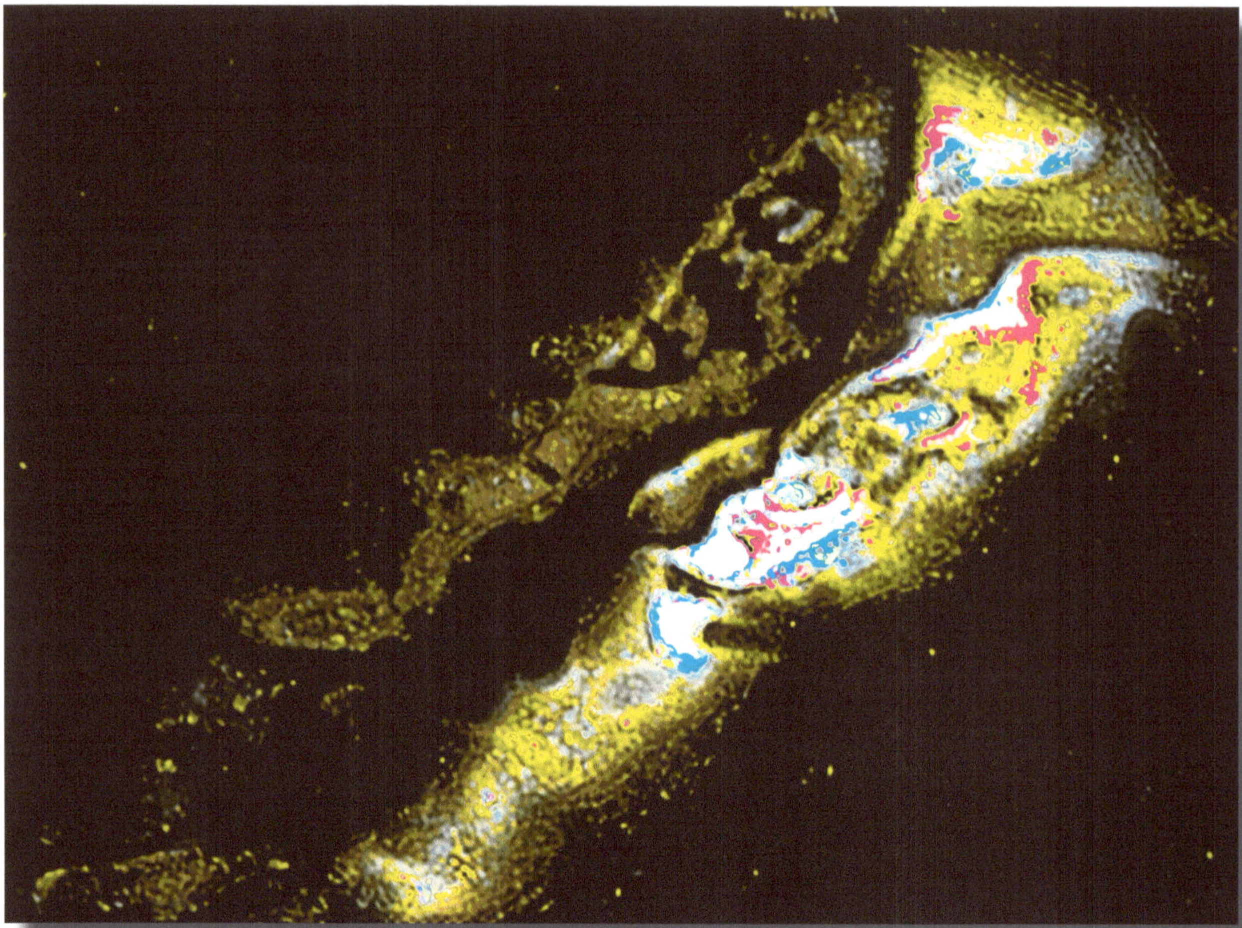

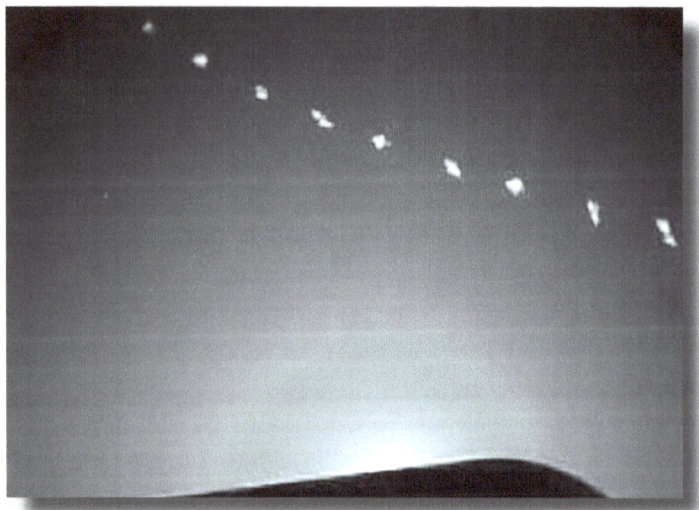

Another UFO was caught on web-cam on October 28, 2009 at 12:29 p.m. (**see left**). HandyAvi software offers the option to capture a meteor track across the sky as one composite photo composed of multiple video frames. However, with respect to UFO photography, this composite photo function in HandyAvi software works equally well with capturing UFO tracks across the sky. This feature was turned on to show a UFO passing by the web-cam eye as a composite of several video frames combined into one photograph. The UFO was passing by at a speed where stacking could not be used, as the UFO is "skipping" to a new position between video frames. This "skipping" or "jumping" of a UFO from one point in space to another is a very common feature of a UFO in flight.

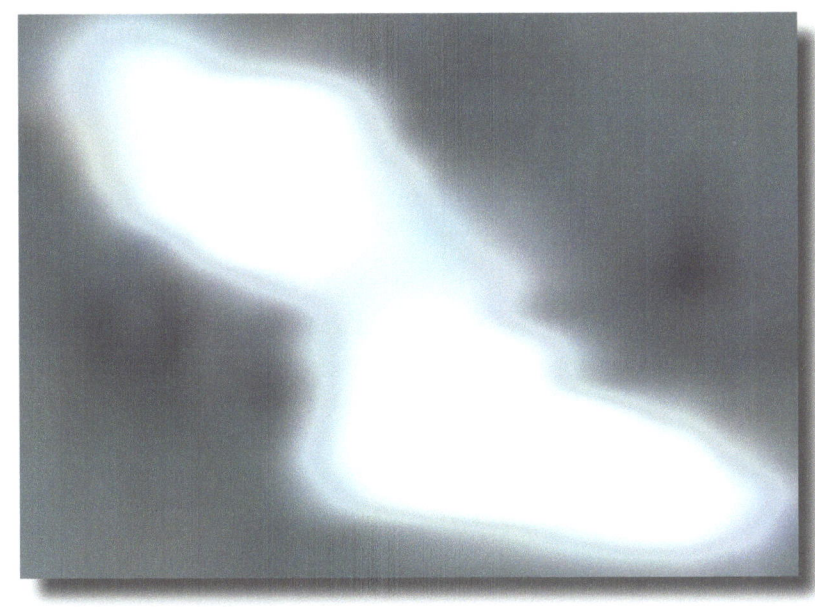

The UFO was blown up 100 times to produce this image (**see left**). After processing the image in GIMP (**see bottom photo**), you can see that the central portion of the UFO is clearly visible in near infrared. This easy to see portion of the UFO is surrounded by a much larger structure that does not reflect much light in near infrared as the UFO is composed of different materials. For example, some of the material reflects infrared light and some of the material absorbs light in that portion of the spectrum (or is reflected away from the web-cam as per our discussion on optical gratings).

The next UFO was seen on November 7, 2009, using the solar obliteration technique (**see top figure next page**). Again, the black painted top of a barbecue was used to block out direct sunlight shining into the web-cam eye. The image was automatically captured with HandyAvi, and expanded 50 times to produce the second blurry image seen on this page (**see bottom picture next page**). The near IR web-cam was modified on this date by taping a LEE gel filter Full C.T. Orange + 0.6 neutral density filter over the web-cam lens to reduce the glare of the sun by two F-Stops.

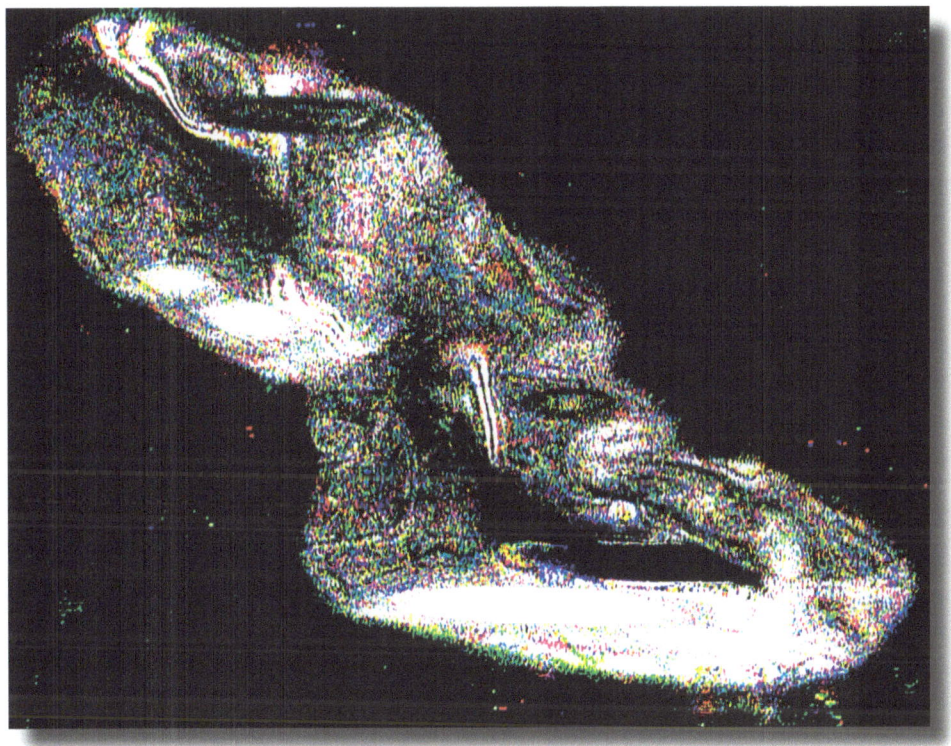

Neutral density filters can be quite expensive. Using a LEE filter design edition filter pack is a quick and economical way to test how to reduce sun glare at different levels of light before purchasing more permanent glass neutral density filters.

As you can seen from the resulting processed image (**see next page, photo rotated 90 degrees clockwise**), LEE neutral density filters produce better pictures of highly reflective UFOs. Highly reflective UFOs form part of the menage of UFO craft flying above our planet.

In this instance of recording this UFO, I was actually looking at the computer monitor screen just after setting up a near infrared web-cam in the direction of the sun. Within a few minutes of setting up my hunt for UFOs, I was surprised by the sight of this particular UFO (**see left**) as it flashed by the computer monitor, and immediately rewound the video after seeing this unusual craft.

This UFO was very unusual with respect to the mirror-like surface of the craft, which was unlike any UFO I had previously seen in the past three years. I spent several hours processing the image. The resulting image, after processing with GIMP, shows remarkable clarity and detail, capturing the mirror-like surface of the mother-of-pearl like appearance of the outer skin of this UFO (**see next page**).

Note the optical grating surfaces, seen in the middle area of the UFO on the next page, make it particular hard to process the middle area of this particular UFO. Often, when there are obvious optical gratings areas on a UFO, these areas will appear as a dark grey, or alternatively, as rainbow like sequences of colors, showing that light is being reflected and refracted away from sight.

You have to work with the "Curves" adjustment function in GIMP or Photoshop, sometimes making tight careful adjustments with the Curves function with respect to the narrow bands of light frequency being reflected and refracted in these optical grating areas of a UFO, in order to bring out details.

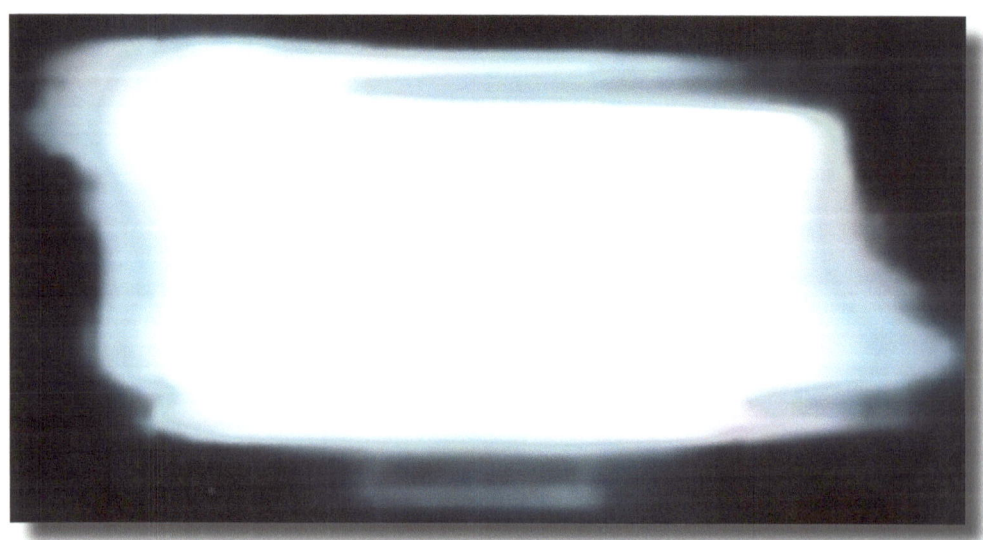

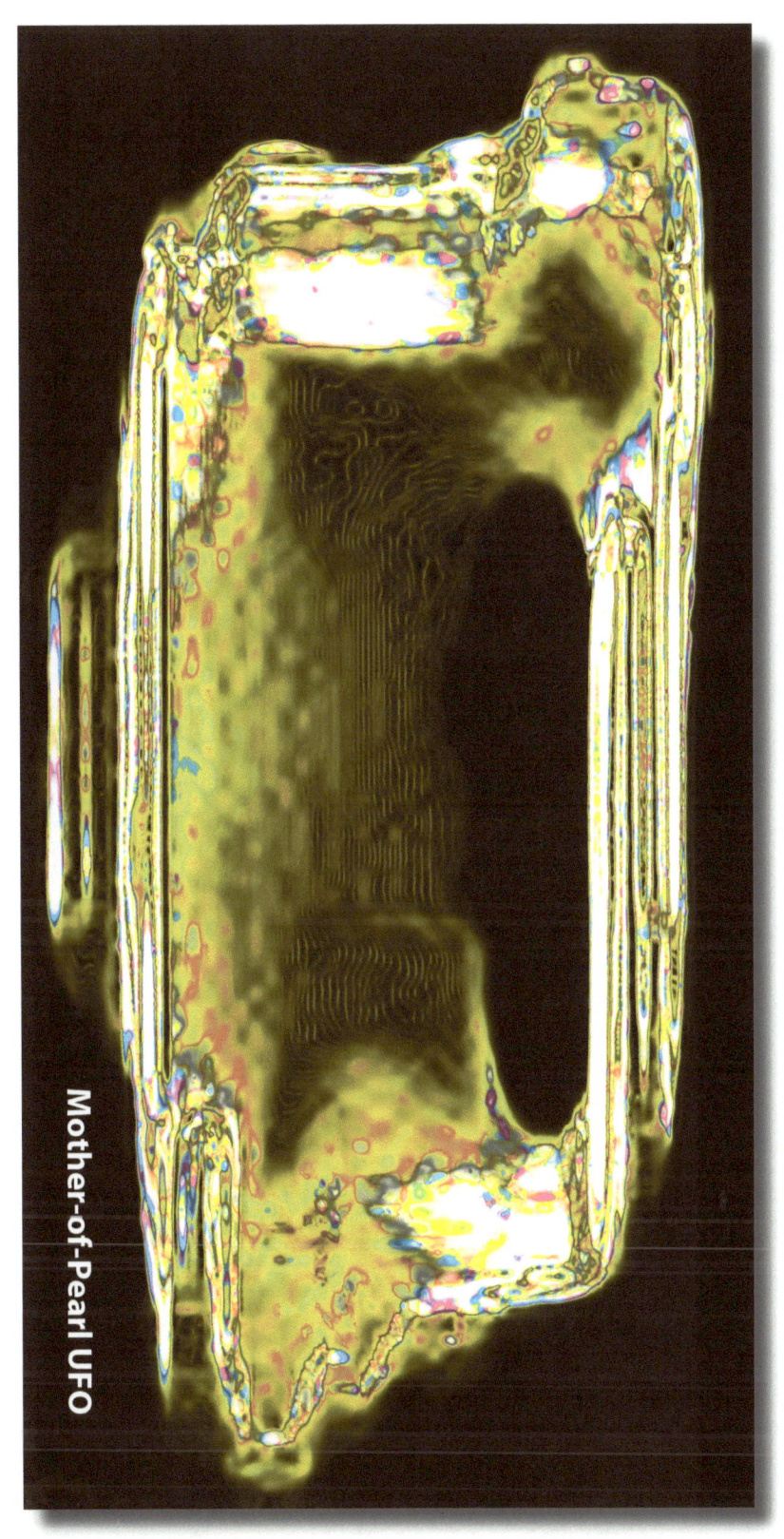

Mother-of-Pearl UFO

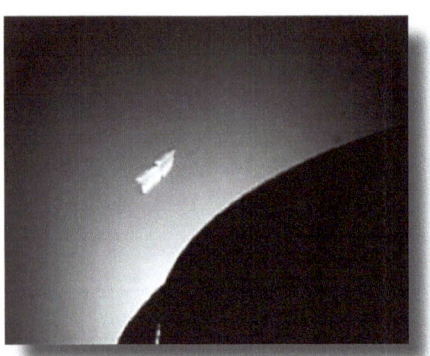 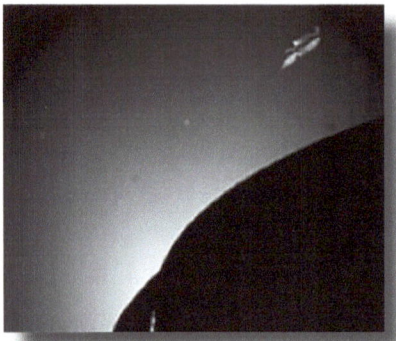

On November 9th, 2009, at 11:42 a.m., the following close flying UFO was automatically captured by HandyAvi during a twenty minute UFO hunting session. The cloudless day provided perfect conditions for using HandyAvi automatic capture of UFO video. The UFO was likely within about 350 meters of the near infrared web-cam and moving at a rate where only two frames were captured in sequence (**see above images, zoomed UFO photograph below**). Once again, the barbecue top was serving the purpose of blocking the sun as per the John Bro Wilkie method. The image was then rotated 90 degrees to show more of the UFO when expanded 30

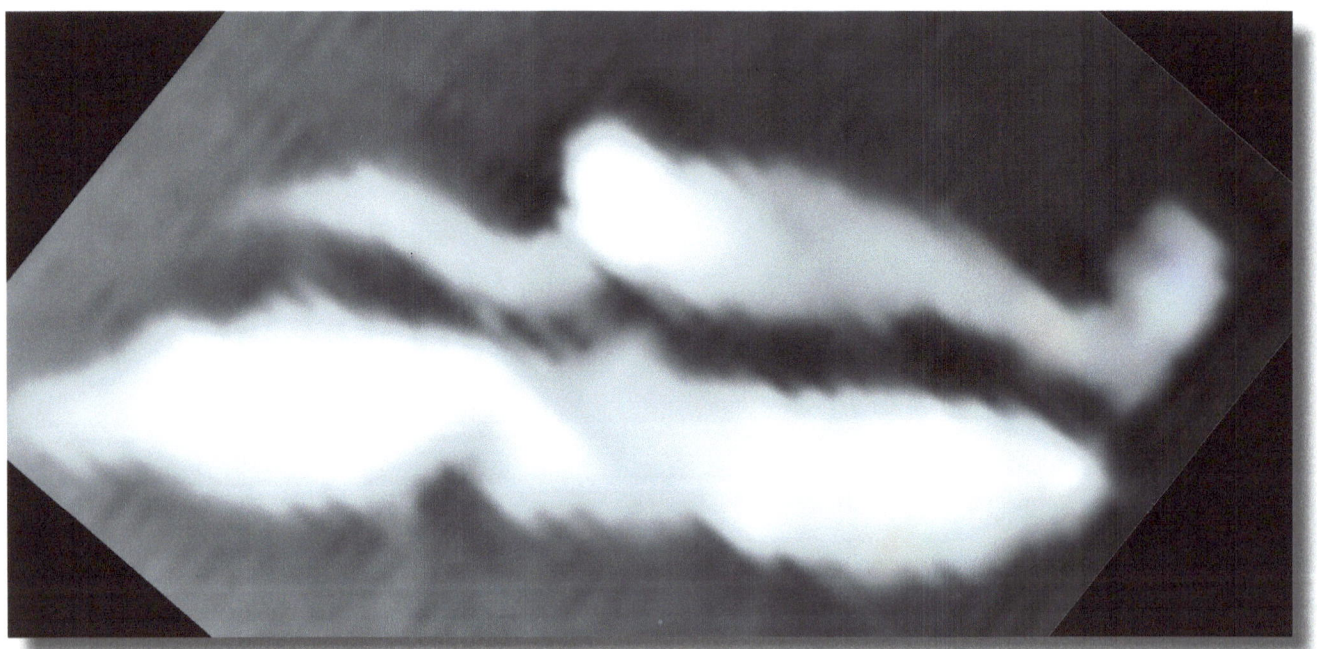

times in IRIS software. Further processing of the image in GIMP resulted in the very clear image of an organic looking UFO (**see large UFO image located on next page**).

Note the small objects surrounding the larger UFO. These objects are not image artifacts. These smaller objects represent small miniature flying probe type UFOs that are often associated with larger UFOs. These smaller, presumably robotic UFOs, often are seen in near infrared video surrounding larger UFOs. As an opinion, my belief is these small probe craft are a type of "sensor net" that the larger UFOs deploy to expand the ability of the larger UFO to collect data and to sense changes in the environment around the main UFO craft. It is not an uncommon event to record hundreds of these smaller probe type craft around larger UFOs. When recording near infrared video, sometimes these smaller probe type craft will come within a few feet of the web-cam eye as these probes look over a geographic area.

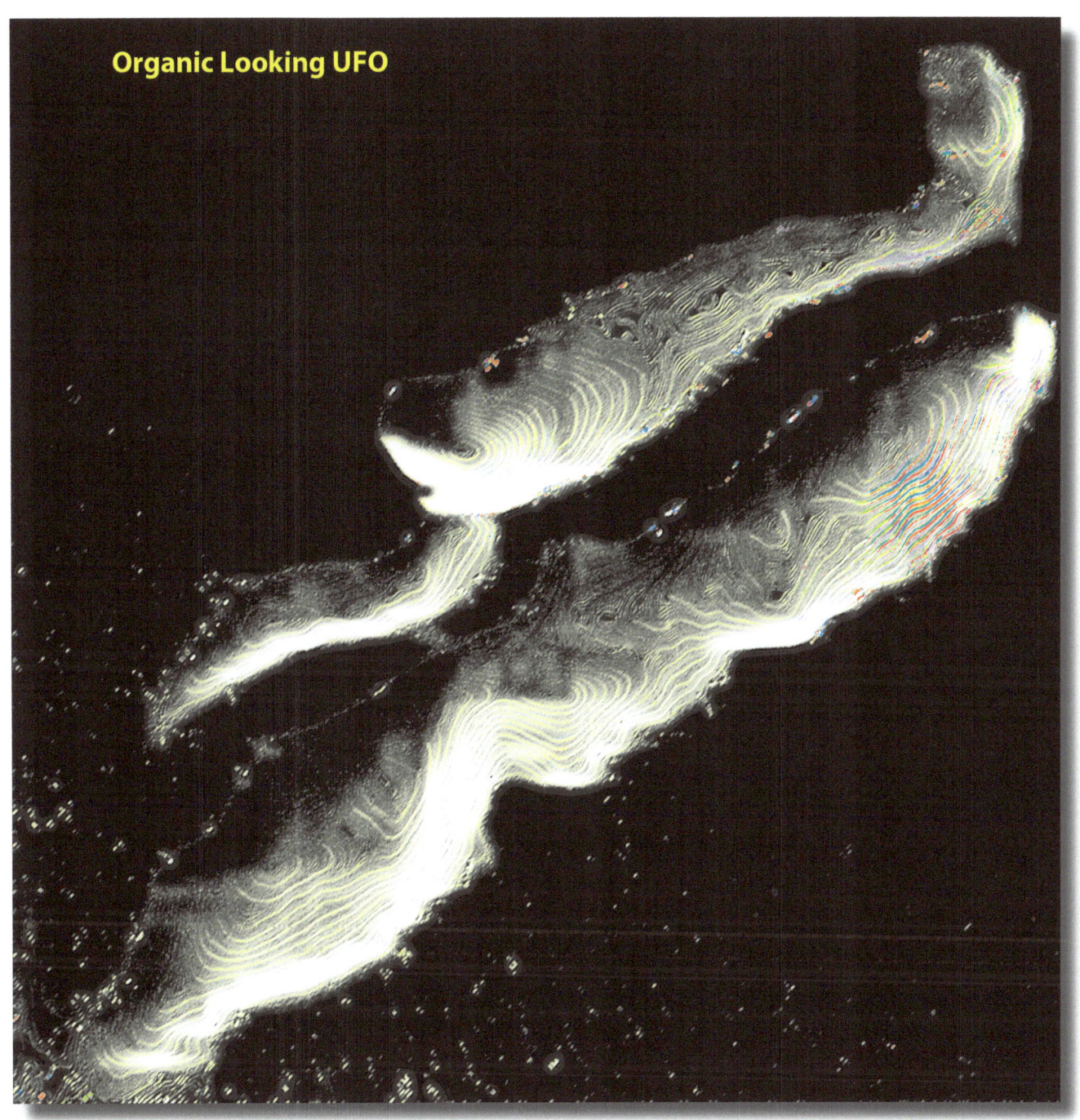

Organic Looking UFO

The following photographic image was extracted from a daylight video taken on October 19th, 2009, showing a UFO probe craft (**see left**) that is above a chimney. The UFO is barely visible underneath a wooden crossbar of a window in this near IR web-cam shot extracted from video.

Note the flying probe is actually pointed towards the frame of the window, suggesting that the probe is looking back at the author while he is photographing the probe-UFO.

Again, this type of occurrence of a probe looking over an area can be pretty common — check out a UFO in the sky, and that UFO may be checking you out right back using

smaller probes.

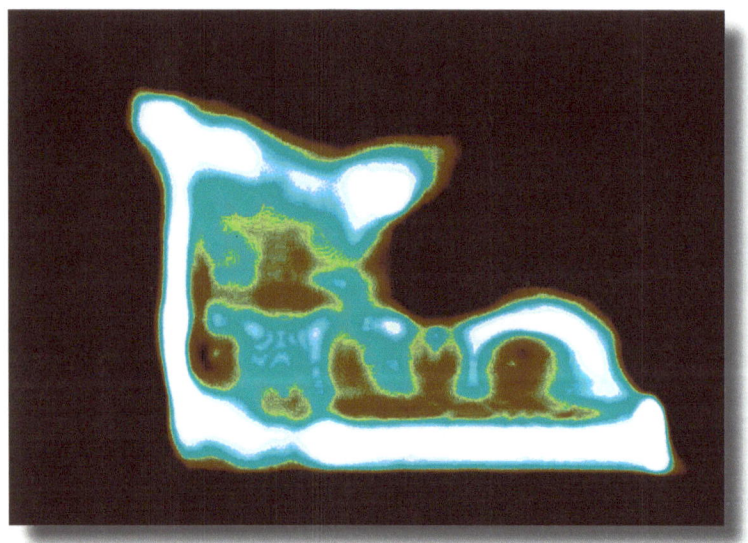

This web-cam frame was then blown up 60 times, and enhanced to reveal an image of a small triangular UFO craft that is not more than two feet in width when compared to the chimney in the picture (**see close up probe photo left**).

Probes seem to represent a low risk strategy by aliens to examine areas before larger, possibly crewed alien craft arrive on the scene. These probes are incredibly fast and often can be seen, as noted before, travelling in masses of hundreds before the arrival of larger UFO craft. Considering the numbers of probes seen, such as the smaller probes surrounding the UFO on the previous page, it is likely that the larger UFOs can collect enormous amounts of information on the ground activities of people by deploying these astoundingly fast and agile flying probes, which by design appear capable of looking into every nook and cranny.

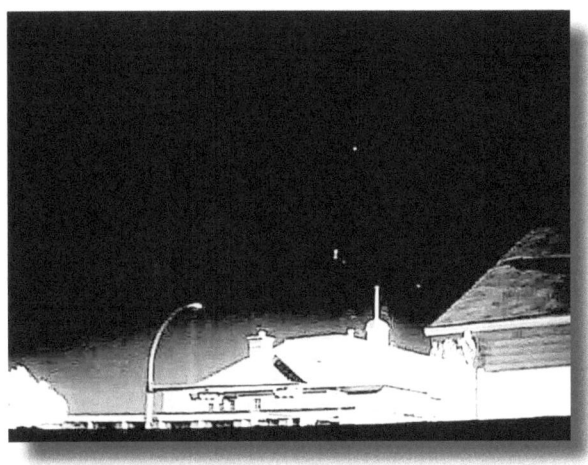

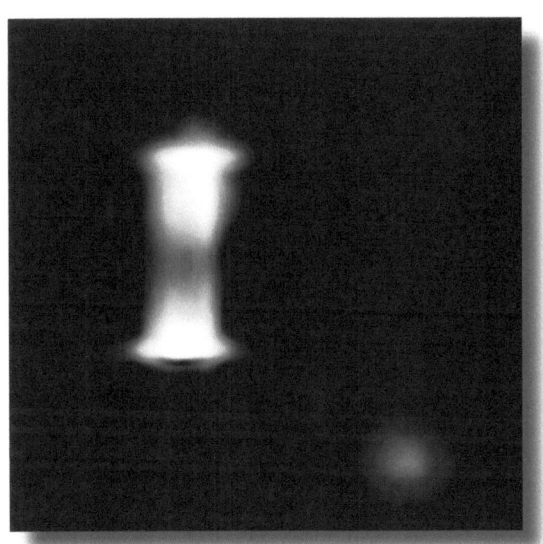

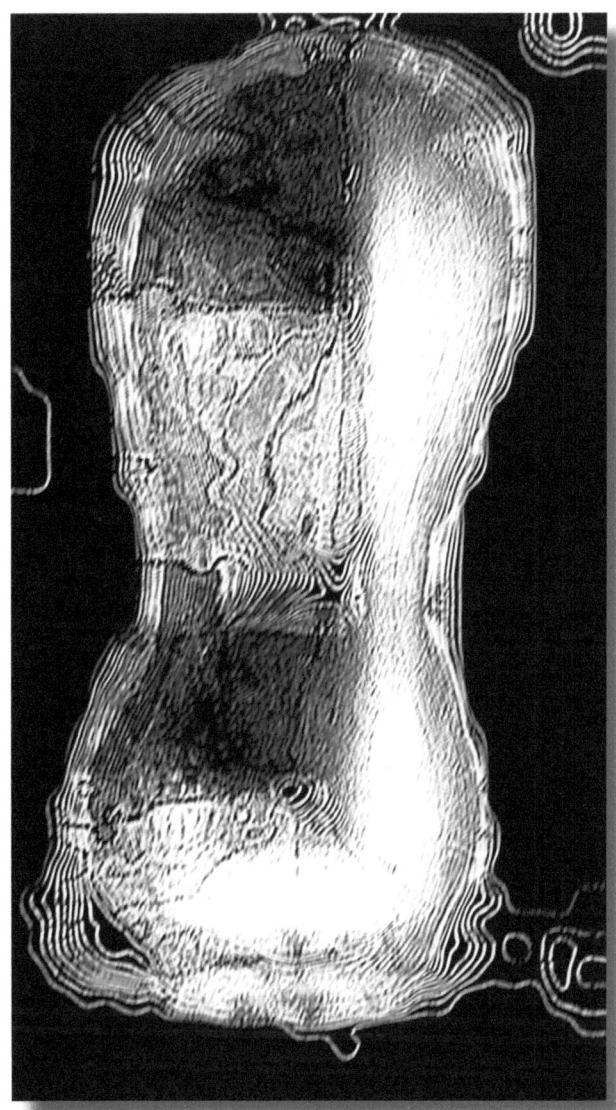

The next set of pictures (**see to top left original photo from video, zoomed photo above, further zoomed and processed photo to right above**) shows you a photo extracted from a video of about 15 UFOs that swarmed over a school building on October 21th, 2008 at 1:52 p.m.

One of the UFOs looked like an hourglass figure, which suggested initially that it was one UFO towing another UFO below it. But when the photo was processed for detail, the image shows that this was a single UFO with an hourglass shape to its structure. The craft also shows stria, or etched lines, which resemble fresnel lens shapes built into the skin of the UFO. These etched lines, as previously discussed, provide light bending optical stealth hiding ability for a UFO.

UFOs also display an incredible variety and variation with respect to shapes that suggests several different species are building these craft. Over the next pages, I show some of these unique craft.

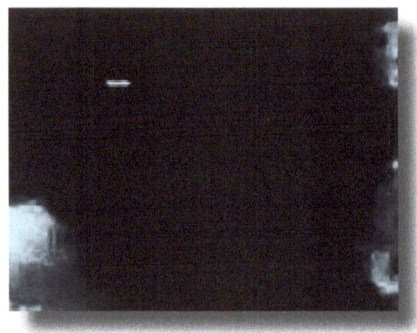

The UFO to the left was extracted from a video taken on March 17, 2010 at 3:10 p.m. This rod-like UFO was moving relatively slowly just below the cloud base in a North to South direction above a busy intersection. The original photo at the top of the page has been expanded 30 times to reveal the UFO images below (**see lower left and right photo, turned 90 degrees clockwise to fit the page, image to the right was color enhanced**).

The following UFO (**see top next page**) was seen on a near infrared web-cam on February 11th, 2010, at 11:37 p.m. The craft flew in an

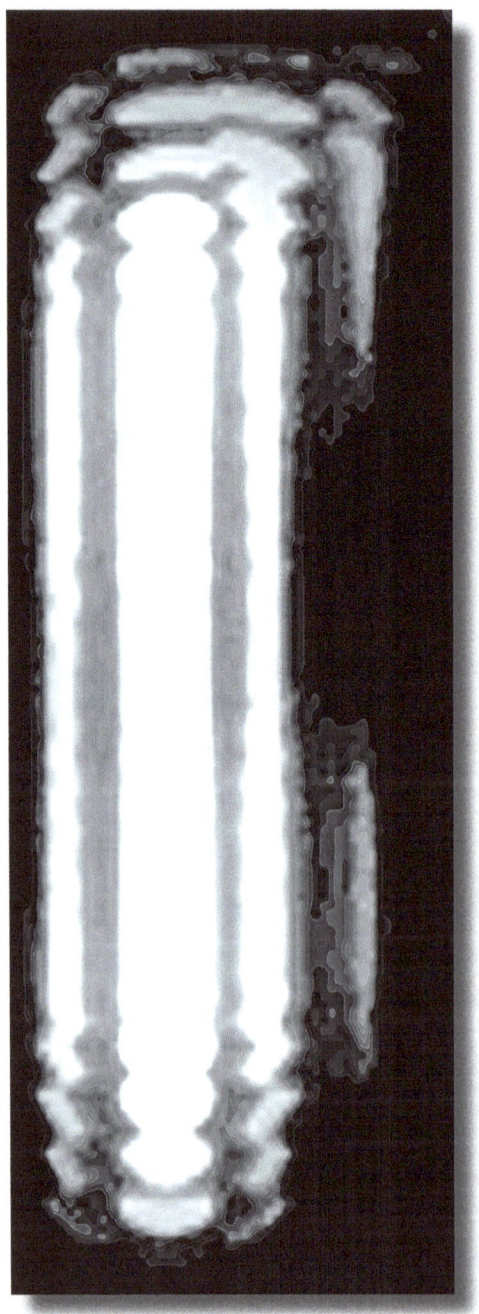

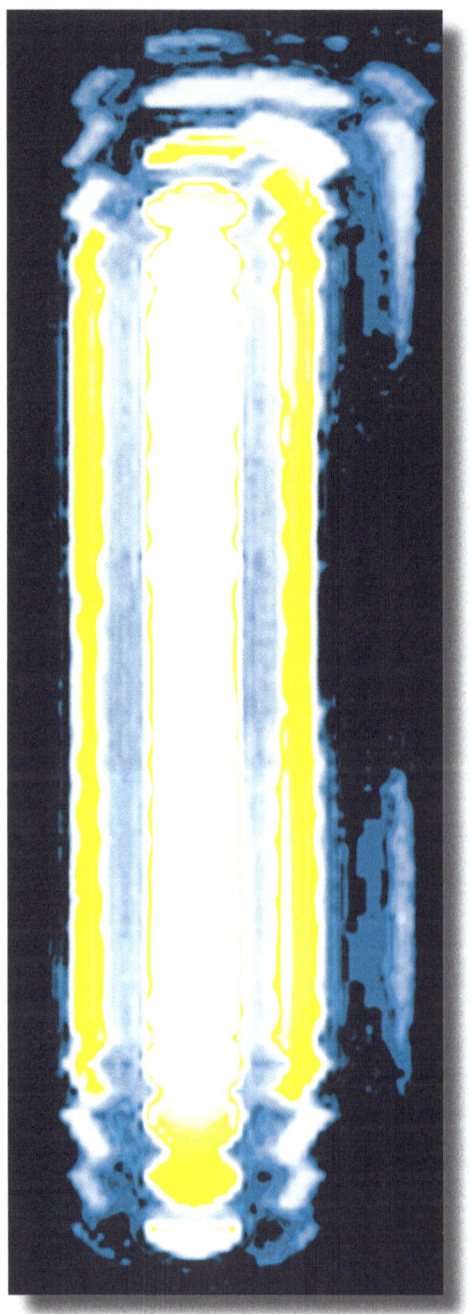

ascending line from East to West, taking about 3/4th of a second to cross the sky from horizon to horizon. The UFO reminds me of an ancient hieroglyph. Note the processed figure shows some sort of machinery or being inside the upper half of the craft (**photo at bottom of page, figure outlined in yellow**), but

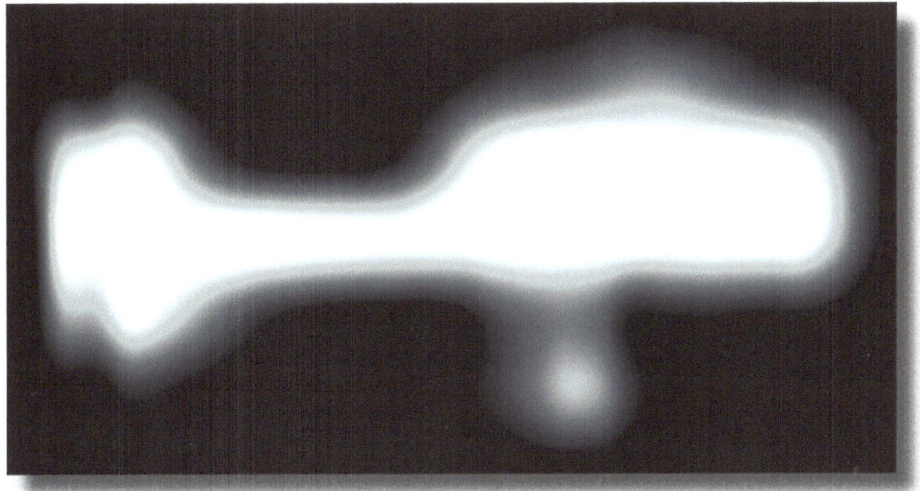

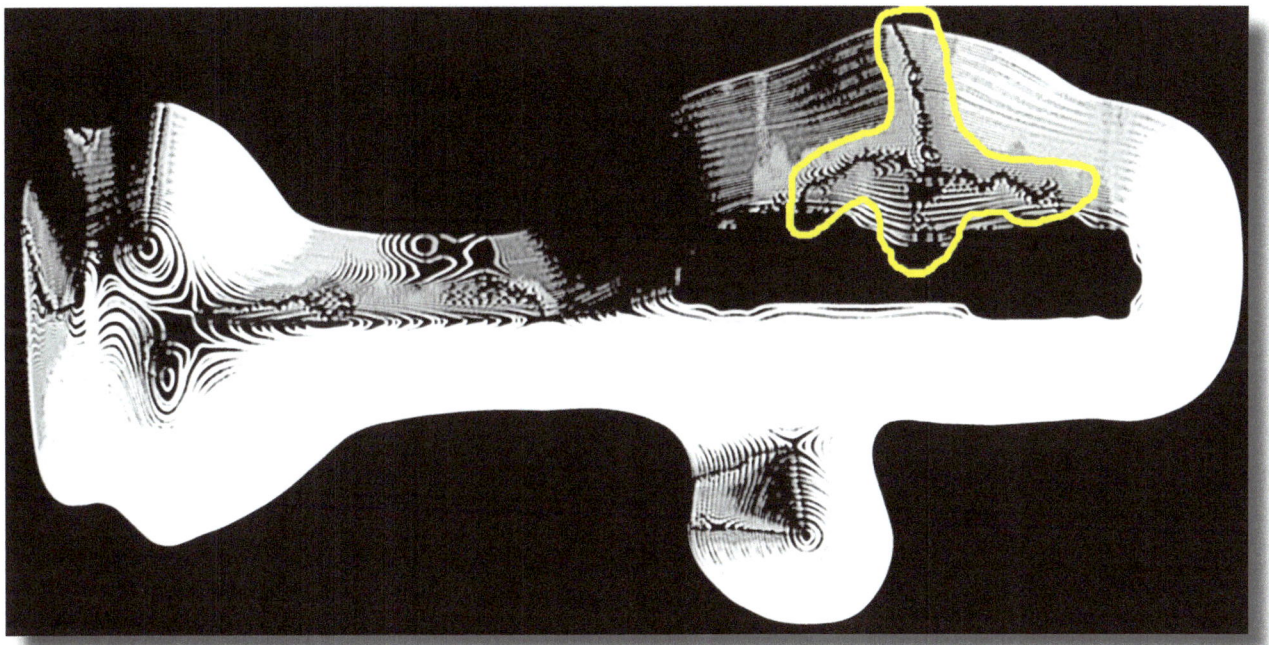

at this time I am unable to classify this figure as to whether it is a machine, or a being. My assumption is that this is a piloted craft, and that only a portion of the pilot (machine or being) is visible due to the stealth suit of the pilot interacting with the overall stealth of the UFO. What I see in the photo is a creature, which can be either a machine or a living being, with bilateral symmetry as indicated by two arms on the being which appear to be manipulating some form of control panel. Your interpretation of this photo may be entirely different, and as equally valid.

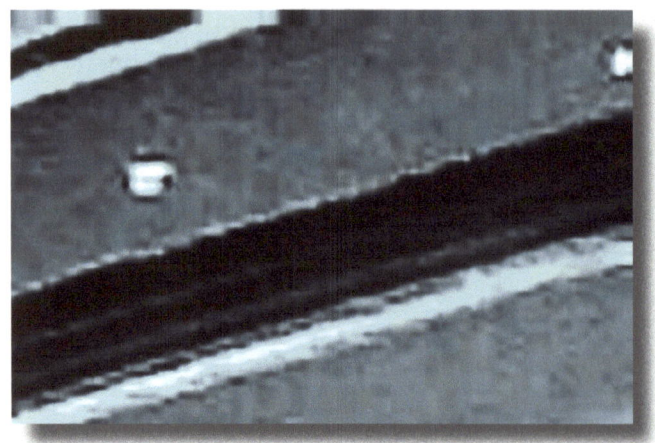

The next near infrared web-cam image (**see left**) was caught on video on March 14th, 2010 (see upper photo on this page) at 1:23:14 p.m. through an eastward facing window. You can see structures, possibly machinery, within the upper half of the UFO (**bottom photo, no pilot visible**).

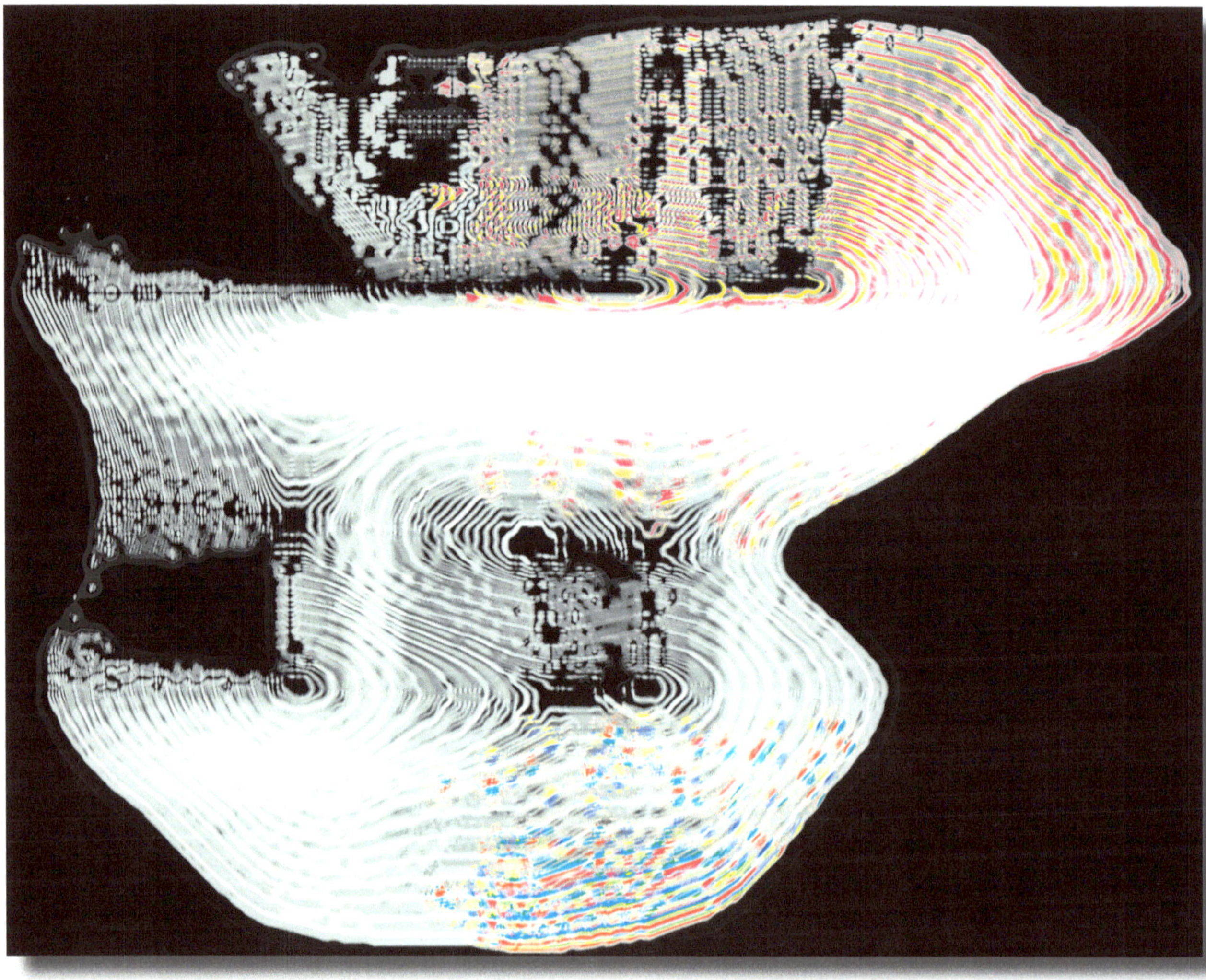

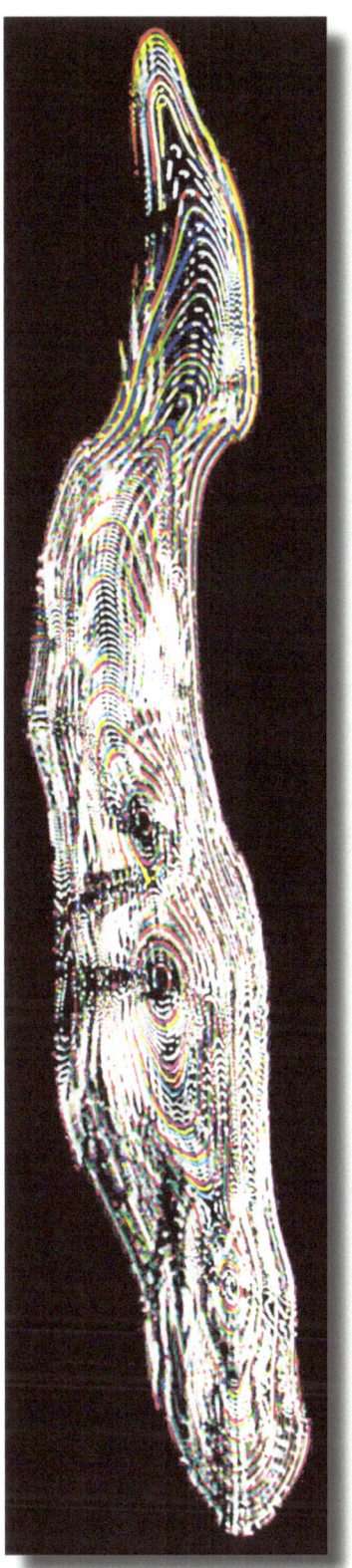

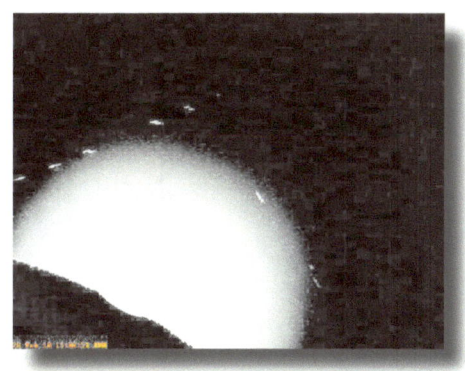

The composite meteor track/ UFO image (**see right**) shows a UFO with an organic appearance, almost resembling some form of sea creature, which was captured skipping across the sky on March 13th, 2010, 11:03:55 p.m. The photo (**see left, photo rotated 90 degrees counterclockwise to fit the page**) was expanded 50 times to reveal a fascinating craft which appears to be composed of fresnel lense like layers and almost transparent components that are emitting colors in blue, green and red. Expanding the middle section of the photo another ten times, you can see a detailed look (**see below**) of the incredible complexity of this craft's optical stealth.

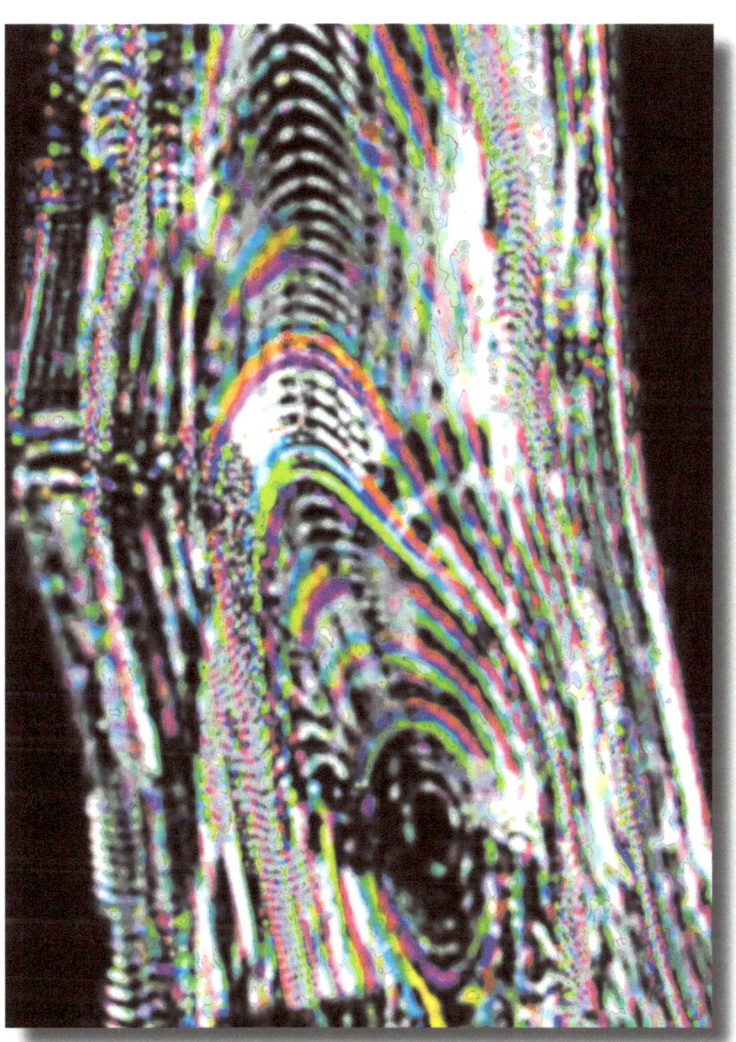

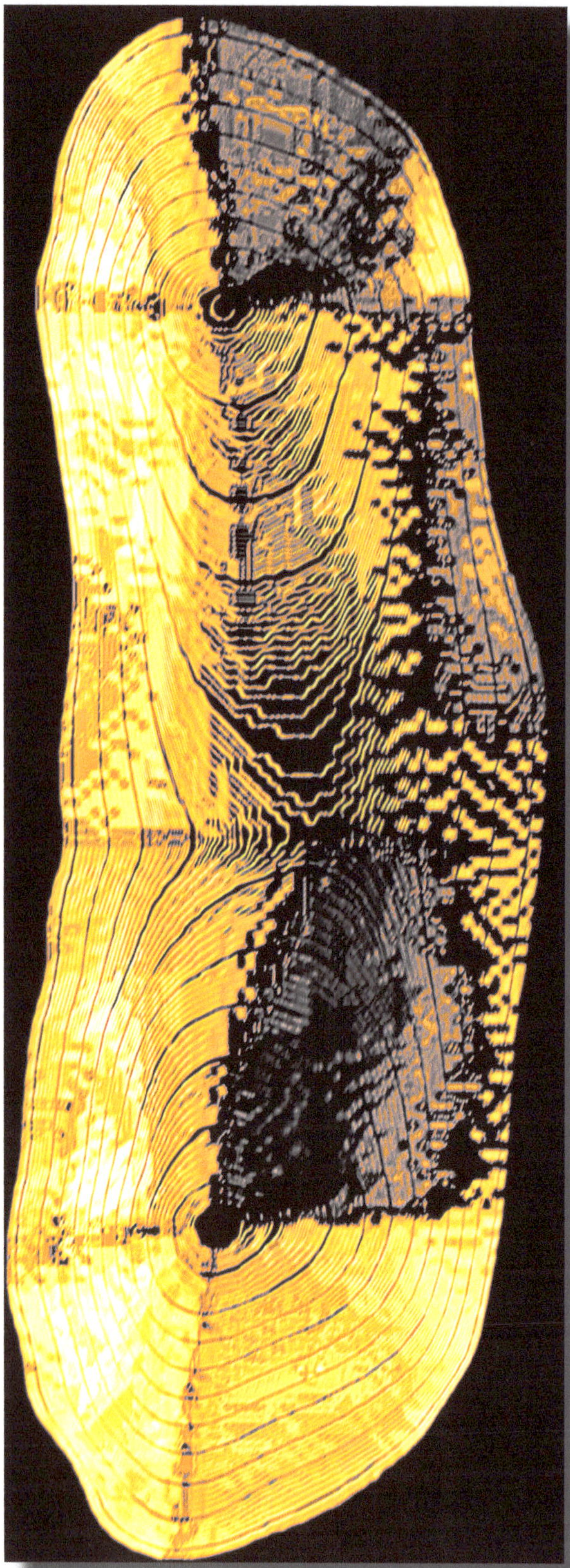

This UFO near infrared image was captured automatically by Handy Avi (**see above**), and shows a golden colored UFO that looks more like a classic UFO shape as portrayed in Ufology. The golden UFO (**see left, photo rotated 90 degrees clockwise to fit page**) was expanded 300 times to reveal a fascinating craft which appeared in the skies to the east of a major Canadian city on March 17th, 2010, 2:40:20 p.m.

This UFO vaguely resembles a Grey Alien UFO shown later in this book in the chapter on aliens.

Chapter 10: Night and Day UFO Photography

A photograph is memory in the raw.

Carrie Latet[1]

UFO Hunting at Night

At night you can mistake UFOs for known objects such as planes while UFO hunting. During nighttime UFO hunting, you should expect to see planes which use red and green navigation lights. Aircraft navigation lights are placed in a way similar to that of marine vessels, with a red navigation light located on the left wingtip leading edge and a green light on the right wingtip leading edge. A white navigation light is placed on the tail of each wing tip. High-intensity strobe lights are located on the aircraft to aid in collision avoidance. Navigation lights in civil aviation are required to be turned on from sunset to sunrise. High-intensity white strobe lights are part of the anti-collision light system, as well as the aviation red or white rotating beacon. The anti-collision light system (either strobe lights or rotating beacon) is required for all airplanes built after March 11th, 1996, for all flight activities in poor visibility, and is recommended in good visibility, where only strobes and beacons are required.[2]

However, and here is the rub: UFOs at night, can and do sport red and green lights as a cover to look like planes. In addition, these type of UFOs will also either put out motor sounds to sound like a prop plane, or will be silent. That being said, UFO craft will generally have much larger green and red lights compared to plane navigation lights. The author has also seen night UFOs emit a blue light, which is not a navigation light that can be mistaken for plane lights. Other known night objects which can potentially confuse the UFO photography hunter are the planets, for example planets such as Venus. Over the years, NASA has used Venus as a possible explanation for UFO sightings. It is an easy enough mistake to make since after the moon, Venus is the brightest object in the night sky.

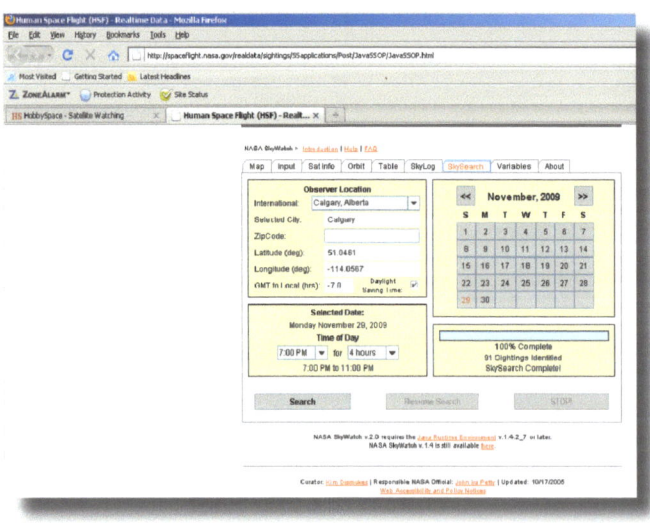

Along with misidentifying planets for UFOs, orbiting satellites can be confused as UFOs. As a general rule, satellites will appear as a small light in the night sky that always takes a few minutes to travel in a straight line course from one horizon of the skyline to the other horizon. That being said, if a light in the sky that looks like a satellite makes a ninety degree turn or more at night, that is a sign you are looking at a UFO. Fortunately, there is help in identifying UFOs using a website that NASA provides for satellite watchers (**see online program screen shot left**). If you input the link below into an Internet browser, you will be able to

---

1   Found at: http://www.quotegarden.com/photography.html
2   Found at: http://en.wikipedia.org/wiki/Navigation_light

use an online NASA program that shows where and when satellites appear in the night sky:

http://spaceflight.nasa.gov/realdata/sightings/SSapplications/Post/JavaSSOP/JavaSSOP.html

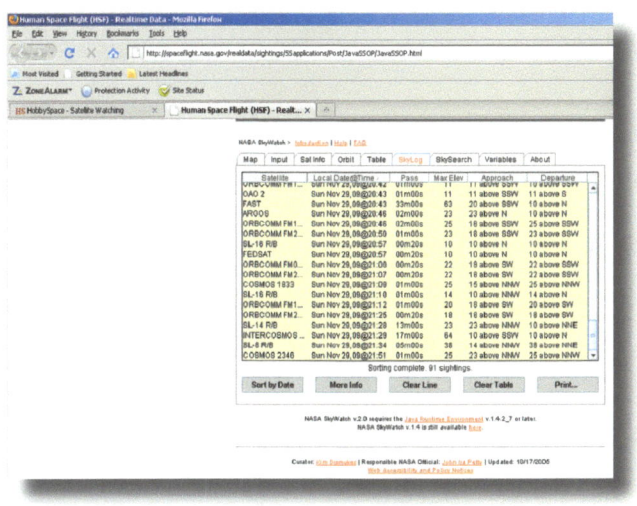

On the NASA site, if you click on the tab labelled "Sky Search", you can set your home location (**see left**). More importantly, the online NASA program can be set to search during the time at night when the UFO hunter will be watching the skies. This program can track when any given satellites will appear, and how many satellites in that period of time will appear over your skies. The program will even tell you when the satellites will depart from your skyline.

If you click on the tab labeled "Skylog", you can see a table of satellites. This table shows the satellite arrival time and can be imported into Excel or Open Office Calc. Saving the table in Excel will allow you to later cross reference the satellite times to prevent mixing up a satellite with a UFO, for example a known quite distinct object, such as the ISS (International Space Station) will appear on this table.

Identifying Venus, Planets and Stars

In terms of locating Venus in the night sky, Stellarium is a free program which contains the locations of 600,000 stars and planets and runs on Linux, Mac and Windows systems. This program is a straightforward way to check on points of light in the sky to make sure that you are potentially not mistaking a planet or star for a UFO. You have to set your home location in the program, and the program will then set up a night sky within your computer which will allow you to identify known night objects such as planets or stars. This program can be downloaded from: **http://www.stellarium.org/**

Another star gazing program called Cartes du Ciel can also be used to identify known night objects such as stars and planets. This program is downloaded from: **http://www.stargazing.net/astropc/**

Nighttime UFO Pictures with Cameras and Video

Subjects in low light, night scenes, or point source lights in the sky such as stars and UFOs, are hard to capture without being familiar with manual modes on cameras. An important concept in photography regarding low light is understanding ISO. In traditional (film) photography ISO (or ASA) was the indication of how sensitive a film was to light. ISO was and is measured in numbers (you've probably seen them on film canisters, i.e. 100, 200, 400, 800, etc). The lower the number, the lower the sensitivity of the film and the finer the grain in the shots you are taking.

In digital photography ISO measures the sensitivity of the image sensor. The same principles apply as in film photography. The lower the ISO number, the less sensitive your camera is to light, and the finer the grain in the resulting photograph. Higher ISO settings are generally used in darker situations to get faster shutter speeds, for example an indoor sports event when you want to freeze the action in lower light. However the cost is noisier shots.[3] Overall, the best image quality is usually obtained at the lowest ISO setting on your digital camera.

Recording conditions under low light means that light captured by the CMOS or CCD sensors will be minimal. In order to increase light captured by CMOS and CCD sensors on modern cameras, you have to do the following in manual mode on the camera:

- Increase the aperture on the camera;

- Increase the length of time the sensor is used to record (not easy when a UFO travels across the sky);

- Increase the ISO of the CCD sensor which will increase noise in an image;

- Automatic Focus (AF) works poorly at night and poorly tracks moving objects, so focus has to be set manually.

Also to note, in terms of getting better quality images at night, there are certain conditions that make night photography difficult:

- Taking pictures under a light source whose brightness, color, or pattern keeps changing, i.e. UFOs flicker, shine brightly, and change patterns at night;

- Taking photographs under fluorescent lighting;

- Trying to take pictures and video of small subjects;

- Camera shake or subject blur under low light;

- Auto-focusing while the subject is out of focus, i.e., UFOs are always blurry by design, and;

- Blur from hand shake tends to increase when your shutter speed is slower under low light conditions and when a tripod is not used.

Manual Camera Modes

In order to be successful at nighttime UFO hunting, you have to become familiar with using manual mode on a camera. More often than not, the UFO hunter who succeeds in taking low light photos, does so by practicing with their camera's manual functions, in controlled low light conditions before trying out UFO photography in the field. Prior to starting, find out what works best for your camera using manual mode settings, before going outside and trying low light UFO photography.

Take for example, the photograph on page 99 of this book. In this instance, near infrared light was not used when this photograph was taken with a Canon EOS T1i camera. Rather, the author used low light photography methods shown later in this chapter.

However, at night it is good to remember to use slower shutter speeds. Try to set your camera shutter speed slower than 1/30th of a second or much lower and raise your ISO on the DSLR camera to 800 or higher. If you can, always try to use a tripod to help reduce camera shake induced blur in photographs

---

3 **Definition of ISO**, found at: http://digital-photography-school.com/iso-settings

and video.

As mentioned previously, another thing to remember is to use manual focus at night. Automatic focus on cameras does not work well in low light conditions. There is nothing more frustrating with respect to nighttime UFO hunting, than watching a UFO fly by in the sky when the automatic focus is unable to achieve focus on the UFO due to low light conditions. In low light conditions, manual focus works best to capture a UFO photograph or video.

By manually setting focus on the DLSR camera right at the beginning of the night, you avoid the automatic focus problem. By setting "focus" on manual for infinity, you then have a camera ready for UFO action at night. Keep in mind the street lamp focus trick for focusing web-cams which works equally as well with a camera to obtain good focus. And if your zoom lense allows you to lock the zoom focus (where you can lock the zoom on infinity), lock it. A previously focused camera is especially handy if a UFO is flying in slow fashion over an urban area, and you just have time to grab your pre-focused camera and start shooting.

With night shoots, pictures are often taken in "raw mode" where there is more work post-processing pictures later. Therefore, it is better if your camera supports taking dual jpeg and raw photos at the same time. In particular, photos saved as "raw" are better than jpeg saved photos for changing the picture later using curves, white balance and levels functions. However, a jpeg picture is quicker to process, while photos taken in raw mode, can be adjusted later to bring out much more detail in underexposed dark photos.

Overall, the best tool to use at night is a camera tripod. But for those on the fly, handheld shots, to reduce shake in a picture, lean your body on a solid object (building or fence), then take the photo. For those action photos of UFOs moving at night, lean against a wall and hold the camera on the object while sweeping the camera at the same speed the object travels. Holding the camera steady on the object as it flies across the sky reduces motion blur. A trick to steady your hand, while taking the picture, is to take a deep breath and let out half a breath, then hold your remaining breath to steady your hand while holding the camera on the moving or floating still object.

To have success with this method takes practice. Practice this half breath out, hand sweep method at night on known objects, such as moving cars, to get the method down pat. It helps to practice taking photos using the half breath method with a Liveview screen preview. Liveview offers instant feedback and you can take as many photos as your camera memory card allows, while deleting blurred photos.

A DLSR camera will typically offer anti-shake capabilities in the lens or camera body. Turn on anti-shake during night time UFO photo work. Even a tripod mounted camera can be thrown off by shake from setting up equipment on an unstable platform, such as a wooden deck. Image stabilization technology (IS), as offered in the Canon camera lenses along with other name brand cameras, greatly helps by reducing shake in photos taken at night. Image stabilization is one of the best features to have in a DLSR camera during night time UFO video and picture taking. I carry an extra battery pack for longer night time viewing sessions, and keep image stabilization on all the time.

In terms of blur in photos due to shake, it is more of a problem when using zoom lenses. To reduce this problem, get yourself a good tripod. A tripod is a must have item for taking UFO photos at night.

Setting Up a Tripod

Using image stabilization can only take you so far. Image stabilization permits you to choose a lower shutter speed and it can mean a crisp shot is taken rather than a blurry shot during twilight

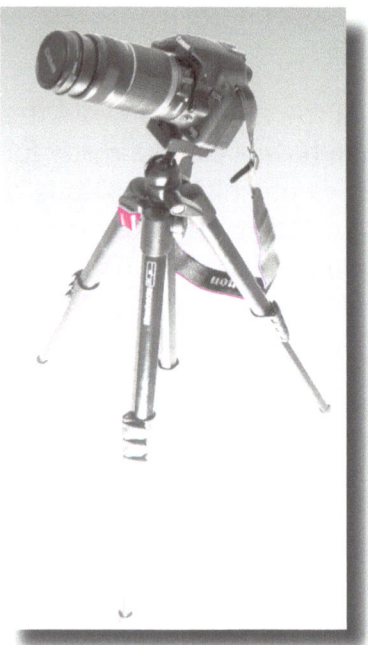

or night. A decent tripod is one of the best items to use when taking night photos. A good tripod ensures a camera can stay still even for longer shots taken at night. Tripods allow night time shots where the shutter stays open longer. Even these longer shots can come out razor sharp when the camera is mounted onto a tripod. All DSLR cameras have a female socket on the bottom of the camera where you can screw a camera onto a tripod mount. Some tripods offer a wedge plate mount feature that installs on a camera bottom. This plate then snaps into the tripod itself. This system offers you one of the quickest ways to mount a camera onto a tripod. And while the nicest and smoothest tripods are not cheap, the simpler, casual use ones can be as low as $20.[4]

The tripod that I use for UFO shots is a Manfrotto tripod (**see left**). This brand of tripod has a ball bearing type swivel and wedge plate mount. The camera is joined to a metal plate and the camera and plate snap onto the tripod.

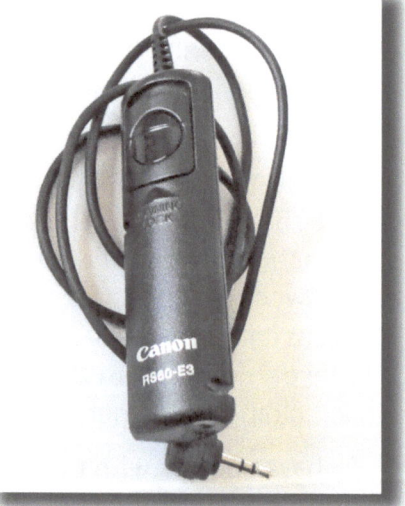

You can reduce camera shake even further by picking the right kind of surface to set up the camera and tripod for taking night photos, for e.g. concrete surfaces, asphalt, and lawns all provide solid surfaces. By placing the tripod on solid ground and turning the image stabilization feature on, you are provided with a better chance for taking clearer shots. You can also hang sand weight bags off the tripod in order to remove camera shake quickly.

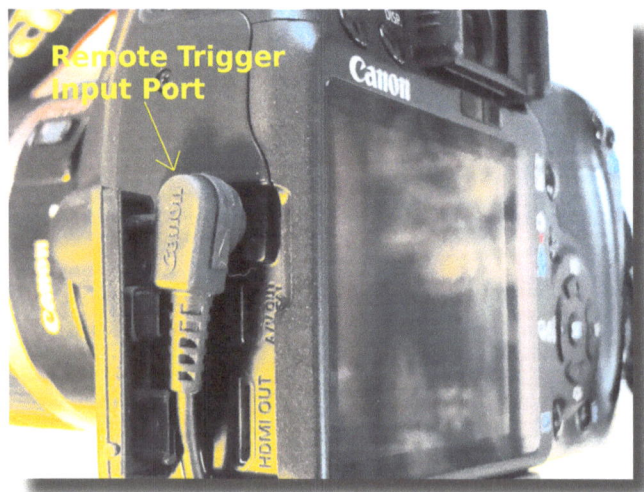

Remote Trigger Input Port

If you are keen to an extreme to remove shake for extra distance photo shots, you can purchase as an accessory, a remote trigger. Either a wire or wireless trigger can be used. With the Canon Remote Switch RS-60E3 (**see upper right**), the trigger can be plugged into the port shown (**see left**), to trigger the Canon EOS T1i in a remote manner. The wireless version of a remote trigger uses the infrared remote control sensor seen on the front of the Canon EOS T1i DSLR (**see top next page**). The remote wireless trigger allows the wireless triggering of the Canon camera as far as 16

---

4   Pogue, David, **Digital Photography the Missing Manual**, page 78

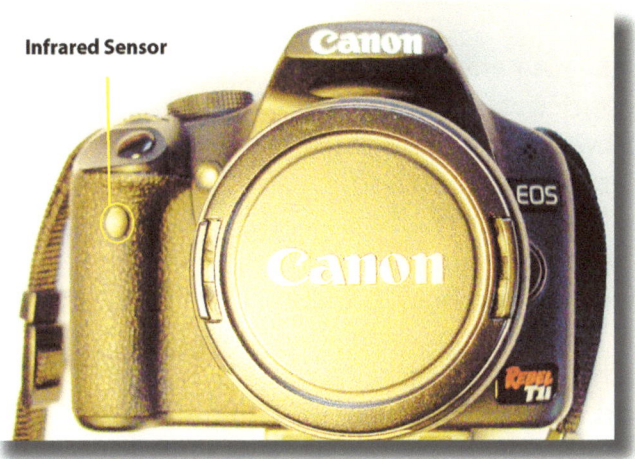

Infrared Sensor

feet away. The Canon EOS T1i also provides the option to use a USB cable and the EOS utility software program (included with Canon EOS T1i) to remotely take photos from a camera controlling laptop through a USB connection. The EOS utility software has been designed for people who take photos by joining their DSLR camera body onto a telescope eyepiece in order to take photos of the night sky. The sky is the limit in pursuit of a better picture!

Processing Nighttime Photographs Using Photoshop

Some degree of noise is always present in any electronic device that transmits or receives a "signal." For television, this signal is the broadcast data transmitted over cable or received at the antenna. For digital cameras, the signal is the light which hits the camera sensor. Even though noise is unavoidable, it can become so small, relative to the signal, that it appears to be nonexistent. The signal to noise ratio (SNR) is a useful and universal way of comparing the relative amounts of signal and noise for any electronic system; high ratios will have very little visible noise whereas the opposite is true for low ratios.[5] When there is a high ISO setting on the DSLR camera then the camera is more sensitive to light. However, there is a trade off: more noise in a picture. The noise itself comes from a few key sources on the camera, such as heat from the camera circuits, and from another type of noise called "luminescence".

One of the quickest ways to deal with this unwanted noise in night time UFO pictures is to use programs such as Photoshop and GIMP to process noise out of the pictures. GIMP, offers free plug-ins, such as the wavelet denoise plug-in found on the Internet at: **http://registry.gimp.org/node/4235**

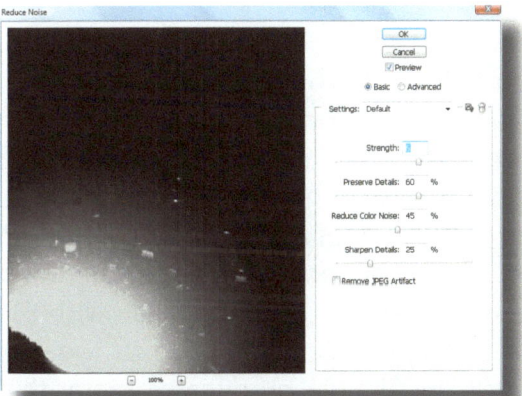

One approach to use in Photoshop is the Noise Reduction Filter box (**see left**). This mode in Photoshop contains four sliders in "Basic" mode which helps with noise reduction, i.e. strength, detail preservation, color noise reduction and detail sharpening. You can find this noise reduction filter in Photoshop under: Filter> Noise >Reduce Noise. The "Advanced" mode provides channel-by-channel noise reduction for more complex work, although "Basic" ought to provide a simple interface that delivers results.

Yet another approach is to reduce noise by taking camera raw photos (you can set the Canon EOS T1i to take raw or dual raw/jpeg photos), and manipulating the raw photos later in software packages such as the Adobe Photoshop "Camera Raw" screen to reduce noise. As a side note, Adobe has a raw update file for many camera brands for Photoshop, found at: **http://www.adobe.com/products/photoshop/**

5   Found at: http://www.cambridgeincolour.com/tutorials/image-noise.htm

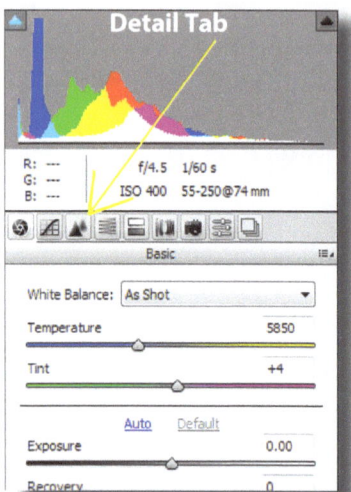

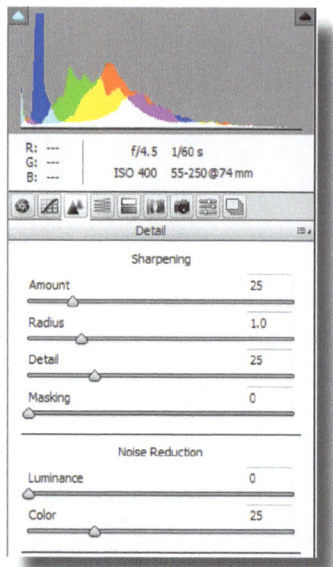

cameraraw.html

Double clicking on the camera raw file taken by the camera, in order to call up the "Camera Raw" screen, allows you to apply an interesting denoise feature in Photoshop. In the Adobe Camera Raw screen, there is a denoise feature, which is found as a feature in Adobe Bridge or Photoshop as a histogram on the "Detail" tab. Clicking on the detail button will call up the detail tab screen (**see left, detail button pointed at inside the Camera Raw screen, see right, detail tab screen**). A denoise feature is also offered as both "Luminance" and "Color" Noise Reduction sliders on this "Detail" tab. Luminance noises appears in photos as white flecks, while color noise appears as color specks that tend to appear randomly in the picture. Move the sliders to reduce the noise.

Nighttime UFO Pictures

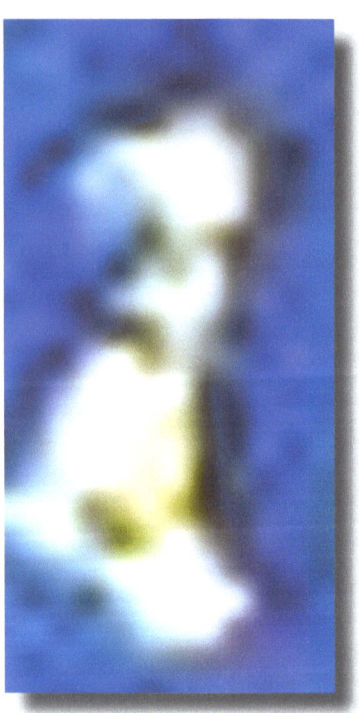

For years I have taken nighttime photos of UFOs using methods previously discussed in this book. And with that experience, I have come to the conclusion that the Canon EOS T1i DSLR is not best in class for nighttime photos. And in spite of great IS features of Canon DSLR, the Canon is still not the best for night photos. In fact, a simple point and shoot, the Fujifilm E510, is a better choice for taking night photos of UFOs than the Canon EOS T1i (**see picture to left, UFO picture taken with Fujifilm FinePix E510 in April, 2007**).

In particular, it is a known fact that some Fujifilm point and shoot cameras from around circa 2004 to 2005 tend to beat other brands when it comes to its talent for taking clear night time photos. In fact, the Fujifilm FinePix E510, despite a low end feel to this point and shoot camera, takes better close distance UFO photos at night than the Canon, despite this old camera having 1/3rd the pixel count of the Canon EOS T1i. With the Fuji, UFOs come out brighter, cleaner and more clear as photographs. Time and time again, I was able to process UFO photos taken with the Fujifilm FinePix E510 and break through UFO stealth due to the fine nature of the photos. In subtle ways, Fujifilm has produced cameras that are better at night time photos for UFOs than other brands.

In addition, a DSC-W300 Sony point and shoot camera was tested late last year for UFO photography. This camera did poorly in taking night time UFO photos. The DSC-W300 has a low light capable near infrared tuned Superhad CCD sensor. This type of chip, the Superhad chip, is noted in the UFO field for its ability to pick up UFOs (Superhad CCD sensor can peer out as far as 1200 nm in near infrared, further into the near infrared than other types of CCD sensors). For example, Nightshot camcorders use Superhad CCD sensors and are often used for UFO spotting. However, surprisingly the Fujifilm FinePix E510 took better UFO pictures than the Sony.

Canon Camera EOS T1i

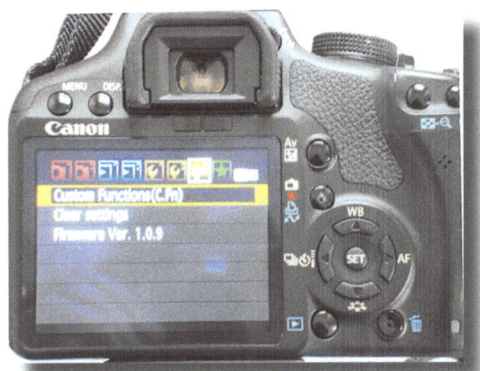

Taking pictures of UFOs at night with the Canon EOS T1i DSLR can be done a few ways. One way is to set up the manual controls to take a longer exposure picture of UFOs without using the on-board flash. This entails setting an ISO number of 800 or greater. With higher ISO numbers, you get higher noise in the Canon camera, so be sure to set up the Canon DSLR to reduce noise in the photos being taken. Setting noise reduction in the Canon EOS T1i involves pushing the "menu" button on the Canon EOS T1i (the uppermost left button when looking at the back of the camera), and using the arrow key pad on the "Set" menu, and pushing the right arrow key to reach "Custom Functions". Then push the SET button and change it to option "2" for strong noise reduction (**see two photos to upper left and right showing setting of "Custom Functions" in Canon EOS T1i**). You can then manually set for longer exposure photographs, from one thirtieth of a second or slower, making sure the DSLR is on a tripod to reduce the chance of shake and by doing so, lowering the chance of blurry pictures. At this point you may want to try some UFO photo hunting at night, and capture UFOs that may by chance come

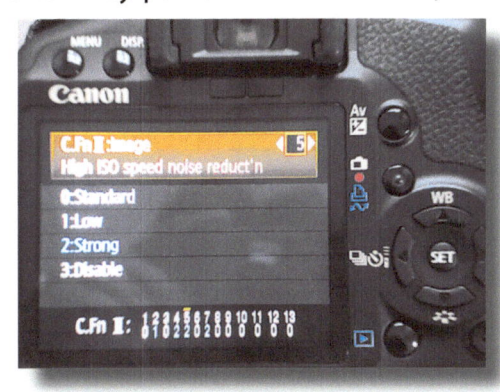

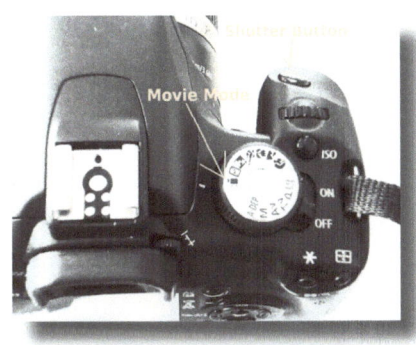

by, or try to take photographs of UFOs that may be hanging still in the night air. Another quick trick: set the DSLR to a mode suitable for taking photos at night, such as setting the camera to movie mode (**see left**). You can then simply take single photos on movie mode at night by pressing the shutter button rather than the movie "Liveview" button. With "Movie Mode" the DSLR will adjust itself for nighttime conditions without any additional manual adjustment. In movie mode, the viewfinder will not work, but with practice, you can quickly turn the DSLR off, locate the UFO in the viewfinder, turn the DSLR back on with the camera set on movie mode, and track the UFO using Liveview to take photos or video. This UFO photograph (**see right**) resulted from taking a photo in "Movie Mode".

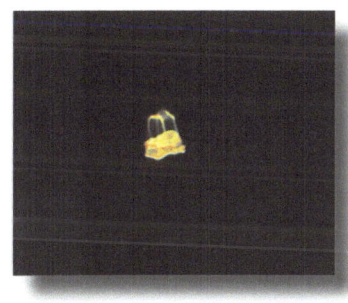

The UFO photo was taken in movie mode as single picture rather than a video, using a kit lens (EF-S55- 250mm F/4 to 5.6. lense). The UFO was slowly moving in a southward direction in the air. Using "Movie Mode" on the Canon T1i, sets the camera to an ISO of 1600 at night, with a plus 1/3rd compensation, which produces decent night shot pictures

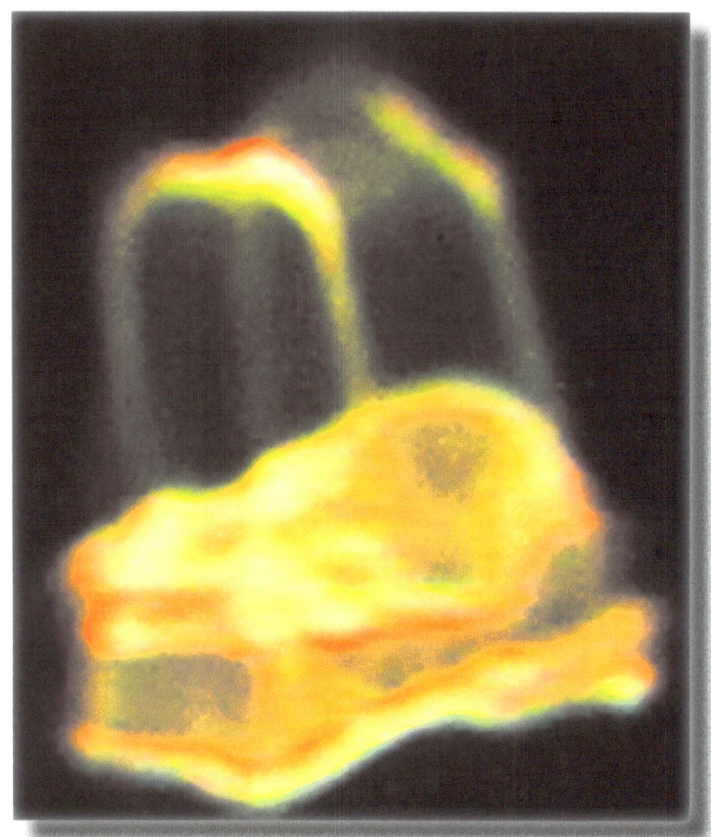

of UFOs. The UFO was quite close to the DSLR, so the enhanced picture (**see left**) was only blown up in IRIS software 8 times using bicubic resampling and contrast adjusted to bring out details. Often, I will alternatively take UFO video and photos at night using the "Movie Mode" setting. Using the half breath out, hand steadying technique, and by leaning against an outside wall of a house, you can sometimes take wonderful photos of UFOs as single shots in Movie Mode. The UFO (**see below right**) was taken on October 5th, 2009 at 8:09 p.m. using a Canon EOS REBEL T1i, ISO 1600, F 5.6, Center Weighted Average

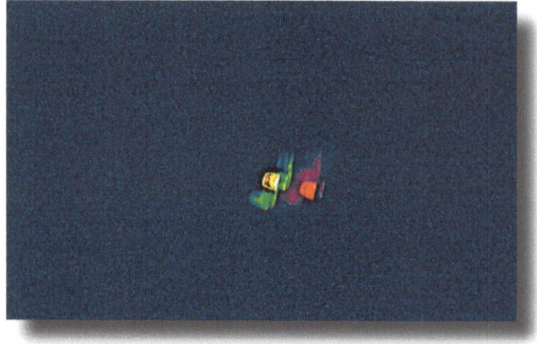

Metering Mode, no flash, exposure time of one half a second. This very clear photo of a UFO flying through the sky was taken using Movie Mode on the Canon EOS T1i camera. In particular, you can see the UFO looks like a flying lego block. Also, there are two large square lights or windows on the UFO which because of the hand steadying technique, are not blurred by movement. When the UFO is blown up (**see right**) twenty times, the details of the UFO are quite clear as a result of using the method of the half breath out, hand steadying technique. Finally, a UFO photograph (**see next page**) was taken using a combination of breathing and hand steadying techniques, with only one leg of the tripod resting on a bookcase, to take this shot of a UFO out of a window early in the morning. You can sometimes combine use of a tripod, with the breath and hand steadying technique, to take amazing UFO photos.

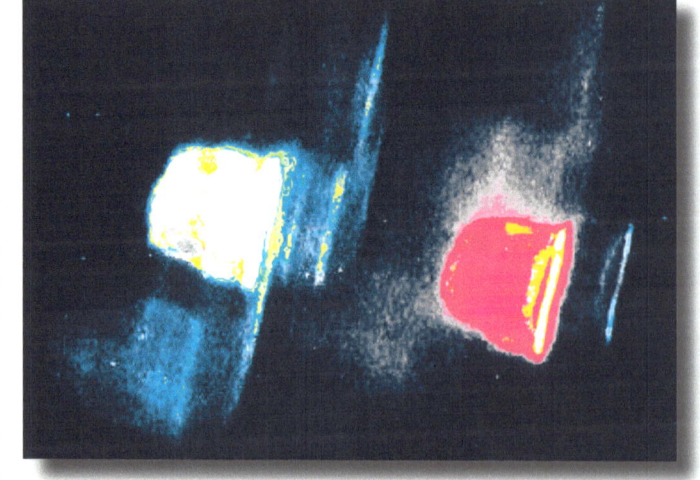

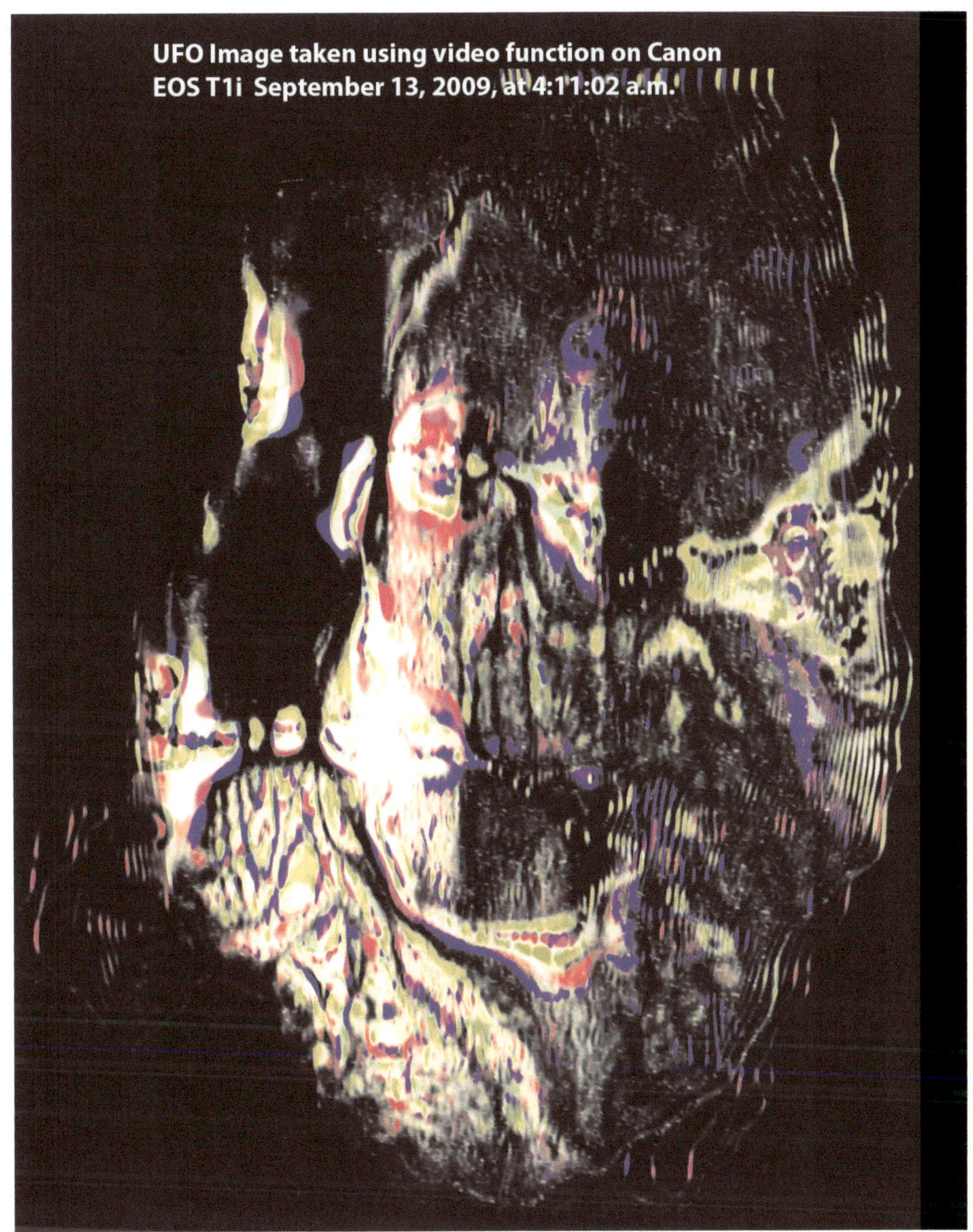

UFO Image taken using video function on Canon EOS T1i September 13, 2009, at 4:11:02 a.m.

Daylight UFO Photographs Using the Solar Obliteration Method

Using the Solar Obliteration Technique and high definition Movie Mode on the Canon EOS T1i camera, you can obtain regular light photographs of UFOs during sunny and mostly cloudless days. In this case, unlike night photography described in the previous section, the Canon EOS

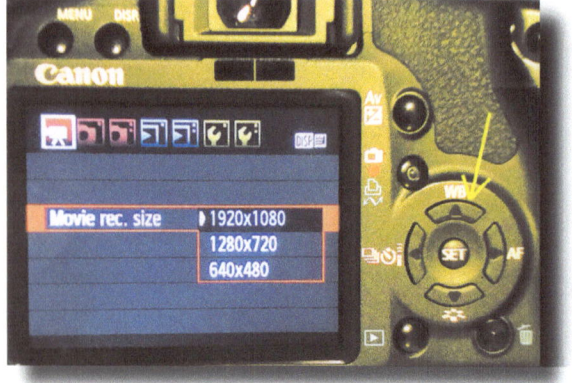

T1i is used entirely as a high definition video camera.

To turn on the high definition video mode, set the camera to movie mode. Next, press the "Menu" button on the back of the Canon EOS T1i camera. Then select , using the arrow key pad, the option for "Movie rec. size", press the "Set" button and use the arrow keypad in the back of the camera to select "1920 x 1080". Select the "Set" button again to select "1920 x 1080" (**arrow key pad pointed at with yellow arrow, see left**). Once these modes are set, adjust the manual focus for infinity by focusing on a distant object.

Then place your camera on a tripod and adjust the camera position according to the previous section on positioning cameras when using the Solar Obliteration technique. From there, click on the "Live View/ Movie Record Button" on the back of the camera to start recording video (**see right**).

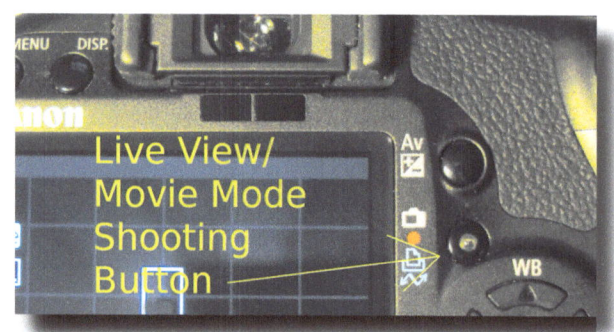

I tend to record in five minute segments, review what has been recorded in Live View on the back of the camera and delete video clips inside the camera that do not contain UFOs. For the most part, UFOs are seen on sunny days generally after about twenty minutes. Your experiences will of course vary depending on location and the weather in the area that you live.

For example, the following fifteen photos were extracted from several video clips taken in September of 2009. Starting with the photographs on the next page, the first picture is the original, while the second photo in sequence of right to left is blown up 140 times. The third picture shows, after enhancement processing of the picture in GIMP, that the UFO is emitting a hologram showing alien symbology (**bottom photo, see next page**).

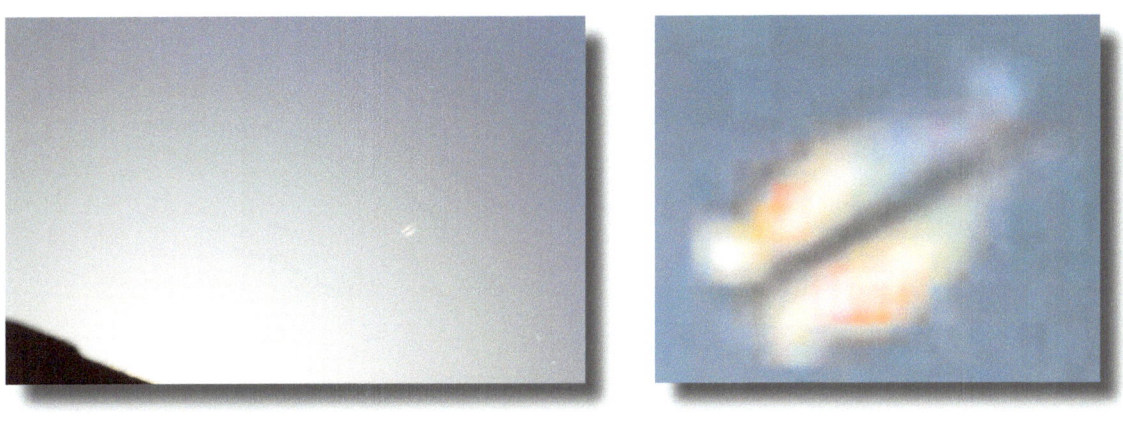

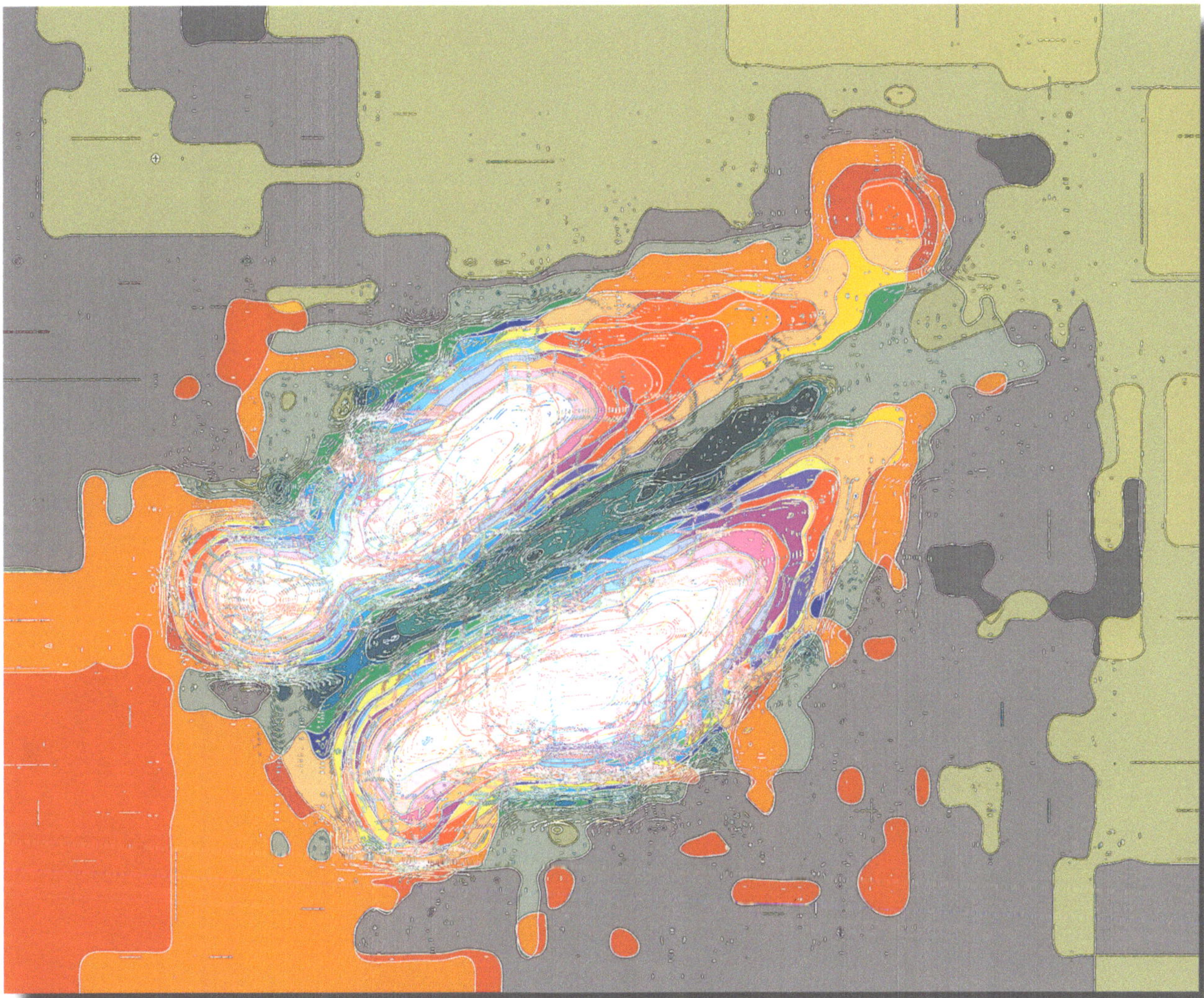

I have arranged a set of six photos (**see next page**) extracted from video which show different UFOs recorded during one solar obliteration session, and the second set of six photos shown on the same page are blown up shots of UFOs taken from the top six video extracted photos.

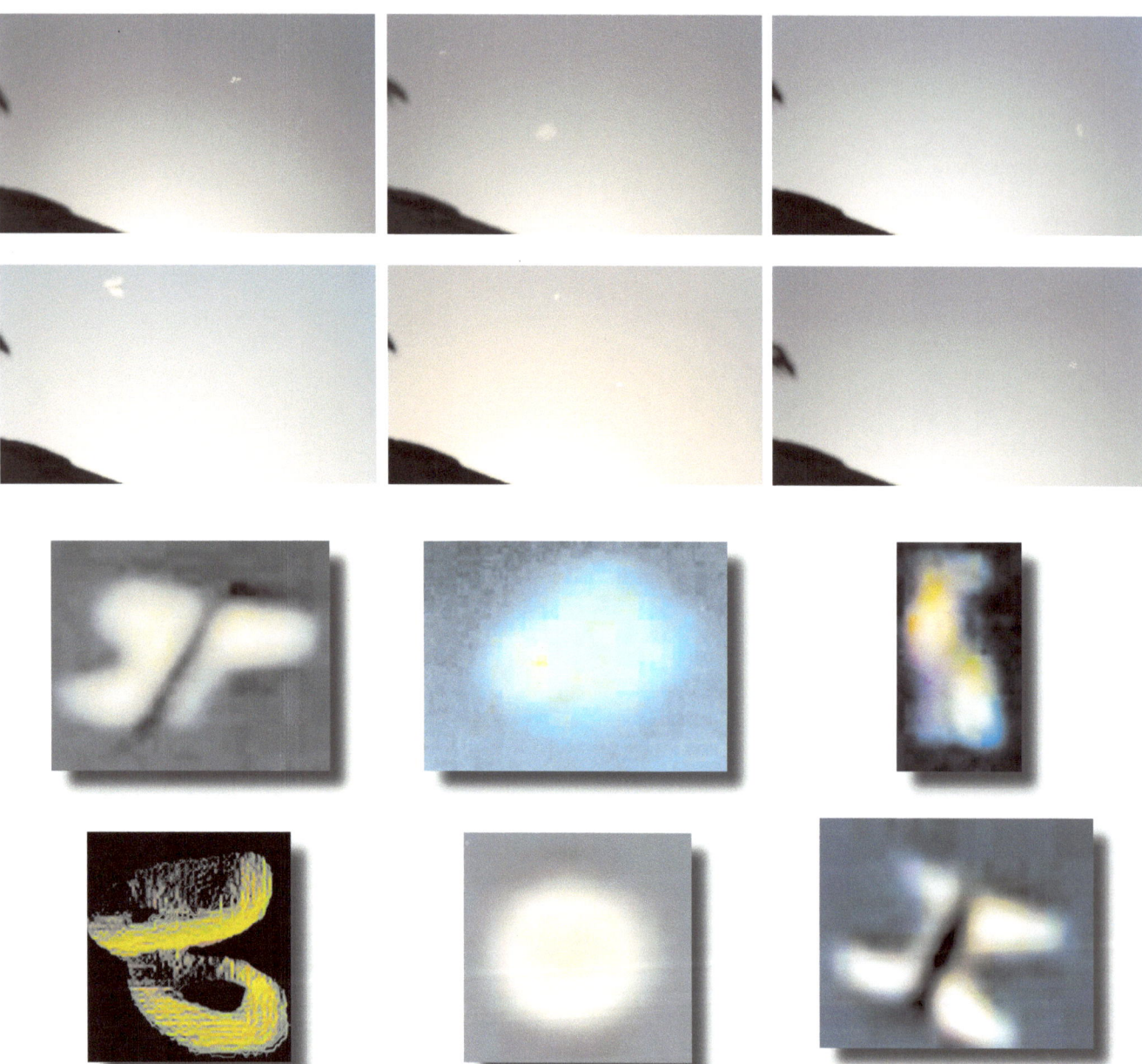

UFOs: Stealth Hologram Helicopter or Planes during Daylight Viewing

UFOs during daylight hours will occasionally emit a hologram which makes the UFO craft resemble a black or dark to medium blue helicopter, grey helicopter, or prop plane. Unlike other types of UFOs, this type of UFO will show up on cloudy days, foggy weather, or when it is snowing. In particular, this type of UFO appears to be designed for slow flight, where it loiters around at close range to observe people. Recognizing that a plane or helicopter is perhaps a stealthed UFO, is a matter of observation. In this case, your camera tells more of a story about the real shape of the craft than your eyes. A litmus test as to whether or not you are observing an alien craft is to take a photograph and see if you are looking at a real human aircraft, or a hologram that surrounds a UFO. A hologram stealthed UFO will show up in a CCD based camera photograph as a blurry object with an entirely different shape, while your eyes will just see a plane or helicopter. This is a strange experience for the person who first looks at the photograph in Canon Live View and sees a blurry object with a strange alien shape, and then looks up to see a plane or helicopter with their eyes. In this case, rather than think of a camera as just a camera, think of a camera as a type of analytical instrument that can test to see if a helicopter or plane is real or is a UFO surrounded by a hologram.

There are only a few visual signs that tell you that the object being seen is not a real plane or helicopter. For instance, black hologram helicopters will in full sunlight have a slight tint of grey. These hologram-helicopters will carry ultra bright and very large diameter spotlights below and to the rear of the hologram UFO craft. In addition, these helicopters or planes will have a mirror like, very reflective appearance when sunlight reflects off the craft. In a photo processing sense, it seems impossible to break through the hologram aspect of these UFOs as they appear to be, by design, the highest form of steathed UFO.

UFOs stealthed as planes are easier to spot than stealth helicopters, for example, almost without fail, the tail section, wings, and the nose section of a stealthed UFO will look odd in appearance compared to a real plane. The wings will be too thin, the tail section will be too small, and the nose of the plane will be too pointed to be a regular plane design for a prop plane. Another aspect to consider is that stealthed UFOs, seen as planes or helicopters, ignore human economics with respect to the cost of flying helicopters and airplanes.

Take, for instance, the Bell 206L4. To rent a Bell 206L4 costs anywhere from $1,100 to $1,400 U.S. dollars an hour in the U.S. midwest. A light plane usually costs less per hour to run, but the cost is still significant. Because of the high expense of running a Bell 206L4, these helicopters will tend to take passengers from point A to point B.

Other than when a helicopter is doing a city wide police search, these highly expensive aircraft will tend to go in straight lines to and from destinations. Such highly expensive craft do not tend to loiter around for hours flying in circles. So if you see a plane or helicopter flying around for hours on end without refueling, then you may have a stealthed UFO hiding in plain sight, as a fake helicopter or plane in the sky. For instance, a Bell 206L4 with a ferry tank can last 3.7 hours in the air, however the author has seen UFO stealth helicopters resembling the Bell 206L4 on station for five hours or more. These UFO helicopters tend to show up around the time people are travelling to and from work.

The ultimate test to see if these are real helicopters or planes as compared to the UFO stealths is easy. Take a DLSR camera, focus the camera on a distant object on the ground, put the camera

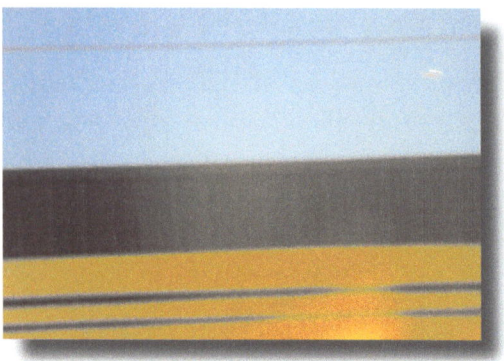

on manual focus to achieve a reasonable infinity focus for the camera, aim the camera at the plane or helicopter and take a picture. If the camera is in focus, and the object in the air is close, and you are carefully tracking the helicopter or plane to remove motion blur, then it is reasonable to say that you should have sharp, clear photos of the helicopter or plane.

If, after focusing the camera carefully before taking the photos, and applying the hand steadying technique outlined in the Canon EOS T1i section on night photography, the aircraft photo ends up blurry with a 3-D look, then you are viewing a UFO stealthed as a helicopter or plane.

A stealthed hologram UFO airplane, even if you swear with your eyesight that it is a plane, generally looks like the picture at the top of this page when the image is processed (**see left top figure and zoomed figure to left**).

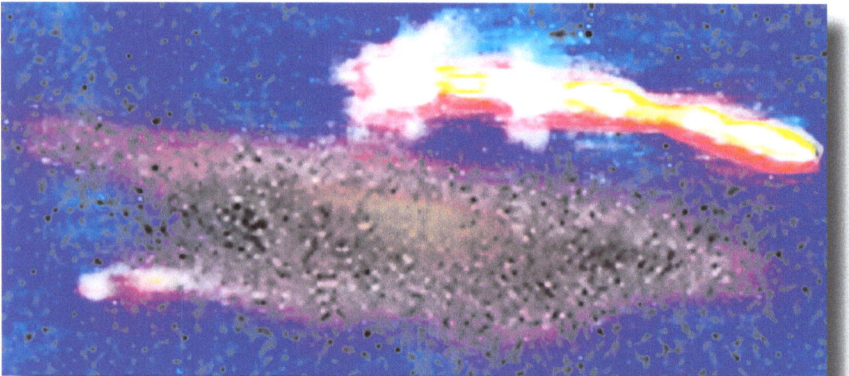

For example, when the author viewed this UFO using his eyes on January 28th, 2010 at 8: 36 am in the morning, the craft looked like an airplane (**see image below expanded 30 times, automatic levels adjustment applied, series of sharps applied to photo to bring out 3-D visual stealth of UFO**) with a peculiar shape to its wings and nose. Using the Canon EOS T1i camera, a photo was taken of the craft. The photograph revealed the true nature of this vehicle was a UFO emitting a hologram designed to emulate the appearance of an airplane.

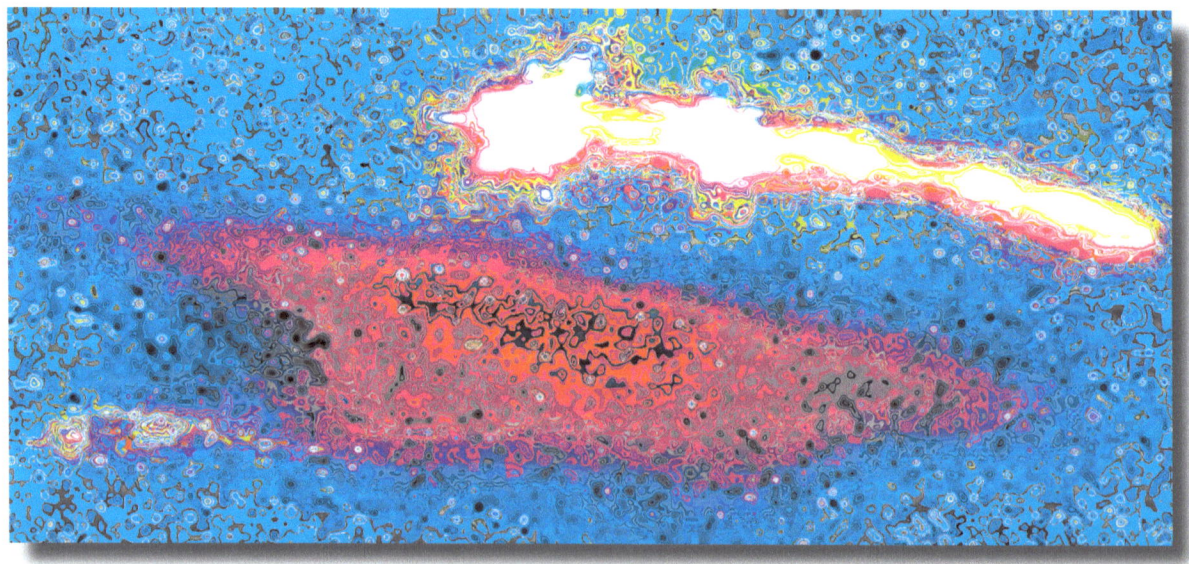

A Further Look into Nighttime and Morning UFOs

The following pages takes a deeper look into the various UFO vehicles that have flown the night skies above a major Canadian city in the year 2010. The photograph (**see right**) was taken on April 4th, 2010, at 9:40:26 p.m., and shows a UFO. This UFO was recorded on the Canon EOS T1i Canon camera in movie mode with a 250 mm zoom lens. Using very advanced free software, Virtualdub, the UFO was both deshaken (some of the shake from this handheld recording was removed from the video electronically), and was zoomed by 500 percent. As an observation, this UFO seems to be one of the rare repeated recorded UFOs

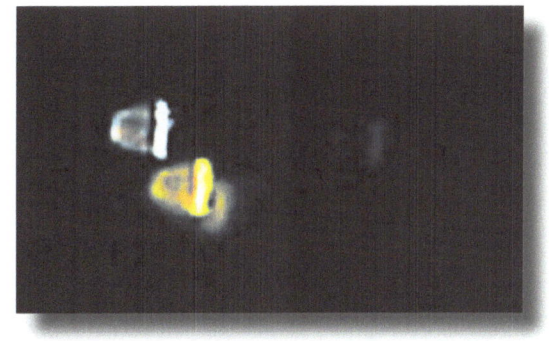

seen at night. I have seen and recorded in video this particular type of UFO several times, and this craft seems to be always on the move as opposed to hovering.

With respect to this UFO, my belief is that this type of UFO is likely a pilotless machine, as I have never recorded an instance where alien life was observed on this craft. Generally, this particular machine tends to blink between yellows, blues, and reds, and will tend to fly over an area in a repeated fashion in an oval shaped flight pattern. The repeated nature of this craft's flight gave me several chances to record this vehicle flying overhead. The following next few pages show other types of UFOs seen and recorded, from hovering type UFOs to UFOs of ambiguous shape.

Hovering UFOs will generally hover within a few hundred meters of a given area of sky for several hours, and will tend to slowly move at a pace of a few meters every twenty minutes or so, moving either with the star rotation pattern in the sky, or, as is often seen, moving in a direction counter to star rotation or in some random direction, moving closer or further away.

A close up of this same UFO noted above is seen to the right, where the photograph extracted from video has been expanded a further 30 times.

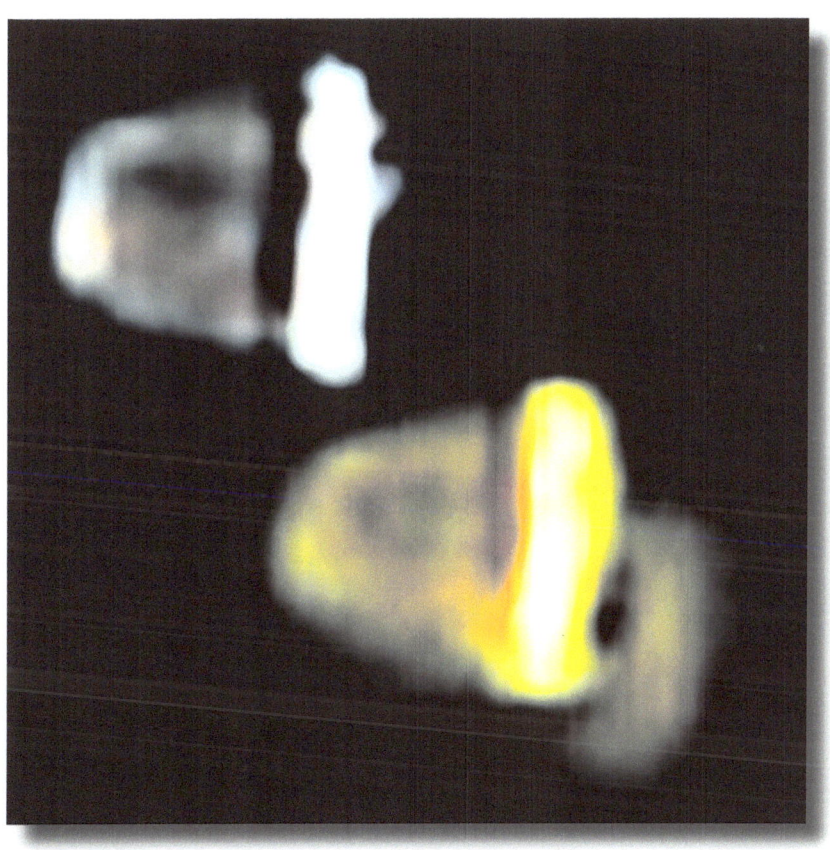

The UFO seen on this page was viewed on April 4th, 2010, and was rapidly rotating and hovering, while resembling the wheel of a car spinning, with the long axis of the UFO perpendicular to the horizon. Another feature of this UFO was that it tended to bob erratically, slightly up and down, while spinning and flashing between blue, yellow, red and green colors (**see expanded image below, original photo extracted from video to the right**). The bobbing motion could not be attributable to camera shake, as the camera was positioned on a tripod resting on a solid tile floor.

This particular UFO hovered over the nights skies of a major Canadian city for several hours, without notice by the local population. UFOs will typically place themselves just at or

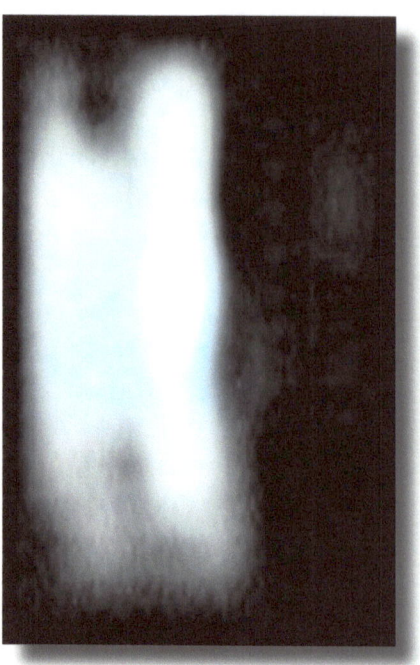

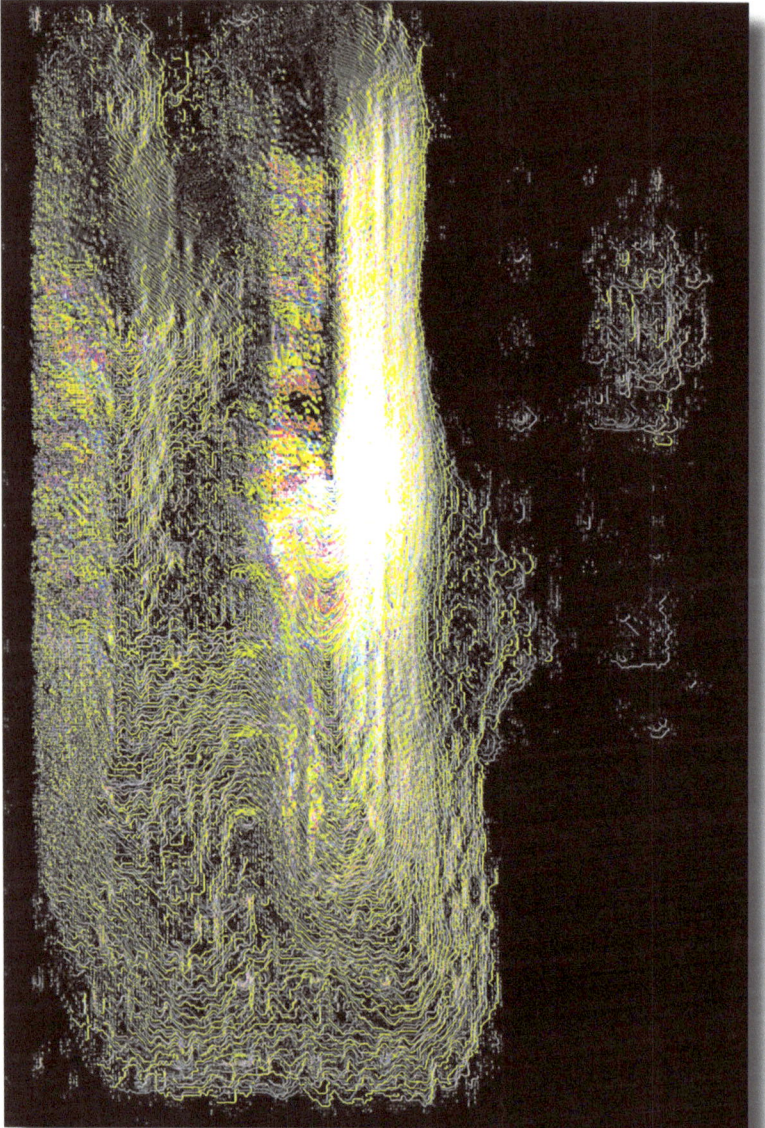

slightly above the cloud base while monitoring the population below. The UFO will typically find "holes" in the cloud base, and will place itself in these areas so as not to appear as a foreign object against a cloud background at night. The idea here also seems to be that a UFO will to place itself at a height where people will not notice the object, while at the same time placing itself at an altitude from which it can carry out some form of monitoring activities on the population below.

The end result is if you were to look at this craft without the aid of photographic or video equipment, the object would resemble a very bright star. But by using long range zoom coupled with software based bicubic zooming of video (using programs such as Virtualdub — a topic for a more advanced photography book on UFOs), a detailed image of the craft can be obtained combining the power of zooming in software, and zooming

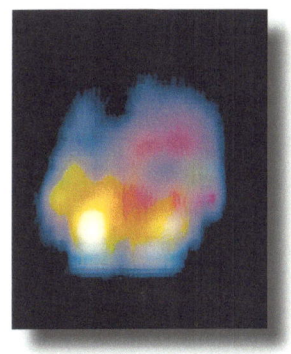

with a camera's zoom lense.

The next colorful and detailed UFO (**see original UFO from video left, blown up photograph from video, see below**) was taken again on April 4th, 2010 at 9:48:46 p.m. Rather than rotating quickly, this UFO flashed a frequently changing pattern of colors, from red, green and blue (mixed with some yellow high-lights). This craft also was bobbing randomly in one spot in the night sky. A composite photograph, composed of several layers of different states of colors and shapes of this UFO was built up in Photoshop. This technique is more or less equivalent to the super-resolution technique, except building up a composite photograph manually allowed me to fine tune the composite photograph for detail by layer. The final composite photograph of this UFO (**see below**) shows the fine detail that can be achieved using composite techniques and Photoshop. Notice the shaped lines on the surface of this UFO, as per our previous discussion on UFO camouflage. During daylight and during night, these shaped lines or optical gratings, tend to make this UFO blurry when viewed. This UFO had no visible portals or observation ports, suggesting that this was not an occupied machine. The UFO hovered for several hours.

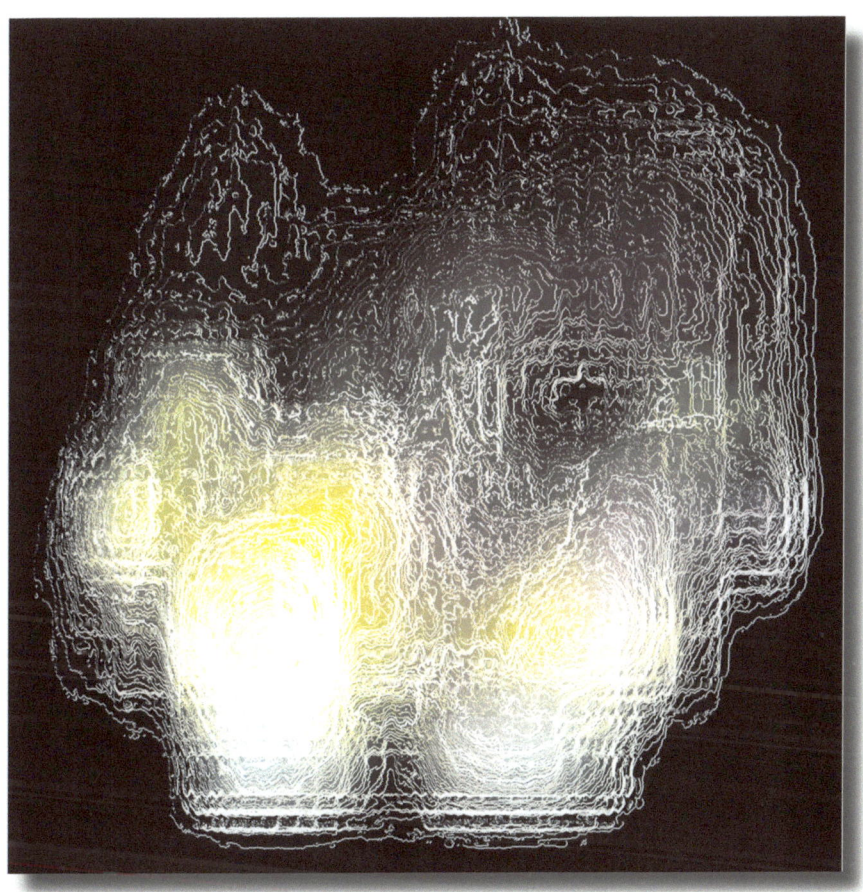

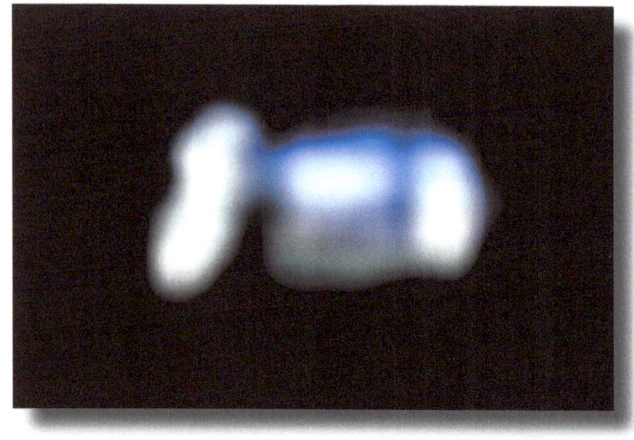

As you can see from the previous UFO, and the UFO to the left (**observed on April 6, 2010, 9:19:04 p.m., image zoomed 700 percent below**) many UFOs appear to have an organic appearance, as if the craft themselves, were each individually grown to a unique shape and pattern.

Standardization, which is the benchmark of how humans presently carry out the manufacture of vehicles (air, water or land vehicles), is really a reflection of the inflexibility of our industrial process to making things with unique shapes for each unit of production. A human engineer will spend his or her professional life often creating products that conform to a limited set of industrial processes. Changing the shape of a product in our society means changing the industrial process, at great expense, to make that new shape. On the other hand, alien technology with respect to industrial processes, appears to be adaptive to basically any shape.

Or, another explanation presents itself. In a larger universe, one composed of many different species, multiplicity of UFO shapes suggests many sources for those shapes. The extreme variability of UFOs in shape is suggestive of unique manufacturing processes from different points of origin. This is a more likely explanation with respect to the amazing variety of differently shaped UFOs visiting this planet. UFOs visiting our planet likely come from many different species of origin. Multiplicity of shape is really a function of diversity in visitors to this planet. Earth appears to be a "place of interest" as reflected in the unique vehicles. From the perspective of photography of UFOs, the visually recorded instances of these visits shows as an almost never ending parade of uniquely shaped vehicles, which appears to defy human classification of repeated instances of the same shaped vehicles appearing twice or more. The only exception to this has been the UFO shown on at the start of this book section, which is the only UFO that I have seen more than twice in a row on different dates of recording videos at night or during day.

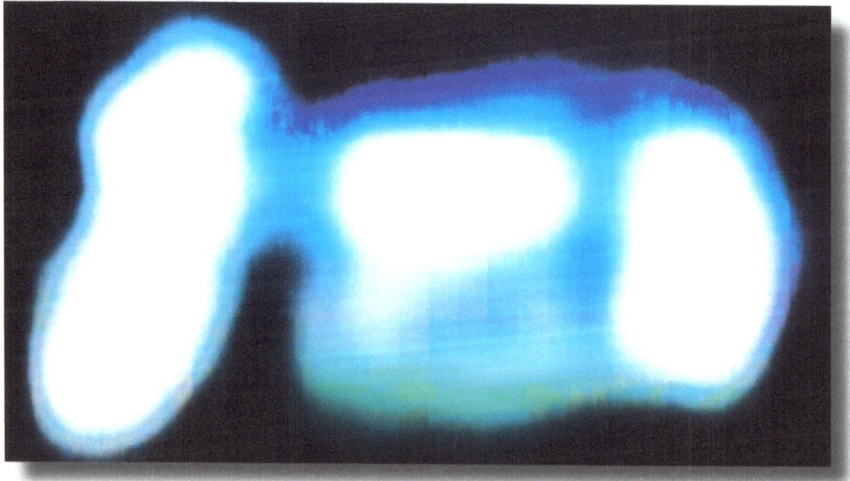

Whatever the case, the end product of this diversity is unusual sights to be photographed, (**see below image processed from previous page UFO, rotated 90 degrees counterclockwise, zoomed 1200%**), such as the photo of the UFO from the previous page, processed for detail below and showing the rather organic looking nature of many UFOs. What follows is a speculative discussion on what is being seen.

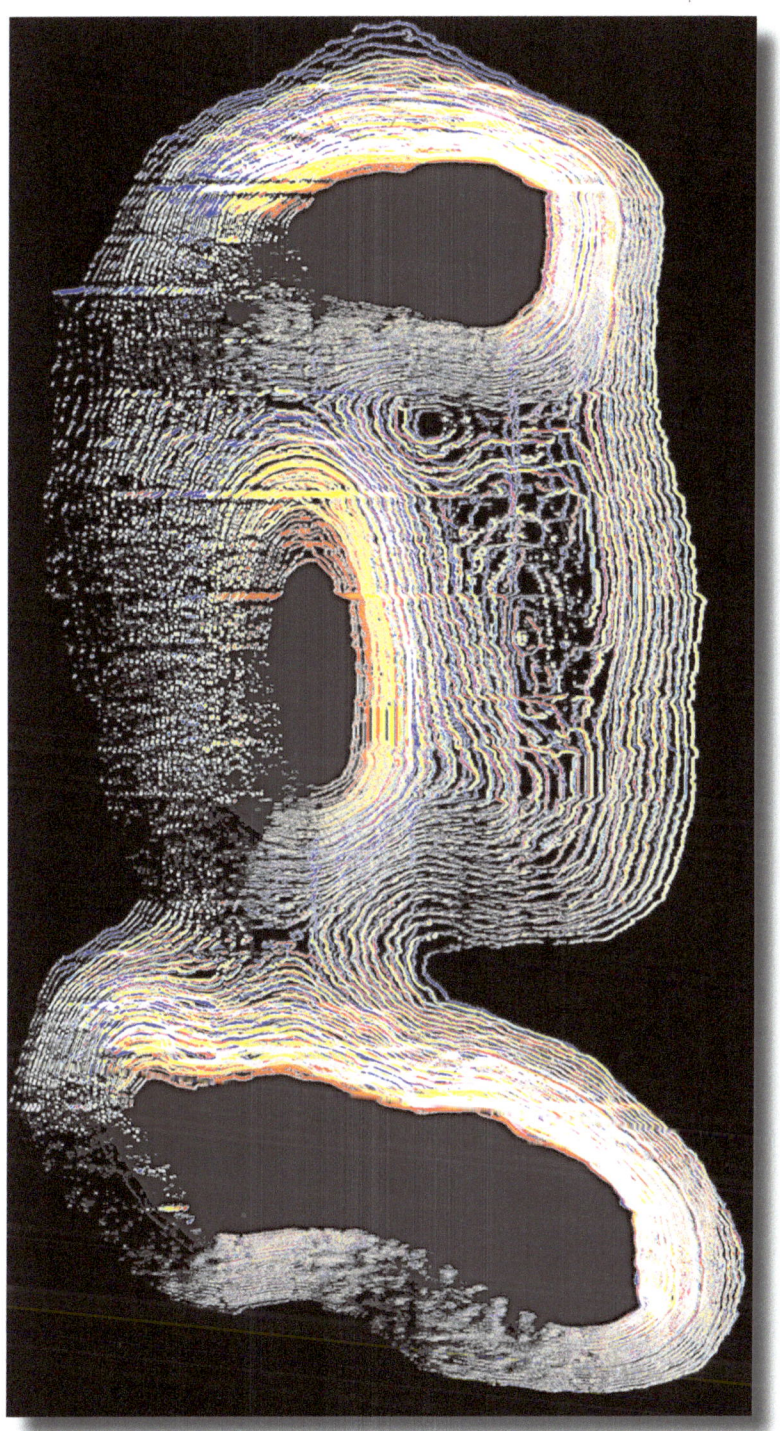

Whether or not UFOs come from either a diversity of origins, or from a superior creativity of thought with respect to manufactured vehicles shapes, UFOs do have the commonality, or standard, to which the majority seem to adhere, which is, each of these uniquely shaped vehicles deploys optical stealth systems so that these craft are not noticed very often by people. This use of optical stealth appears to be the one constant in the variety of vehicles seen and recorded by myself over the past three years. The fact that these vehicles are "stealthed", which is no doubt a worrisome thought to several militaries across this planet, is a commonality which at least allows a start to classifying UFOs in some manner. Another commonality that may allow classification of UFOs is that these craft often emit symbols that relate to mapping of people on the ground.

In the next few pages, UFOs that project "maps" of city areas in 3-D will be discussed further, and examples of a different UFOs projecting 3-D visualizations of a city park will be shown as a series of different UFO photographs. As discussed before, UFOs often appear to communicate "maps" of areas of high people concentration on the ground, using projected 3-D maps that reflect people carrying out activities seen from the air, such as walking pets.

The UFO below was seen hovering in the air at night on April 15th, 2010, at 9:24:52 p.m, recorded with a Canon EOS T1i, and zoomed 1200 % with VirtualDub software in combination with a full 250 mm zoom on the Canon EOS T1i camera. A UFO is seen floating over a major city in Canada, and technically appears to be communicating using symbolic "map" geometry language on the skin of the craft. Using our trick of reprojection of the "map" message on the UFO, onto a human satellite image, it can be seen

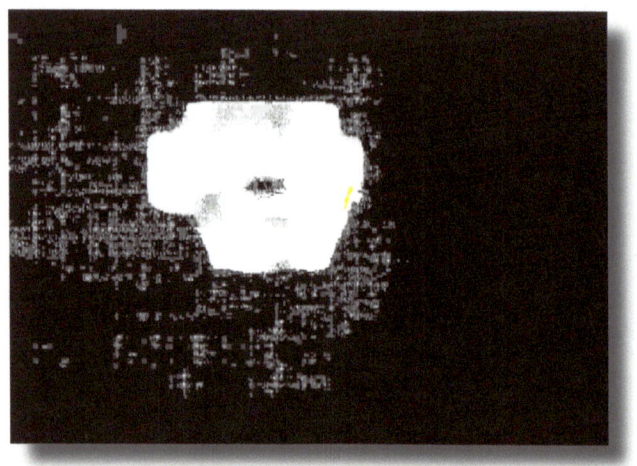
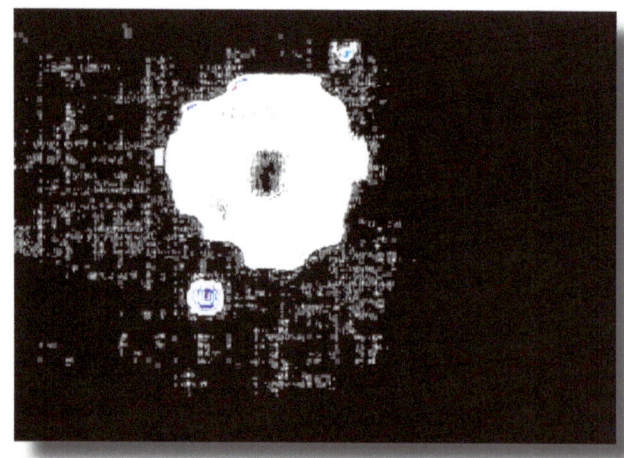
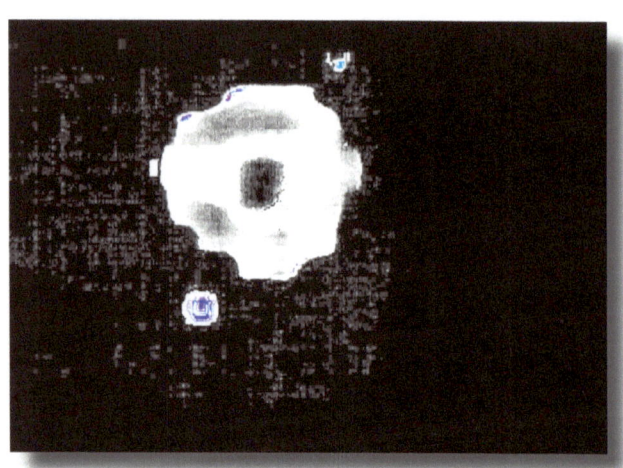
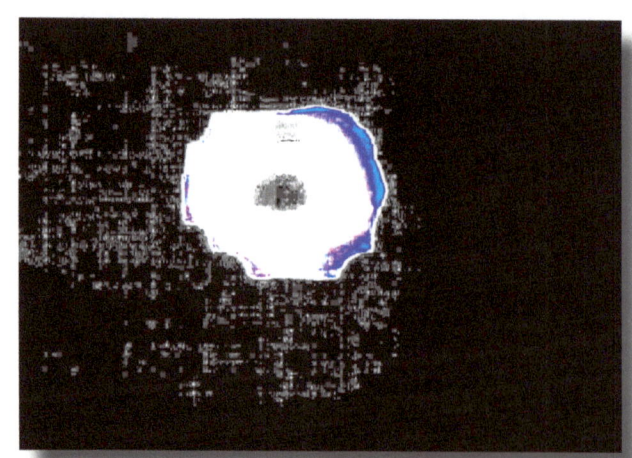
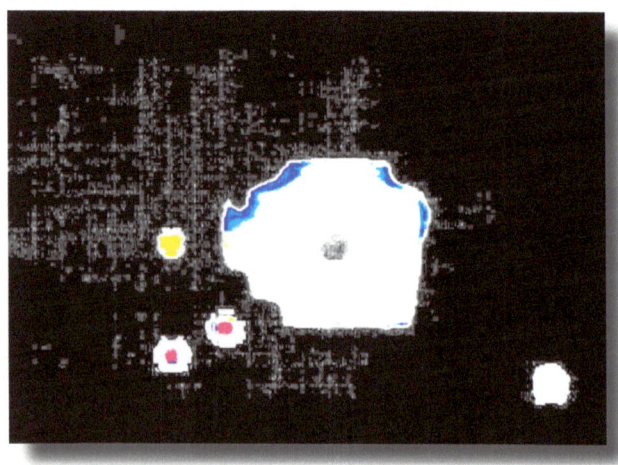
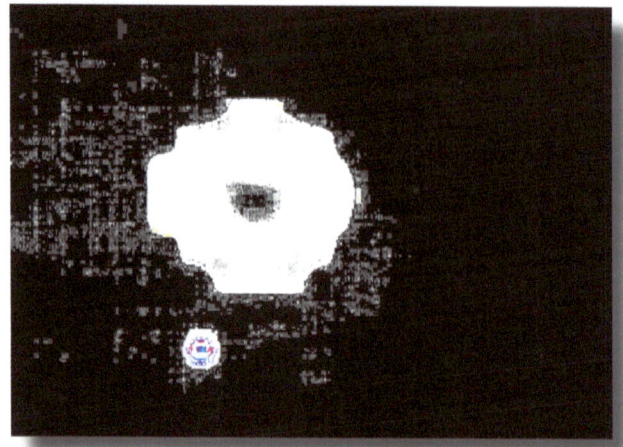

that the message being "written" represents the park below, and the activities of people walking the park. The UFO is projecting a 3-D map on the UFO outer skin which directly relates to the general shape of the park gully below the craft, and human activities in the park. So this is again, an example of the continuous nature of study of this park by aliens, both during a daylight context, and at night. See below series of photographs, taking the UFO "map symbolic" message from the previous page, inverting the image, and reprojecting the message onto the ground below, with increasing transparency, or

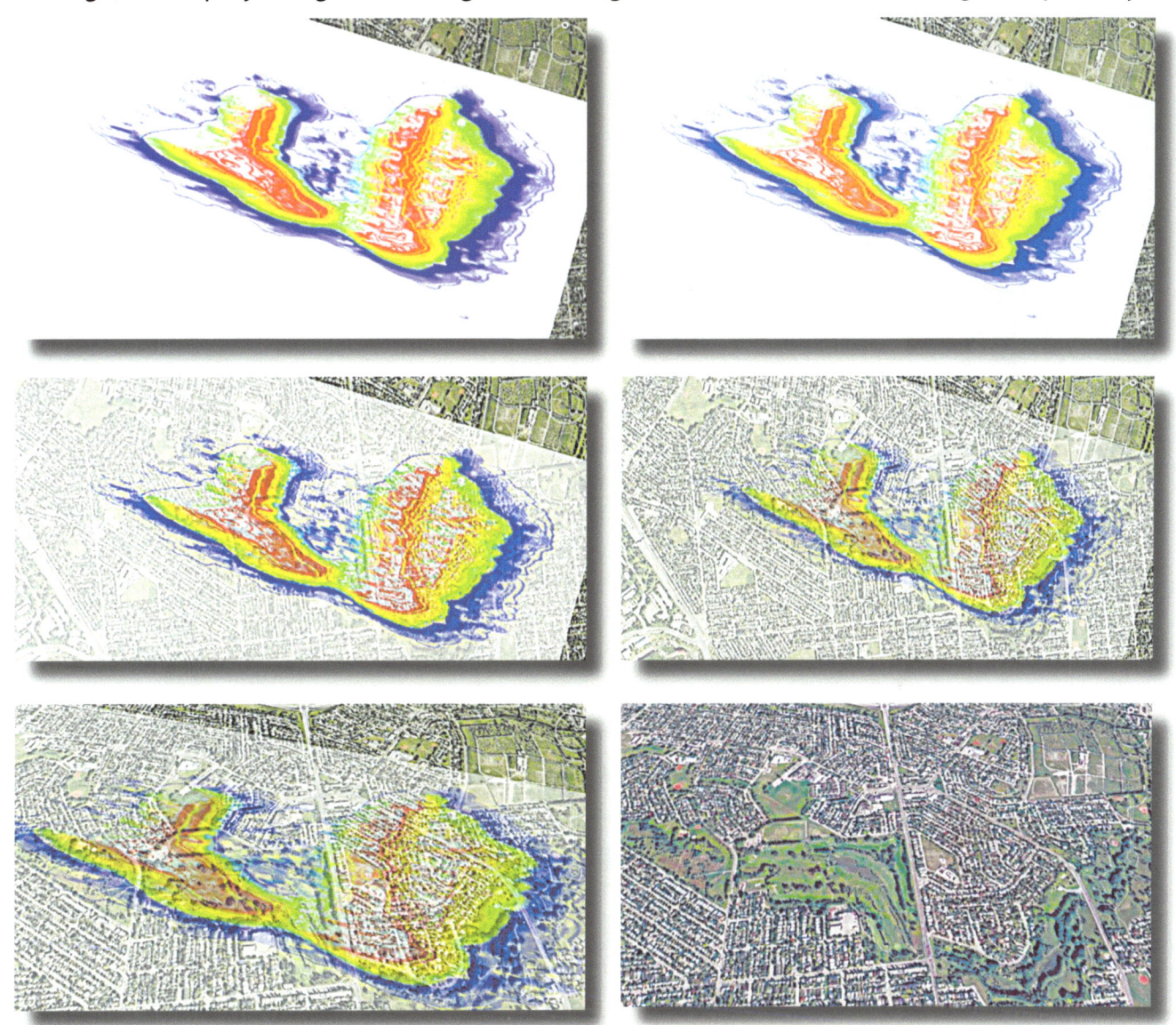

alpha channeling, of the white in the image to show a satellite image I have put underneath the UFO image for comparison purposes. Obviously, the changing shapes on the UFO relate to the park below the UFO.

In fact, some of the UFOs shown on the next few pages also have projections and shapes showing park mapped geometry, emphasizing the point that alien language appears to be broadly speaking, based on geometry, and communication of concepts through active use of geometry and maps.

The UFO below is another instance of a UFO projecting a map of a city park, but this photograph was extracted from a video taken in the morning. The high definition video of the UFO taken on April 18th, 2010, at 5:12:04 a.m.

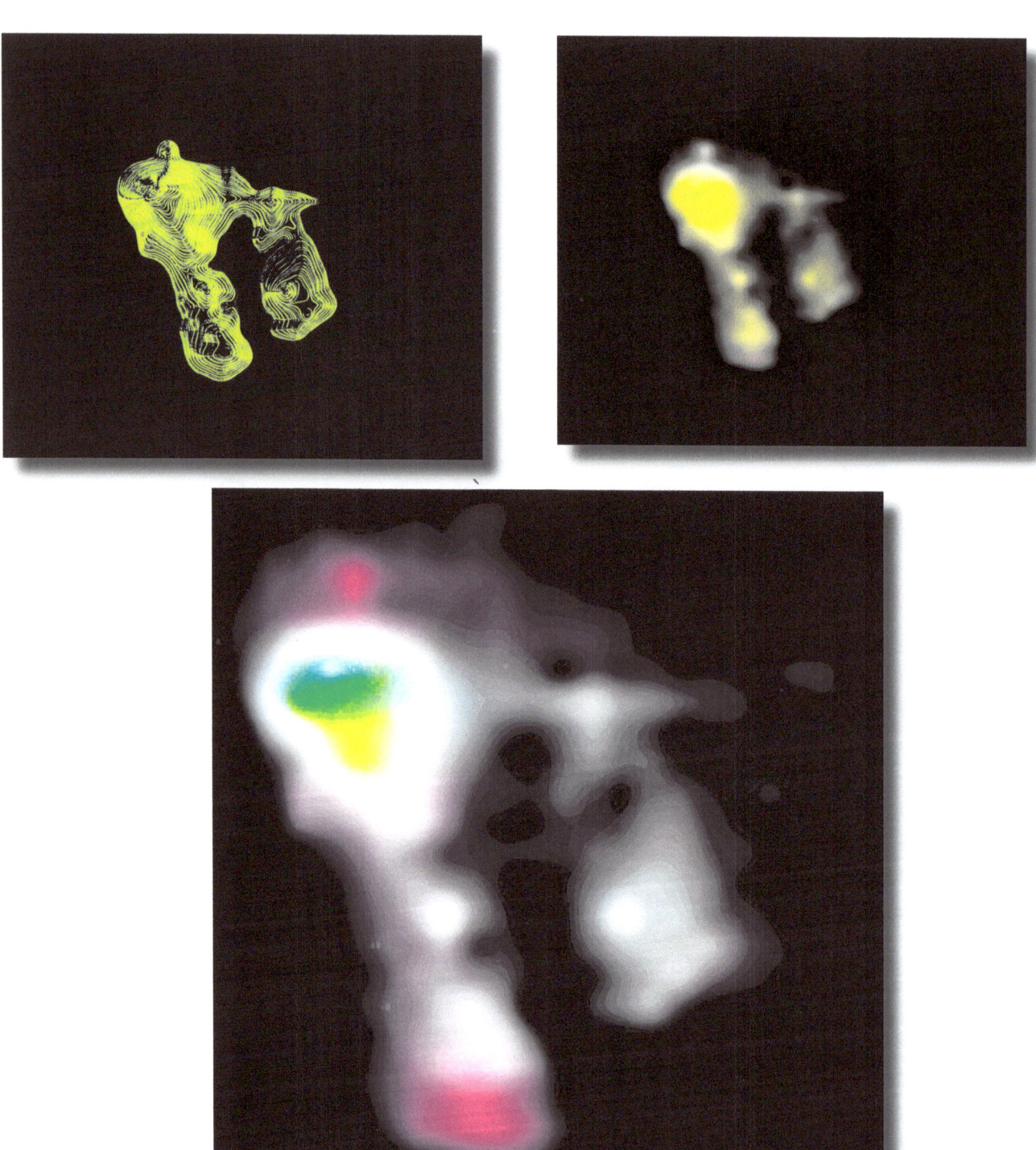

Another instance of a UFO projecting a map of a city park seen on the morning of April 18th, 2010 (**series of photographs below**).

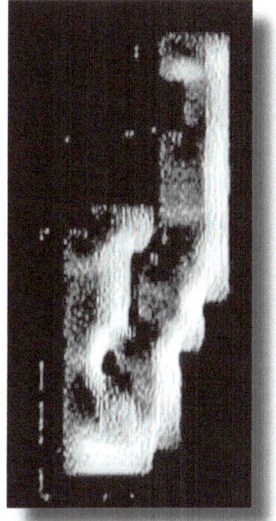 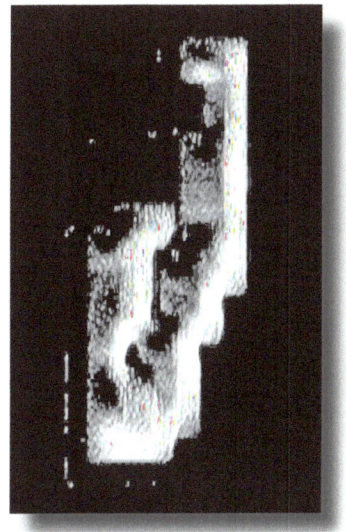

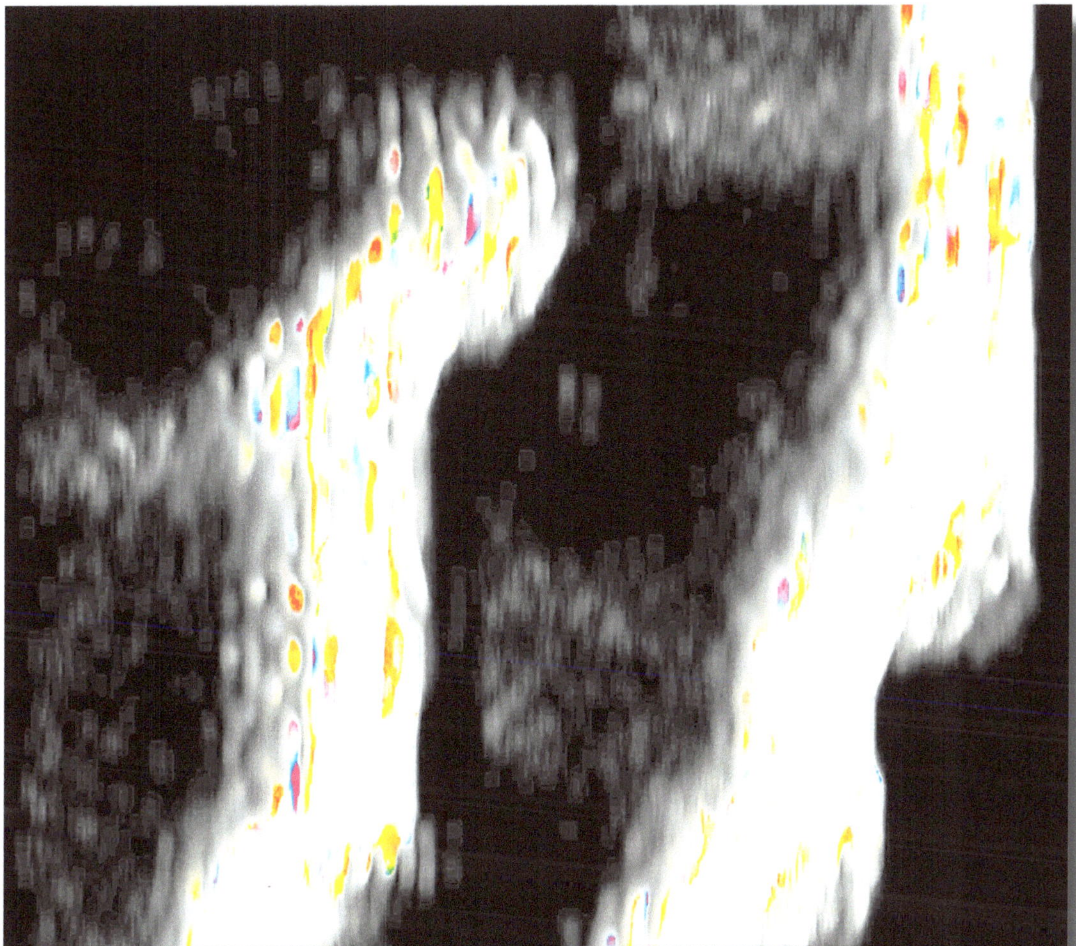

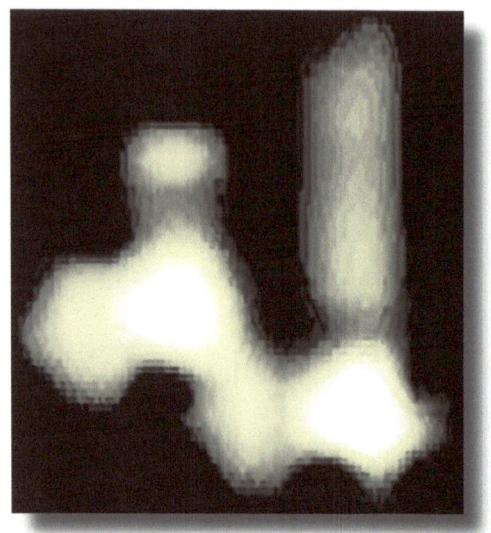

This fourth "map" projecting UFO, was seen on the morning of April 19th, 2010, at 5:20:00 a.m (**see original photo left, and blown up and processed photo below**). The nature of this UFO projected mapping, also brings up the potential of an experiment to develop and understand alien map geometry language. Interested people could carefully analyse satellite photos and compare the satellite image to geometrical shapes projected by the UFO to develop an understanding of the UFO geometry language as related to landforms and structures on the ground. Additionally, activities in the park could be tracked by our scientists to develop an understanding of alien symbols assigned to activities of people. So this book shows a potential entry into both a unique photography study, and also an opportunity for hobbyists and language scientists to develop an understanding of this alien symbolic language through interpretation of objects on the ground as related to symbols projected on and around UFOs. This would be an interesting and exciting socio-exobiological examination of people from an outside viewpoint.

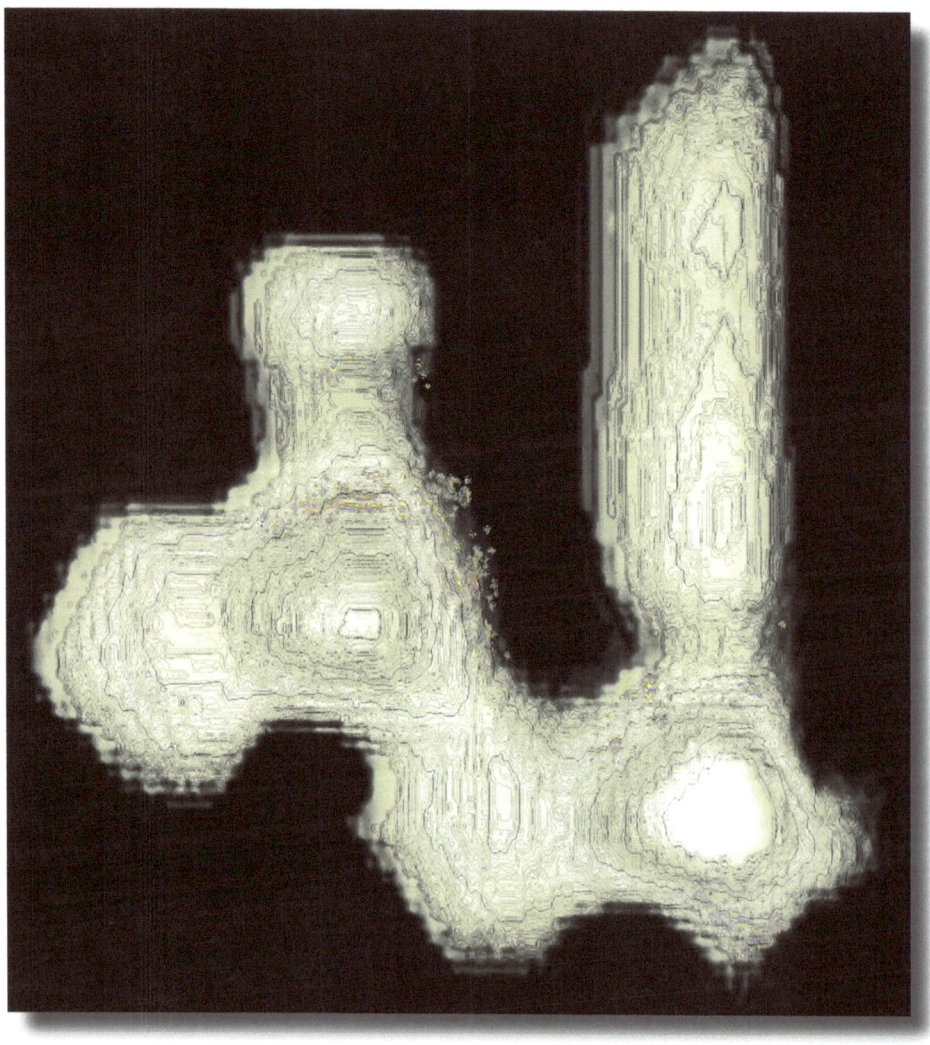

Chapter 11: Aliens

We have your satellite if you want it back send 20 billion in Martian money. No funny business or you will never see it again.

Joke ransom note mailed to Jet Propulsion Labs after 1993 Mars Observer's Failure[1]

Aliens are a rare sight. Meeting or seeing an alien is becoming an even more rare event. By using the National UFO Reporting Center's (NUFORC) 23,000 data point data set and tallying up alien encounters or sightings reported by people across the U.S. from 1939 to the year 2000, you had six times more of a chance of meeting or seeing an alien between the years 1939 to 1950, compared to the years between 1991 to 2000.[2] The graph below illustrates this point.

Meeting or seeing aliens is a less frequent event, but there are occasions when aliens show up in photos and videos. The next few pages will show a small sample of aliens found in photographs extracted from video clips of UFOs flying over a major city in Canada.

Time wise, taking pictures of aliens is the ultimate photography challenge with respect to it being a fraction of a second event. For sheer difficulty, taking a photograph of an alien cruising by in a UFO is a mind boggling mix of luck and preparation. However, in this fraction of a second event, we have

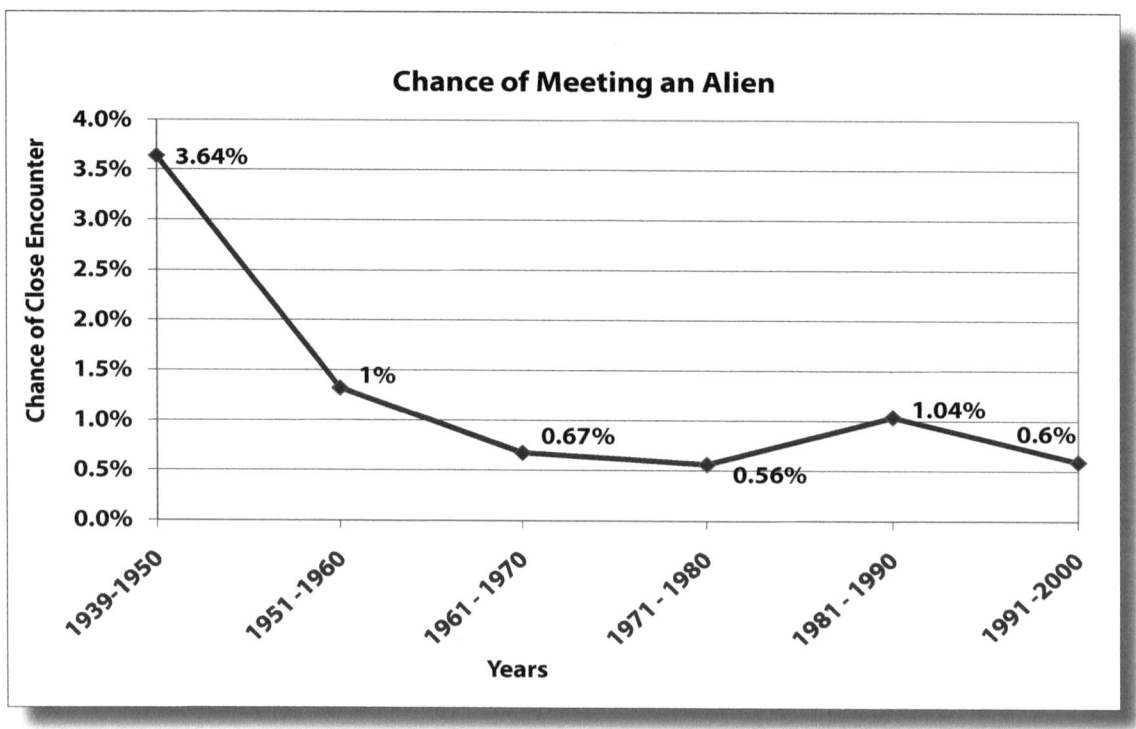

the essence of photography, or what the famous photographer, Henri Cartier-Bresson stated "To take photographs means to recognize - simultaneously and within a fraction of a second - both the fact itself

---

1   Author Unknown, New Scientist magazine, p.4, September 25, 1993
2   NUFORC database, Found at: http://www.nuforc.org/

and the rigorous organization of visually perceived forms that give it meaning. It is putting one's head, one's eye and one's heart on the same axis."[3]

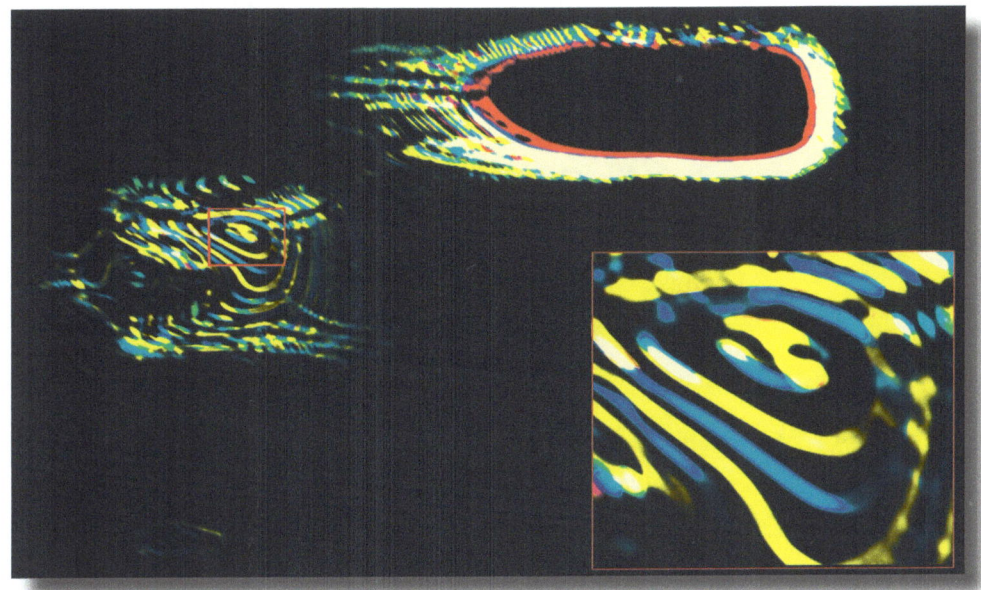

Take, for instance, the masked alien staring out of a UFO portal window extracted from a webcam video recording on May 10th, 2009, at 2:40 p.m (**see left**). A detailed image of the masked alien has been expanded eight times to reveal detail (**see left insert photo**).

As a photographer or videographer, capturing a 1/15th to 1/30th of a second event, of an alien crossing a web-cam field of view, is the challenge, fact, and the prize of UFO photography. Your thoughts then have to go into processing these pictures for detail and quality. My experience has been, that you may get one in ten photographs from UFO video capture with detail and quality. To capture aliens in photographs, you get maybe one alien per five hundred video clips. However, the impact of capturing UFO photos and seeing aliens is the most difficult aspect of UFO photography. You get the sense that belief systems held dear, appear empty compared to the larger universe being captured in video, literally outside your window. There is the impression that these creatures might examine us, and without further notice, leave. Take for example, the photographs of an alien that resembles a garden gnome (**see below**). These photographs were extracted from a near infrared web-cam taken on September 20th, 2009.

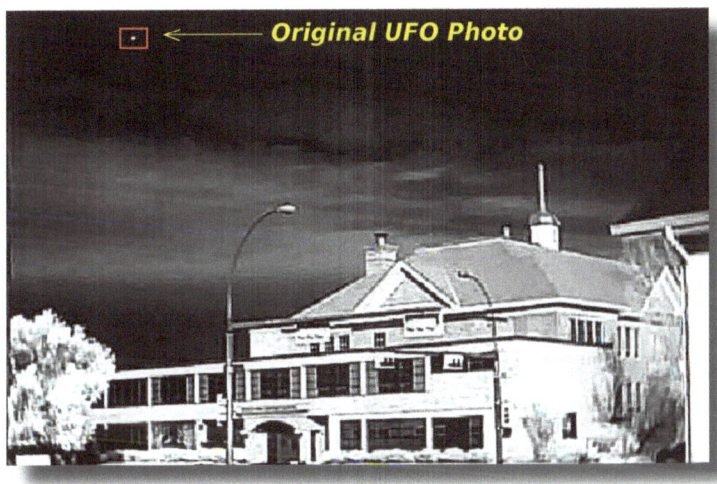

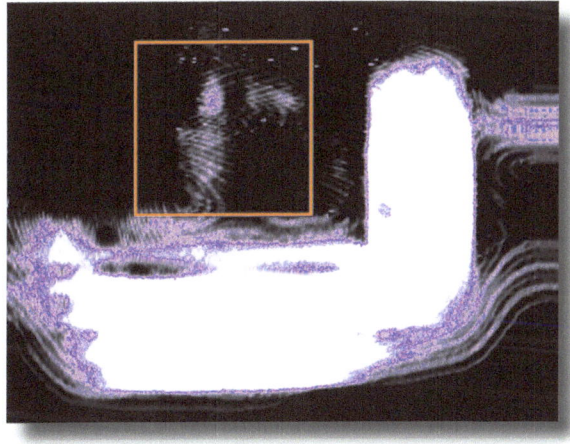

3   Cartier-Bresson, Henri, quote, Found at: http://www.brainyquote.com/quotes/quotes/h/henricarti107208.html

The craft paused for two frames above a school as children played below, then the UFO sped off to the northwest. Nothing in the photos on this page or the following pages indicates aliens want to actually stop for a moment to make contact. All these pictures indicate is that aliens are actively monitoring people, but not with the intent, so far, to stop and communicate with us in an overt manner (**see alien photo below, blown up 20 times**).

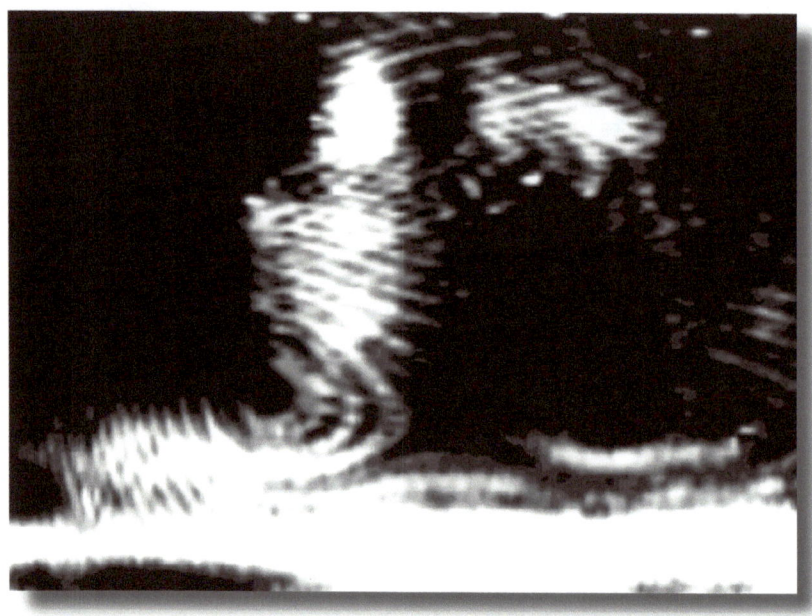

The third alien photograph is that of a grey alien. This is one of the clearest pictures of our very small group of alien photographs that I have taken over the years.

The picture below left was taken on Sept. 25th, 2009, in near infrared. In this footage portfolio, the UFO containing the grey can be seen in the photographs below at the bottom of the page. The UFO paused for three frames in the air (**see original photograph extracted from video below left, blurry blown up photo lower right**), and with the use of the stacking technique, to clear up the picture, you can see the grey's features. We can also see the goggle-type glasses that this alien wore (**next page**). In particular, super-resolution of the picture shows the scan lines of red, green and blue that display when the UFO is emitting red, green and blue colours in sequence, as part of the UFO stealth system. Note the alien, when enhanced, has a distorted nose area on its face (**see blown up photo left, grey in boxed area**).

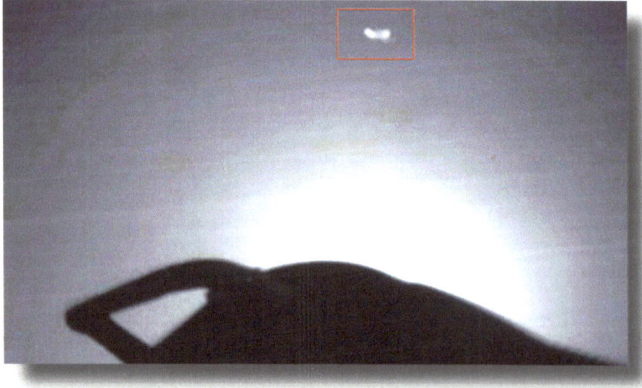

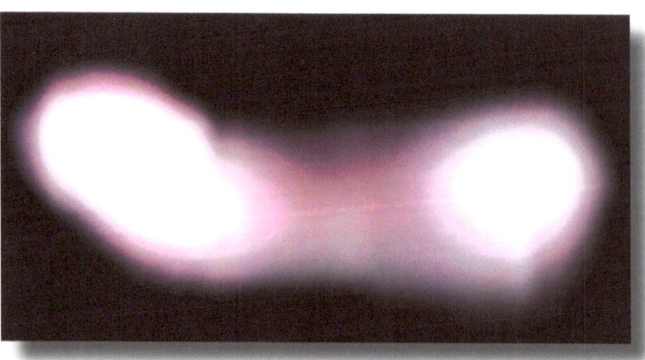

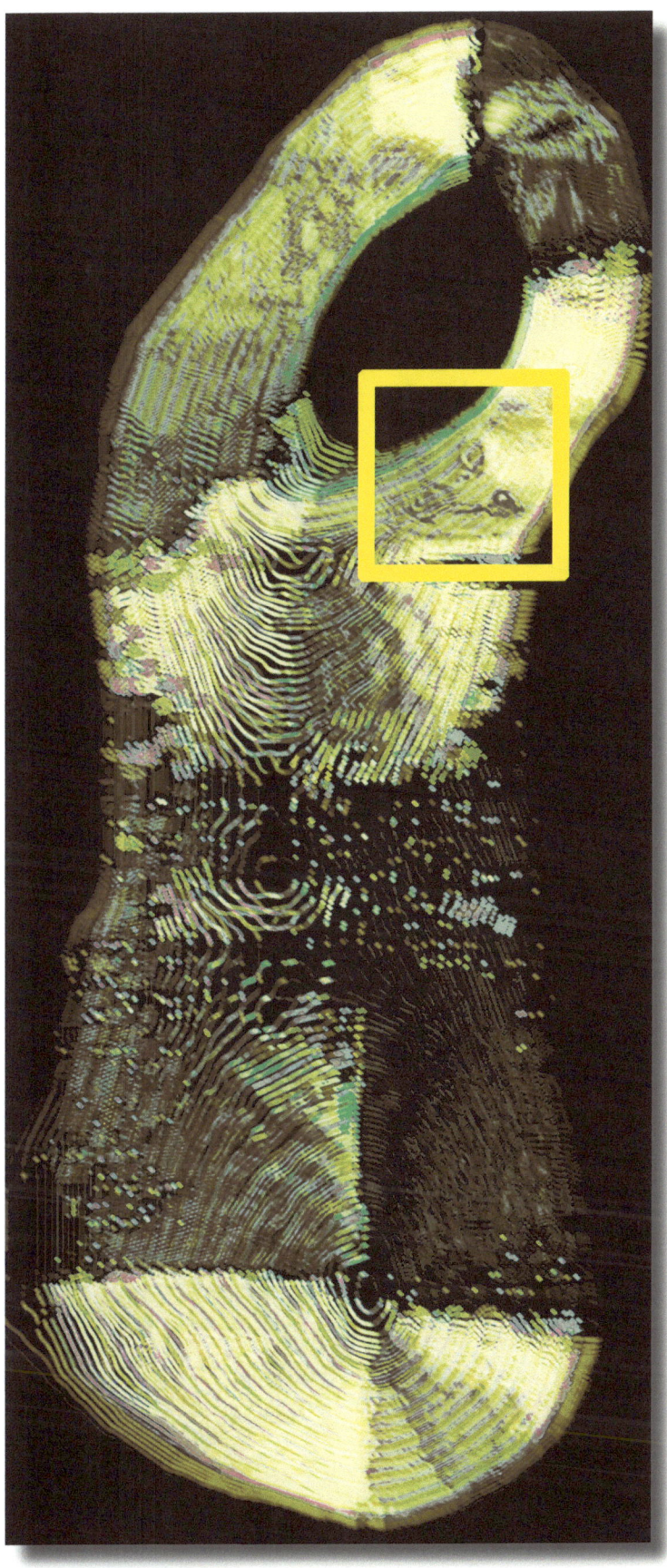

The grey's ship, seen left, is rotated 90 degrees counterclockwise to fit the page.

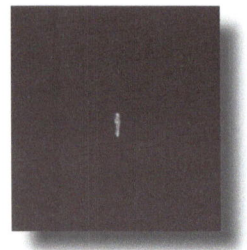

The following photo (**see top left**) was taken on October 29th, 2009, at 4:41 a.m. with a Canon EOS REBEL T1i, using a 55 to 250 mm zoom kit lense at full zoom and an F-stop of 5.6, exposure time was 1/6th of a second, zero bias, and no flash.

In this photograph, the alien is floating still in the night air and is several hundred meters away. The alien photo has been blown up 30 times and the figure has then been further processed in GIMP to extract a little more detail. The alien itself (**see right**) looks a lot like an Egyptian temple figure when compared to an actual Egyptian temple figure (**see lower left**). Broadly and speculatively speaking, one wonders about current views and ideas on Egyptian history when looking at this

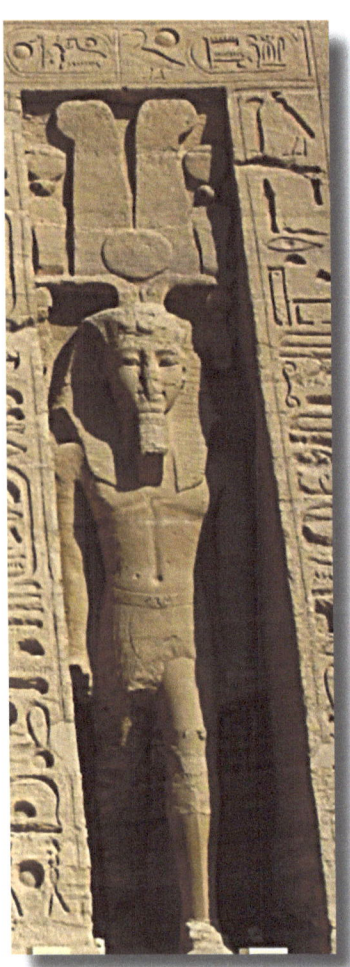

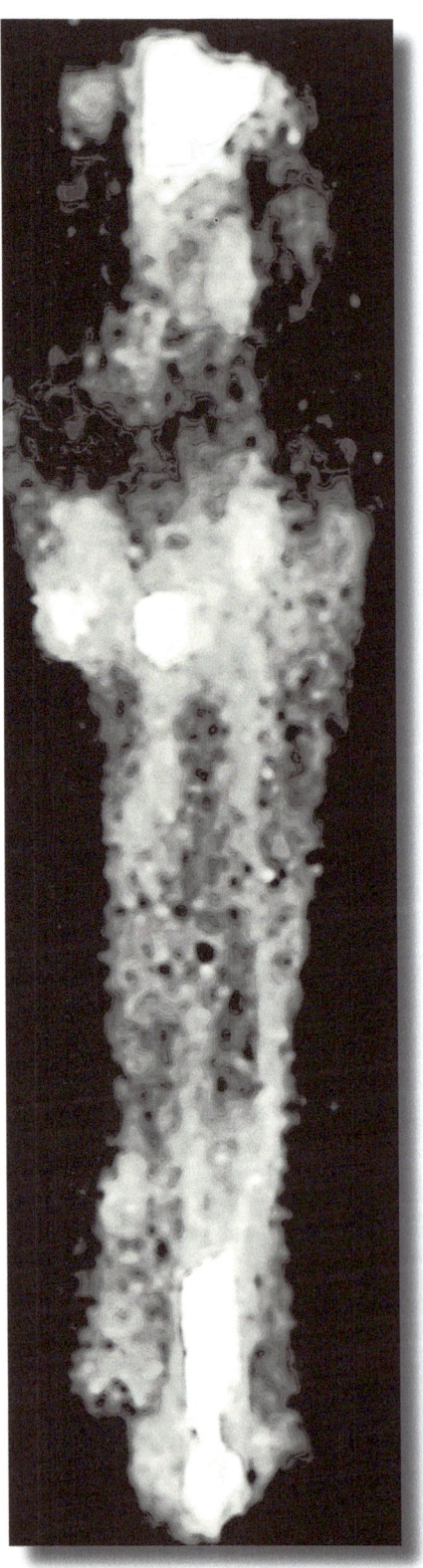

particular picture. Are the common ideas we hold about ancient Egypt true? Is our knowledge on ancient Egypt factual given that its culture is buried in the past, and is only seen through traces of historical records? Were ancient Egyptians influenced by an outside, more advanced alien culture?

Alien seeded culture is not a new idea, i.e. the idea was the basis of the a now defunct TV series, "Stargate".

However, the idea that some of our ancient cultures were seeded with knowledge by an outside alien culture gains a form of context when almost 3300 years after the temple statue to the left was made one sees an Egyptian-like alien in the sky at night.

Built around 1290 to 1254 B.C., the picture to the left is of a statue seen on an outside wall from the Temple of Nefertari, in Abu Simbel, Egypt.

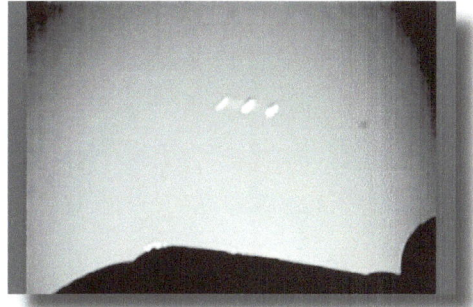

Continuing on in our photographic alien journey, the picture to the left was caught by a near infrared web-cam using HandyAvi motion detection software. A black painted barbecue lid was used to block out direct sunlight as per the solar obliteration method. Three frames of this UFO were caught as it flew over. However, frames from the video were too far apart to apply super-resolution.

To be sure, there are odd events one sees in near infrared UFO hunting. Strange shapes often boggle the mind, and there is generally the feeling you are following Alice down the rabbit hole. But on occasion, surprising details can emerge.

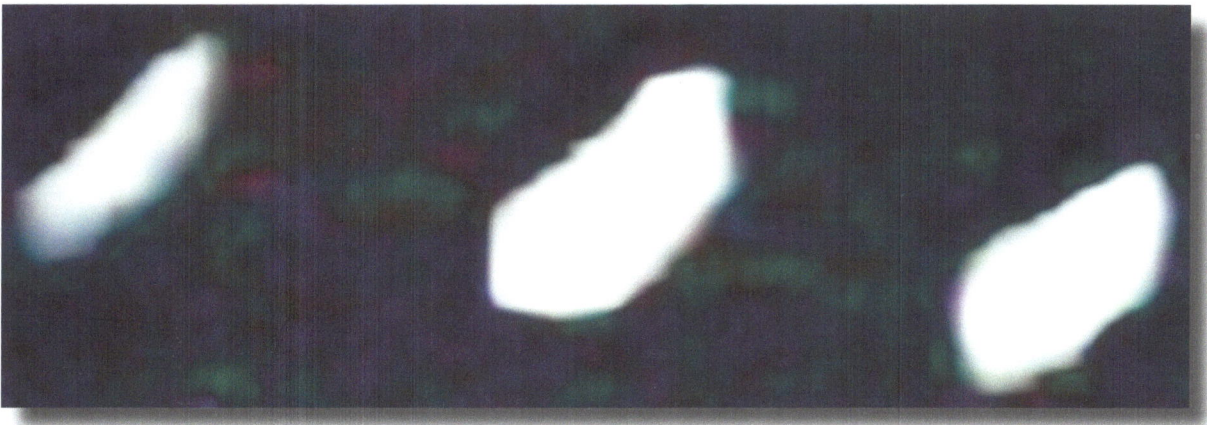

When the central pod on this UFO (**see above**) was processed further (**see next page**) using a mixture of IRIS software to blow the image up 60 times and then processed further using GIMP software, an alien reptile figure is seen looking through a blurry smoke screen of green light which masks the windows on this UFO.

The alien's reptile-like head is outlined by a yellow marker on the photo. If you stare at the image, you will note two eyes on the alien. Aliens, the few that I have seen in my photographs, tend to have some form of goggles which appear to enhance their vision.

There are other alien oddities that have been seen in my processed UFO photographs. The first oddity, as seen on page 123 of this chapter, is that aliens can sometimes be seen wearing masks. The second oddity seen in occasional photographs is where aliens will wear flight suits that match the camouflage of the overall craft. On one occasion, In a video unfortunately lost to a computer virus, a humanoid alien was even noted to be wearing what appeared to be a sidearm, or sidearm-like looking device.

All these alien oddities makes the work of being an UFO photography hunter more like taking a ink blot test, in that aliens do not exactly show a "line-up" profile of the usual suspects. On the contrary, it takes time and study to figure out what is going on in the pictures.

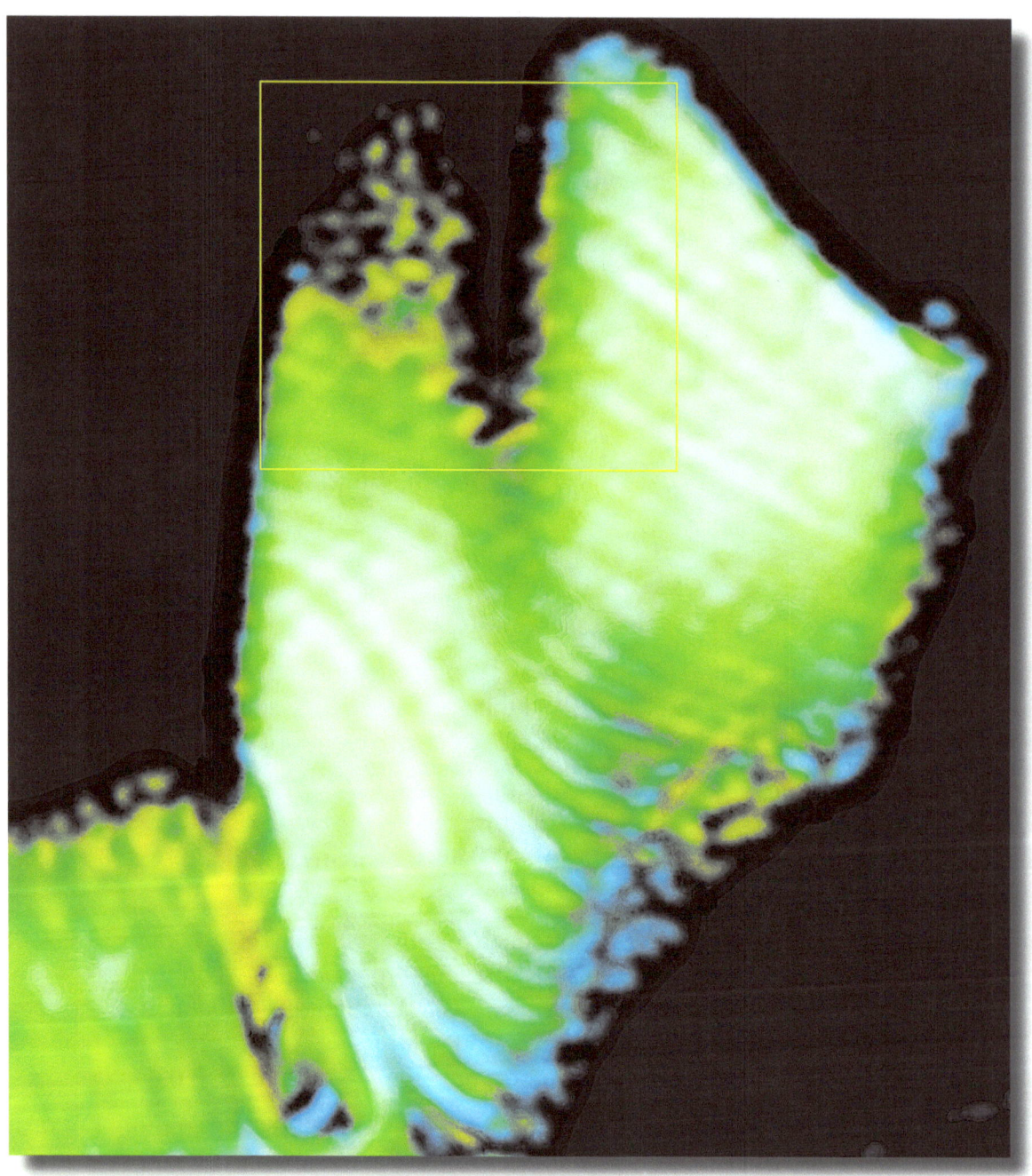

This next picture (**see left**) was taken with the Fujifilm FinePix E510 on January 26th, 2009 at 6:00 p.m. Here, the UFO is floating still in the air. The picture was taken using an F-stop of 5.5, an exposure of 1/2 a second, a 0 step exposure bias, focal length of 15 mm, and no flash with a maximum aperture of 3.1. The second photo on this page shows the UFO blown up 110 times using bicubic resampling in IRIS software (**see middle photograph below**).

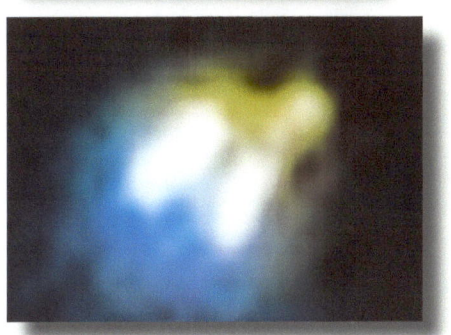

Using the Fujifilm Finepix E510, the UFO was captured as a photograph which when processed, came out in the form of an **anaglyph (see left bottom picture)**. An anaglyph is a stereoscopic picture where the left and right eye images are laid over on top of each picture, but in different colours. In this case, red and blue. With a color gel filter (red, green, or blue) over each eye; the color gel filter for each eye only transmits the image part tasked for that eye while the brain combines the red and blue image seen from each individual eye to see the result as a 3-D photo. It sounds complex, but that is how a 3-D movie works. In other words in the photo (**see below left**), the alien uses something like a 3-D movie screen image to hide itself from direct view. This 3-D effect applies

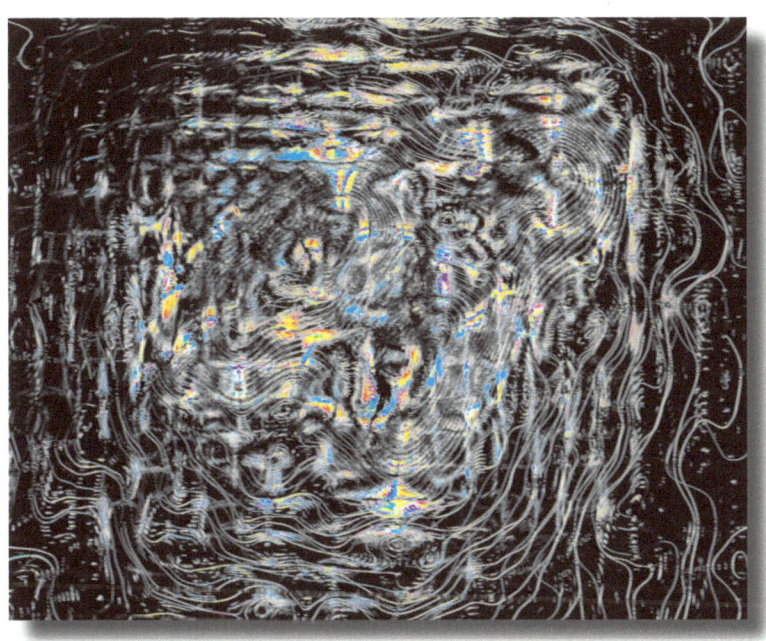

a previously discussed principle of UFO stealth, i.e. using a mixture of red, green and blue colors that mix to form white. However, in this case, the UFO applies a 3-D anaglyph to achieve the same effect of red, blue and green blurring to form white at a distance and thereby hiding the craft and craft interior. If you use the right camera, such as a Fujifilm Finepix E510, you can capture the separate colors being emitted (the Canon EOS T1i is not capable of this feat). Splitting up the colors helps to break through UFO stealth, and if you put on a pair of 3-D glasses, you are able to see a picture of the alien in 3-D. The expanded picture of the alien (**see expanded picture next page, top photo**) will leap into a 3-D image that reveals the disturbing image of a fang-toothed alien.

By wearing 3-D glasses, this effect is pronounced. You can order 3-D glasses for a few dollars on the Internet at: **http://www.3-Dglasses.net/**

Note that the alien also appears to be looking through a telescope-like device and is wearing some sort of cap with lit cables attached to the cap. This can be seen in a desaturated version of the 3-D photo (**see next page, bottom photograph**).

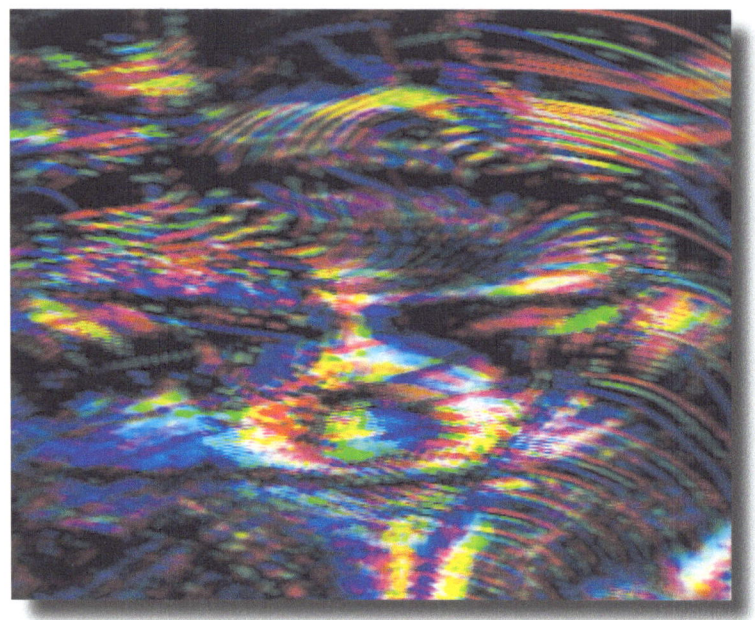

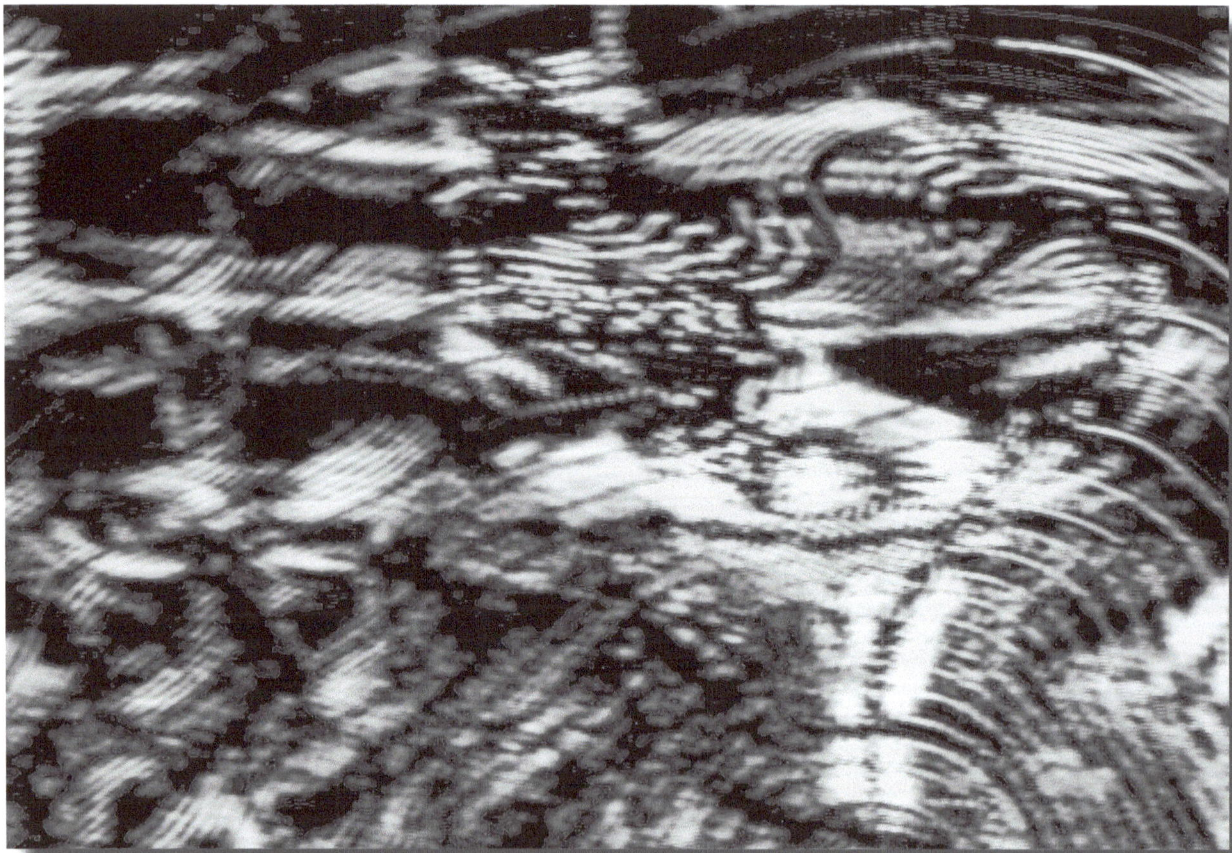

The UFO picture to the right was captured by HandyAvi motion sensing software using a near IR web-cam on January 20th, 2009, at 4:34 p.m. The UFO, as seen on the top edge of the web-cam photograph extracted from video, was enhanced by expanding the photo 30 times and applying a series of photo processing techniques to remove the blur around the UFO (**see below bottom photograph, expanded 30 times**).

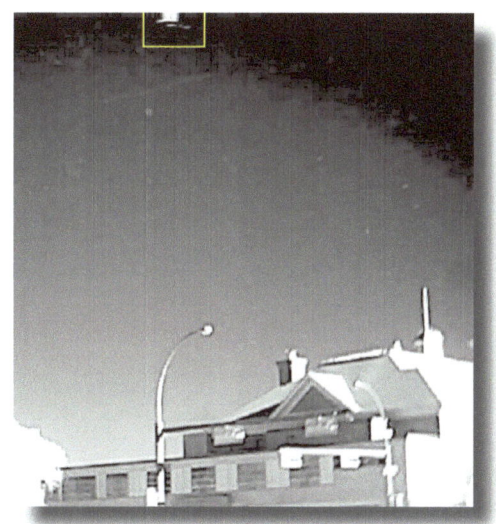

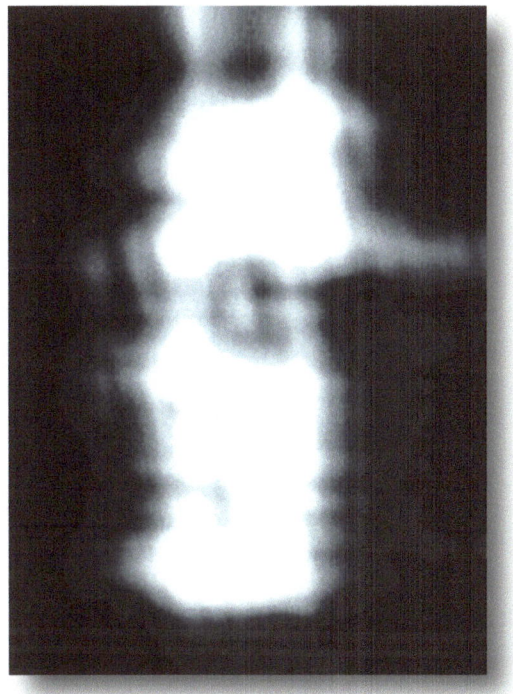

This UFO appears in form to be cage like and presumably some sort of drive unit is seen under the craft. The picture below was expanded 20 more times to reveal a rather strange looking image — a humanoid with goggles peering out the side of the craft (**see left**). The rest of its face is barely visible beneath the layer of UFO stealth around the craft. The form of its face suggests that perhaps this is a non-humanoid alien wearing a human looking half mask.

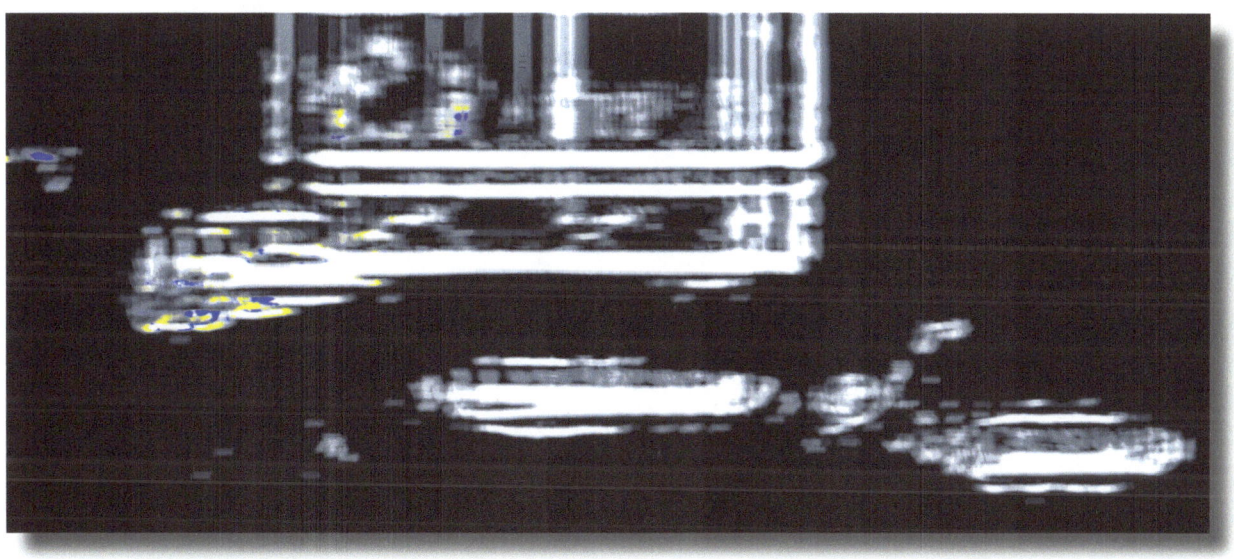

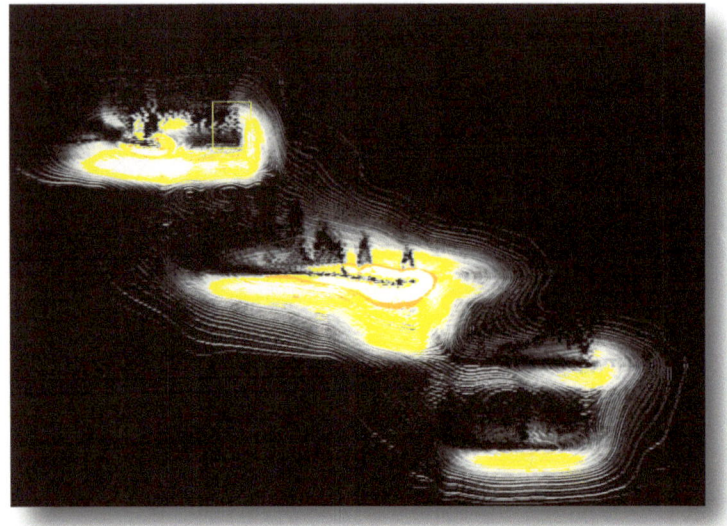

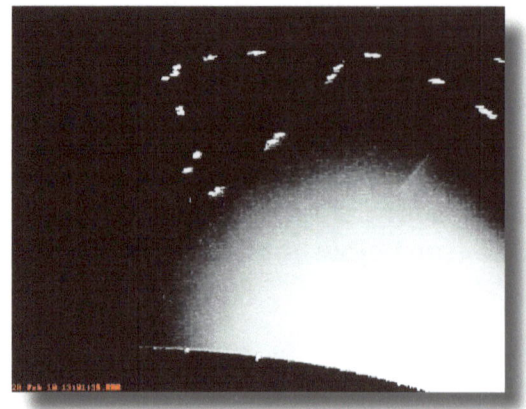

The final alien photo is an Extraterrestrial Biological Entity, or "EBE", which is an alien entity, four feet in height, with wrap around goggle-type glasses that was supposedly first seen at the Roswell UFO crash.[4] The EBE was viewed in a three level UFO (**see above left UFO photo, pilot marked with yellow square**) which was caught on near infrared web-cam video doing an uncharacteristic turn as compared to other UFOs. This uncharacteristic UFO turn is shown on a composite photo of the UFO track (**see above right**). The EBE pilot (**see left**) is barely visible through stealth on this craft. The UFO was recorded on near infrared web-cam on March 5th, 2010, at 3:46:24 p.m. This craft appeared after an hour of almost constant examination of the area by small, pilotless probe UFOs.

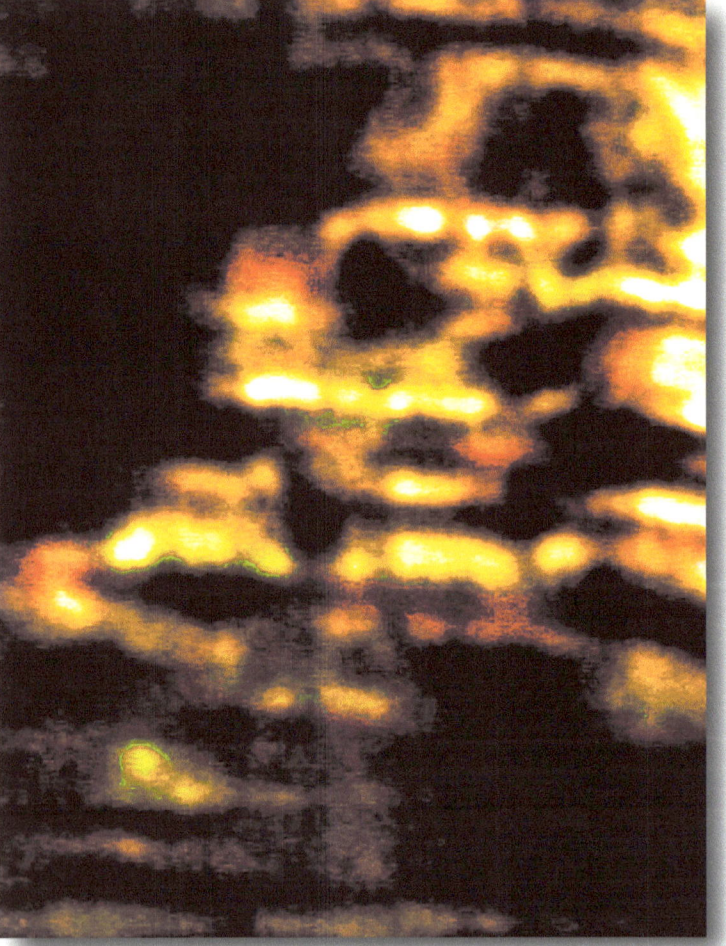

---

4   Extraterrestrial Biological Entity, Found at: http://www.consciousape.com/discussion-topics/aliens-ebes-ets/

Chapter 12: Where to Submit UFO Photographs

Truths are not relative. What are relative are opinions about truth.
Nicolás Gómez Dávila[1]

Submitting Materials to NASA

NASA likes to debunk UFO sightings. How do we know NASA likes to debunk UFO sightings? Try this out as a party trick: type "UFO" into the main search engine of NASA's website at: **http://www.nasa.gov/.** On the second response down, you will get...

UFO Planet

The planet Venus, so bright it is often mistaken for an alien spaceship, reaches maximum brilliancy this week.[2]

After reading through many entries showing where NASA again and again claims people mistake UFOs for planets, Venus or weather balloons, you quickly come to the conclusion that NASA's main mission, other than near earth space travel, is to debunk anything which relates to UFOs.

Submitting UFO Videos to Youtube

On the other side of the coin, NASA shows a great deal of concern with respect to UFO footage showing up on Youtube. For example, NASA has looked at some of my UFO videos. Youtube has a function called "Insight Logs", which tracks other Internet sites that are linked to online Youtube videos. In essence, a record is made of who links to videos on Youtube. From late 2008 to early 2009, NASA linked to the author's video recording of a near infrared web-cam sighting of a mother ship. So it would be fair to say, that NASA does have an interest in UFO phenomena, despite official denial.

Other websites from various armed forces in the U.S., France and Canada have shown up in my Insight Logs (**see Insight Log right**) through **www.militaryphotos.net/**, a website that shares photos and videos to many armed forces within many nations, these sites are:

- defenselink.mil

- army.mil,navy.mil

- af.mil,usmc.mil

- www.defense.gouv.fr/ema

- www.defenceimages.mod.uk

- combatcamera.forces.gc.ca

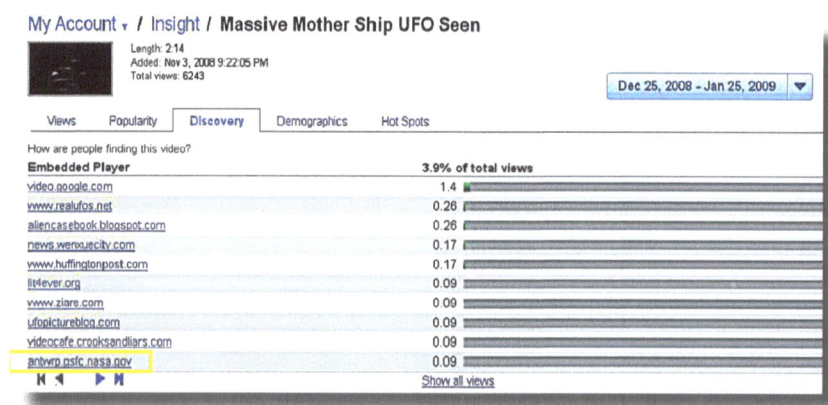

---

1 Found at: http://en.wikipedia.org/wiki/Aphorism
2 Phillips , Dr. Tony, **UFO Planet**, http://science.nasa.gov/headlines/y2004/03may_maximumvenus.htm

However, if you wish to show the public UFOs in a direct manner, you can submit pictures and video to Youtube. Submitting UFO video to Youtube consists of the following steps.

Log onto the Internet and go to the following web-page: **http://www.youtube.com/**

On the upper right hand side of the main Youtube page, there is a "Create Account" link. You will go through a sixteen page, legal terms of "Google Terms of Service and YouTube Terms of Use" that Youtube requires you to acknowledge before account creation, after which, you can submit a password and an email to create a Youtube account.

You have the choice of turning comments "on or off" for the public's comments on your submission of materials to Youtube. However, once your UFO footage is lodged on Youtube, the footage will compete with other real UFO videos and pictures. Your "real" Youtube UFO videos will also compete with "fake" and real UFO images and footage, alongside dead alien "prop corpses" that appear on the Youtube site. These fake computer generated graphics pictures and videos are easy to spot after working with actual UFO pictures and footage for several years. Fake CGI UFOs only serve to lower the standard of genuine UFO photography, giving power to people who try to debunk and confuse the public with respect to real UFO footage. One of the motivations in writing this book was to give people the means to obtain their own direct evidence and experience, without confusion caused by professional debunkers, con artists, and the creators of fake CGI footage who ultimately take away from the fact that these craft visit our planet every day.

Submitting Sightings to the Mutual UFO Network (MUFON)

The U.S. based Mutual UFO Network (MUFON) is a UFO group that has as its mission statement: "The scientific study of UFOs for the benefit of humanity."[3] MUFON's site is well laid out, with templates of UFO forms for writing down UFO sightings. The actor, Dan Aykroyd, is listed on the site as a lifetime member of MUFON.[4] MUFON offers courses in UFO work. The MUFON web page can be found at: **http://www.mufon.com/**

To submit a UFO report, along with UFO videos and photographs of UFOs, click the link on the left hand side of the page titled "Submit a UFO report".

This direct link to this report form is found at: **http://www.mufon.com/reportufo.htm**

By writing the direct link above into a web browser, you will be taken to an online reporting form. The online report form will ask you for your name, address, time of the event, date of the event, email, phone numbers (work and home), country where you live, and whether or not you wish to give the sighting to third parties who may or may not investigate your sightings. Additionally, you can submit a detailed note on the UFO sighting, explaining in your own words what you experienced.

Once on the MUFON site, it takes about ten minutes to upload a three minute video on a high speed ADSL line. After you submit the sighting, you are given the option to submit background on your education, hearing, vision, and any effects noted from seeing the UFO.

Along with these various options, the MUFON site has a cool added feature called "UFO Stalker" which allows UFO sightings to be georeferenced across the earth. Georeferencing means that the sighting is

---

3   MUFON Mission Statement, Found at: http://www.mufon.com/mission.htm
4   Akroyd, Dan, Actor Dan Aykroyd Supports MUFON as Lifetime Member, Found at: http://www.mufon.com/akroyd.htm

put on a map with a latitude and longitude. Once your report is sent to MUFON, the location where your sighting took place will be added to UFO Stalker along with a set of links to any pictures or videos you have uploaded to MUFON.

The National UFO Reporting Center

The National UFO Reporting Center (NUFORC) has been around since 1974.[5] This group maintains one of the best sets of data and information on UFOs in the United States.

UFO reports can be submitted online to the National UFO Reporting Center at:

http://www.ufocenter.com/reportform.html

NUFORC also has a Hotline: **206-722-3000** (use only if the sighting has occurred within the last week.)

GEIPAN

Geipan (Groupe d'Etudes et d'Information sur les Phénomènes Aérospatiaux Non identifiés) is a government body in France which studies UFO sightings in France. If you are in France and wish to report a sighting, GEIPAN can be contacted through the following email: **geipan@cnes.fr**

Note that in France UFOs can go by the term OVNI (objet volant non identifié), but the term GEIPAN prefers to use, is unidentified aerospace phenomenon (UAP).

---

5   Found at: http://www.nwlink.com/~ufocntr/

Chapter 13: Conclusion

"In our obsession with antagonisms of the moment, we often forget how much unites all the members of humanity. Perhaps we need some outside, universal threat to make us recognize this common bond. I occasionally think how quickly our differences worldwide would vanish if we were facing an alien threat from outside of this world. And yet I ask — is not an alien force already among us? What could be more alien to the universal aspiration of our people than war and the threat of war?"

President Ronald Reagan Speech to UN, September 21st,1987

As a hobby, UFO photography derails the notion of human beings existing as the single species in this galaxy. Capturing UFOs on video and with cameras is an exploration of our skies which provides us with a new viewpoint on the notion: "Are we alone?" As a unique hobby, UFO photography tends to put to rest the idea that we are alone in this universe, when in fact, we are now being visited daily by foreign extraterrestrial craft and ET beings.

In particular, UFO photography encourages an evolution in thought from our conception of aloneness in this universe to an understanding that the sky is vibrant with species from other worlds, and filled with unusual craft and sights. In a sense, this understanding of our planet being visited by vehicles and beings of unknown origin is analogous to the historical idea that the world was flat, with the eventual discovery that the world was in fact round. New concepts sometimes take centuries to come to the fore in our collective consciousness. But just as we now regard the historical thought that the world was flat as a bizarre idea, centuries from now the idea of alien races "not" visiting our planet with advanced vehicles will likely be regarded in some future sense as an odd notion of our times.

In a universe filled with life, and life which uses advanced vehicles as captured by the detailed video methods presented in this book, this book shows the beginning steps to a hobby where you can explore the larger universe from you back door. Carrying out the techniques outlined in this book presents you with the opportunity to pioneer new discoveries in an area that has previously been shaded in mystery .

Index

www.ingramcontent.com/pod-product-compliance
Lightning Source LLC
Chambersburg PA
CBHW050718180526
45159CB00003B/1059